The England of
WILLIAM SHAKESPEARE

The England of
WILLIAM SHAKESPEARE

MICHAEL JUSTIN DAVIS

With photographs by Simon McBride

E. P. Dutton
New York

For Jane, Richard and Matt

Remember . . .
The natural bravery of your isle, which stands
As Neptune's park, ribbed and paled in
With banks unscalable and roaring waters,
With sands that will not bear your enemies' boats,
But suck them up to th'topmast.

Cymbeline (3.1.16)

Frontispiece
Bosworth Field (near Market Bosworth, Leicestershire),
battlefield where *Richard III* 5,3-5 is set. Here Richard was
defeated, 1485, by Henry Richmond who, as Henry VII,
became first Tudor monarch.

Copyright © 1987 by Michael Justin Davis

All rights reserved. Printed in Great Britain.

No part of this publication may be reproduced or
transmitted in any form or by any means, electronic or
mechanical, including photocopy, recording, or any
information storage and retrieval system now known or
to be invented, without permission in writing from the
publisher, except by a reviewer who wishes to quote
brief passages in connection with a review written for
inclusion in a magazine, newspaper, or broadcast.

Published in the United States by E. P. Dutton,
a division of NAL Penguin Inc.,
2 Park Avenue, New York, N.Y. 10016.

Originally published in Great Britain by Webb and Bower in
association with Michael Joseph Limited under the title
The Landscape of William Shakespeare.

ISBN: 0-525-24587-1

USA & P

Designed by Giolitto/Pickless

1 3 5 7 9 10 8 6 4 2

First American Edition

CONTENTS

Introduction

This book is about those places where Shakespeare is known to have lived, and venues where the troupe of actors of which he was a member performed during his time as a player. Other places, however important in his day, do not feature.

Documentary evidence exists for Shakespeare's presence in Stratford-upon-Avon and London, and for his company's appearances on tour in Marlborough, Ipswich, Bath, Shrewsbury, Dunwich and all the other provincial places about which I have written here.

It is impossible to know *precisely* when the troupe acted in particular cities, towns or villages, but from those dates that are available I have constructed a chronological framework and built this book on it. The narrative hops from place to place as surviving records dictate: the effect is restless – and so was the life of players. Whether Shakespeare himself went on tour is discussed in Chapter 3.

As poet and playwright he used landscape to place and illuminate people's actions, emotions and thoughts. He did not describe landscape for its own sake; nor does this book. Here, I have tried to re-create places as they were when Shakespeare knew them: country, town and city alive with men, women and children in action.

I have varied the focus according to the amount of detail needed to show precise aspects of particular places. Those important features of life, such as farming, dress, food, religion, disease, travel, unemployment and crime, which must have affected the way Shakespeare lived and which he would have heard talked about, I have discussed in detail as they arise in a particular locality. For instance, from an account of Shrewsbury's food products, a description of meals and diet develops: and from an account of Dover, there emerges a description of group labour.

In a book as short as this, to write about every important topic is impossible. In selecting what to include, I have tried to choose the particular, which is likely to have had an immediate impact on Shakespeare, rather than the general. So, in this book the legal system is not fully described, but the Inns of Court and their entertainments (which involved Shakespeare's company) do feature. The Elizabethan House of Commons is not considered, but the problem of travel for an MP is touched upon: Shakespeare, on tour, may have heard this discussed. The system of Cambridge colleges is not analysed, but the behaviour of students and townsfolk is mentioned: Shakespeare did not study at Cambridge, but his troupe acted there.

To add to the historical flavour of the book, rather than paraphrase I have quoted lavishly, though with modernized spelling and punctuation; and I have prefaced each chapter with extracts which I hope will prove enriching.

I owe a great debt of gratitude to many extremely learned people without whose help I could not possibly have written this book. To them; to numerous authoritative works on which I have relied; to friends who have encouraged and aided me; and to my wife, whose help never fails me, I record my thanks at the end of this book.

Meanwhile, on to Shakespeare's England:

> '*This precious stone set in the silver sea,*
> *Which serves it in the office of a wall,*
> *Or as a moat defensive to a house . . .*
> *This blessèd plot, this earth, this realm, this England . . .*'
>
> *Richard II* (2.1.46–8, 50)

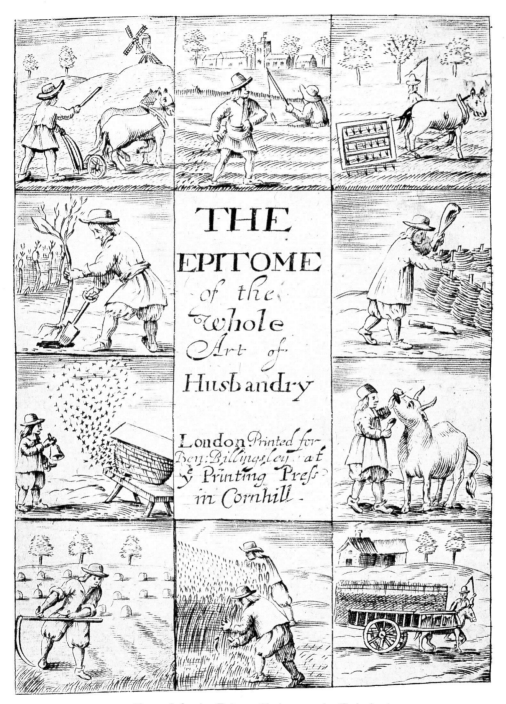

Blagrave's farming *Epitome*, 1669, incorporating Fitzherbert's
far older methods. The farmer's year, from left, top: ploughing,
sowing, harrowing; bottom: scything grass, reaping corn,
carting harvest. Sides, left: planting a fruit-tree; ringing a bell
to make a swarm of bees settle; right: fencing the sheep-pen;
giving a cow a drench from a hollowed horn.

1 THE FOREST OF ARDEN

STRATFORD-UPON-AVON

This song our shire of Warwick sounds;
Revives old Arden's ancient bounds.
Through many shapes the Muse here roves;
Now sporting in those shady groves,
The tunes of birds oft stays to hear:
Then finding herds of lusty deer,
She huntress-like the hart pursues.

MICHAEL DRAYTON: *Polyolbion*

Visitors to England in Shakespeare's day noted an obvious and crucial fact: 'this kingdom is an island'. Consequently, 'no-one can enter or depart except in ships', a restriction helpful to the government: 'orders have been issued to all ports and havens, that no Englishman shall leave without a licence'. So wrote Jacob Rathbeg, secretary to the Duke of Württemberg, with whom he visited England in 1592 when Elizabeth I was queen (1558–1603) and again in 1610 when James I was king (1603–1625). These were the two monarchs in whose reigns William Shakespeare lived, from 1564 to 1616. There is no documentary proof that he ever travelled abroad or applied for a licence to do so.

The county where he was born, Warwickshire, at the centre of England, consisted to the south of 'champaign' – open country – as in Malvolio's phrase 'Daylight and champaign' in *Twelfth Night* (2.5.155) – and the rest of the county, to the north, beyond the River Avon, was woodland. Warwickshire is described in an Elizabethan manuscript as:

'... plentiful both in corn and pasturage, whereby it is well inhabited ... and comprehendeth 158 parishes, whereof there be twelve market towns, and but one borough to the Parliament, besides the City of Coventry.... Next is the Borough of Warwick, the capital town of that country, reasonably well built, with an ancient castle, the chief seat of the earls of that title. Next is Stratford-upon-Avon and Henley, good market towns, and Birmingham, chiefly noted for all sorts of iron tools.'

About fifty years before that account was written the antiquarian and topographer, John Leland, visited Stratford in Henry VIII's reign. He noted that if you approach from London the town stands on the far bank of the River Avon, to the north of which is 'Arden (for so is the ancient name of that part of the shire) and the ground in Arden is much enclosed, plentiful of grass, but no great plenty of corn'. The other part of Warwickshire to the south, beyond the River Avon, 'is for the most part champaign, somewhat barren of wood, but very

Opposite
Anne Hathaway's cottage, one of the cluster of farmhouses that formed the hamlet of Shottery. Hers has twelve rooms.

M Gheeraerts: Elizabeth I; portrait from Ditchley, Oxfordshire, where the Master of Armoury, Sir Henry Lee, entertained her, 1592. Her feet, on a map of England (derived from Saxton's map, 1583), are close to Ditchley. She holds gloves. A sonnet (right), probably by Lee, calls her 'Prince of Light'. She is dispelling darkness.

plentiful of corn'. The river at Stratford is spanned by 'a sumptuous new bridge and large of stone, where in the middle be six great arches for the main stream of Avon, and at each end certain small arches to bear the causeway ... now walled on each side'. People could remember the old bridge, a timber structure 'very small and ill, and at high waters very hard to pass by' so that 'many poor folks and others refused to come to Stratford, when Avon was up, or coming thither stood in jeopardy of life'. Whether as a boon or a menace, rivers were highly respected in Tudor times, and so were bridges.

The 'sumptuous new bridge' – which still carries

vital traffic in and out of the town along the A422, the Banbury road – was the gift of a 'great rich merchant', Sir Hugh Clopton. Born a mile from Stratford in the family manor-house at Clopton, Hugh was a younger son who left home in his youth, headed for London and made good in the textile trade as a mercer. He amassed a vast fortune and rose to be Lord Mayor of London. Some of this wealth he spent on improving his favourite town, Stratford.

In his day, rich merchants who rode about the country on business often paid for the building of bridges and causeways. For his own use Sir Hugh built New Place, a 'pretty house of brick and timber' in Chapel Street in the centre of Stratford, the house eventually bought by Shakespeare, also with money earned in London.

Leland observed that Stratford stands on flat ground seven miles from Warwick and ten miles from Evesham. It 'hath two or three very large streets, besides back lanes. One of the principal streets leadeth from east to west, another from south to north.... The town is reasonably well builded of timber'. (This was the material most commonly used in Tudor times, so the risk of fire was great.) 'There is once a year a great fair at Holy Rood Day', 14 September, when 'a very great concourse of people' gathered for two or three days of business and shopping. 'The parish church is a fair, large piece of work, and standeth at the south end of the town.' Two other important buildings were on the south side of Holy Trinity chapel: a grammar school and 'an almshouse of ten poor folk'.

By Shakespeare's day, the fairs had increased in number. When they were held – and on Thursdays, which were market days – traders occupied spaces and streets in the town centre. Glovers set up their stalls in the most important position of all, under the clock at the Market Cross; country butchers set up theirs on the west side of Chapel St; ironmongers, nailers, collarmakers and ropemakers set up in Bridge Street. Raw hides were sold by the cross in Rother Market. Wood Street was occupied by pewterers, braziers and coopers. At the market house, tanned leather was inspected before being sold, and cheese – of which 'great store' was 'usually brought to the fairs' – was weighed to prevent 'great deceit'. At 11 am the market bell rang and the market closed. Everything had to be transported by road: the River Avon was not navigable in Shakespeare's lifetime.

The chief local industry was malting: the conversion of barley or other grain into malt, by steeping, germinating and kiln-drying, so that it could be made into ale or beer (which differed from ale) or other liquor. About a third of the town's householders did their own malting as a side-line. Shakespeare, towards the end of Elizabeth's reign, was one who did. That was a time of food shortage, when maltsters were accused of hoarding corn which should have been used for bread: the Warwickshire justices wished to ban malting entirely.

In Stratford, as in other corporate towns, each occupation formed its own company. The Bakers' Company was formed about ten years before Shakespeare's birth: and by the time he was seventeen, companies had been formed of Skinners and Tailors; Walkers and Fullers (whose job was to clean and thicken cloth by treading or beating it); Dyers and Shearmen (who sheared the cloth); Smiths; Weavers; an unwieldy company of Masons, Carpenters, Tilers, Thatchers, Ploughwrights, Tugerers (harness-makers), Joiners, Wheelwrights and Coopers; Shoemakers and Saddlers; and Drapers. Every man in the town was ordered in 1597 to join 'one company or other', a measure intended to give practical help to the poor, of whom there were 700 in Stratford four years later.

Soon after James I's accession in 1603, two companies of the wealthier trades were formed. The first was the most important of all the companies: the Mercers, Linendrapers, Woollendrapers, Hatters, Grocers, Haberdashers and Salters. The last company to be formed in Shakespeare's lifetime was that of the Glovers and Whittawers (dressers of white leather, who 'tawed' skins of horses, deer, sheep, goats and hounds, but not those of cattle or swine). Shakespeare's father, John, was a whittawer and glover, but he died in 1601, five years before the formation of the company.

Although the cloth industry was never as important to the Stratford region as it was to Coventry, the decay of Stratford town – population about 1,500 – in 1590 was ascribed to lack of trade in 'clothing and making of yarn, employing and maintaining a number of poor people ... which now live in great penury and misery'.

King's New School, Stratford-upon-Avon: school-room where Shakespeare probably studied, on the first floor, Guildhall. He writes of schooldays as tedious, and a typical pupil is:

'... the whining school-boy with his satchel
And shining morning face, creeping like snail
Unwillingly to school'.

(*As You Like It* 2.7.145)

Gloving, however, centred on Stratford, and in Shakespeare's lifetime the trade was at its height. Men and women of all classes, from the Queen to the shepherd-folk (customers of Autolycus in *The Winter's Tale*) valued gloves. Perfumed (like Autolycus's, 'as sweet as damask roses', 4.4.221), fur-lined, gauntleted, embroidered, tasselled: gloves were of all sorts, fashionable and functional. On special occasions, they were important gifts. At weddings, the bride's gloves – a prized part of her outfit – were given with other pairs to guests and to the two bachelors who led the bride to church.

John Shakespeare's shop, where he sold gloves,

soft leather goods (such as purses, belts and aprons), and fleeces, was in the west wing of his big double house in Henley Street, the home in which his second child and first son, William, was born. The date of the boy's baptism is known – 26 April 1564 – but not his date of birth. Presumably it was only a few days earlier, and as the feast of England's patron saint, St George, is on 23 April, that day has been designated the birthday of England's greatest poet and dramatist.

Stratford, where John Shakespeare was to hold office as an increasingly important public servant, had been granted its first charter of incorporation eleven years before William's birth. There was to be a common council of fourteen aldermen and fourteen burgesses, empowered to make bylaws and headed by a bailiff elected annually from among the council. He was to be clerk of the market, and he and one of the aldermen were to be Justices of the Peace. The council's responsibilities included a weekly market, two fairs and the election of constables, the payment of vicar and schoolmaster, and the maintenance of almshouses.

The poor were a problem and a cause of concern. In those days a pauper was the owner of no more than a table, a chair, a bed and the food in the cooking pot. 'Strangers' who might come to live in the town, make their homes in barns and stables and become a burden on the rates, were unacceptable to Stratford. They were warned to leave. The poor who did belong in the town received coal-money, and in especially hard years the town bought corn and re-sold it at a reasonable price to those in need. In the general depression at the end of Elizabeth's reign Alderman Richard Quiney, a friend of Shakespeare, went to London to plead for a reduction of the taxes and subsidies demanded by Parliament. Stratford, he claimed, was a decayed and impoverished town; and he won the remission.

Stratford was policed by four constables during Shakespeare's lifetime, when the town's population increased greatly, and in his last years the number of constables was raised to six. The constables were elected annually; any man who refused to serve was liable to a fine of £5. Breaches of the peace and absences from church were among their concerns, and they had a special responsibility to prevent fire: a task doomed to failure when the main aids to fire-fighting were leather buckets which the wealthier

'Rehearse after supper the lesson which you will learn
tomorrow morning, and read it six or seven times. Then,
having said your prayers, sleep upon it. You shall see that
tomorrow morning you will learn it easily and soon, having
repeated the same but twice.' (C Hollyband, schoolmaster.)

people were supposed – but often failed – to
provide. Hooked poles were used to pull apart the
timber-framed buildings that were burning or in
danger.

Three fires raged in Stratford during
Shakespeare's manhood. The first, on 22 September
1594, destroyed much of the west side of Chapel
Street and of High Street, Wood Street and Henley
Street (Shakespeare's birthplace is on the east). The
second fire, all but a year later, on 21 September
1595, was concentrated in a block at the town centre
bounded by Sheep Street, High Street and Bridge
Street. These two fires are said to have destroyed
200 houses and the damage was estimated at
£12,000. Presumably Shakespeare's family was in
the town during these fires, although he had become
only an occasional resident. By the time of the third

fire, on 9 July 1614, which destroyed fifty-four
houses and in two hours did damage worth £8,000,
Shakespeare had virtually retired and was living at
New Place. No earlier building of brick and timber
in the town has been recorded. These three fires
were said to have 'had their beginnings in poor
tenements and cottages which were thatched with
straw', many of those dwellings having been recently roofed with thatch, despite an order of 1583
that all houses should be roofed with tiles.

In addition to preventing fires, the constables
were supposed to call monthly meetings of 'certain
of the council and some other honest men', so as to
provide a watch for policing the town at night. In
winter, a bellman patrolled the streets from 11 pm
until 4 am. It was not easy to foster public hygiene: a
dozen years before William's birth, John Shakespeare had been fined a shilling (two days' pay for an
artisan) for making a refuse-heap in Henley Street,
instead of using the 'common muckhill' up the road
towards the country. Two other men were fined the
same day for similar offences. Disease was fostered
by piles of dung, offal and garbage. These attracted

rats, from which the dreaded bubonic plague was carried by fleas to humans. A bubo – a painful glandular swelling – would result from the flea-bite and the patient, ill for about five days, would probably die. A few weeks after Shakespeare's birth, plague broke out in the summer and killed more than 200 Stratford people. One family in the street where he lived, Henley Street, lost four children. There were 254 deaths in the town that year: at least sixteen per cent of the population.

Four years after the muck-heap fine, John Shakespeare held his first public office: he was one of the two 'able persons and discreet' chosen to be ale-tasters. They had to see that ale and beer were wholesome and correctly priced and that loaves were sufficiently heavy. Offenders could be fined, whipped, stocked, pilloried, or humiliated on the ducking stool. John Shakespeare progressed up the ladder of public office and in 1558 he became one of the four constables whose tasks included the prevention of street-riots and the arrest of brawlers.

Some time in the previous eighteen months he had married Mary Arden, and their first daughter, Joan, was born a few weeks before John became a constable. The Arden family, like the Shakespeare, came from villages where they farmed, close to Stratford. Mary was of high yeoman stock or minor gentry and her father owned some 100 acres or more of land in Snitterfield, with two farmhouses. One of these he let to Richard Shakespeare, William's grandfather, while the Ardens lived in the hamlet of Wilmcote, where Mary was brought up. The house is not known, but it would have resembled the building now called 'Mary Arden's House', the spacious old home that a well-off farmer would have had. Snitterfield and Wilmcote are each a little over three miles from Stratford and the same distance apart: Snitterfield is north of Stratford, and Wilmcote, which was then in the parish of Aston Cantlow, is north-west of Stratford. Mary Arden's father, who had asked to be buried in Aston Cantlow, died in 1556. The wedding of Mary to John Shakespeare probably took place in the church there.

Mary inherited from her father his valuable estate: 'all my land in Wilmcote called Asbyes'. His many possessions at his death included oxen, bullocks, cattle, pigs, poultry, bees, bacon, a barn full of wheat and barley, and a house well stocked with oak furniture, bed linen, pans made of copper and brass, and eleven painted cloths (popular substitutes for tapestries) hung on the walls. The paintings showed myths and Bible stories, with rhymed mottoes underneath.

Snitterfield village, where John Shakespeare and his elder brother Henry were brought up, lies in undulating country less than half-way from Stratford to Warwick on the old turnpike road. The farming land is good. Richard Shakespeare's house, rented from Robert Arden, abutted on the High Street. Whereas young John Shakespeare became an apprentice and then a glover, Henry (Shakespeare's uncle) stayed and farmed nearby. He was the member of the family who got into trouble: for violence, for trespass, for debt, for failure to mend the Queen's highway and for wearing a hat instead of a woollen cap, the compulsory Sunday headgear. Felt hats, lined with velvet or silk, had become so much more popular than caps that the cap-makers' trade was protected by law. Uncle Henry was one of those men fined for wearing hats to Snitterfield's large, handsome church. Shakespeare as a boy is bound to have visited him and his wife, Aunt Margaret, at Snitterfield (where those relatives – and almost certainly Shakespeare's grandfather – now lie buried in the churchyard) and to have visited his maternal grandmother at Wilmcote, where she remained with Shakespeare's Aunt Alice. Snitterfield and Wilmcote must have provided Shakespeare with much of his apparently instinctive knowledge of the countryside, husbandry, the farming year and village ways.

Paul Hentzner, a German visitor to England in 1598, remarked that the English soil is fruitful and abounds with cattle, so that 'near a third part of the land is left uncultivated for grazing'. England's 'beautiful oxen and cows' were admired by another visitor from Germany, Jacob Rathbeg: 'they have very large horns, are low and heavy, and for the most part black; there is abundance of sheep and wethers in all parts and places, which graze by themselves winter and summer without shepherds'. William Harrison, an Elizabethan parson whose *Description of England* was added to Holinshed's *Chronicles*, was proud not only of the number of England's 'horses, oxen, sheep, goats, swine' exceeding those 'in other countries', but also of their quality: 'where are oxen commonly more large of bone, horses more decent and pleasant in pace, sheep more profitable for wool, swine more wholesome of flesh, and goats more gainful to their keepers, than here with us in England?'

The horns of our oxen were 'more fair and large' than those in other countries, and many graziers anointed the tender tips with honey when the oxen were very young, 'which mollifieth the natural hardness of that substance, and thereby maketh them to grow unto a notable greatness'. The distance between the tips was often a yard, and the oxen 'themselves thereto so tall as the height of a man' of medium stature 'is scarce equal unto them', said Harrison.

Richard Shakespeare probably owned at least eight oxen, the usual number for a plough. At night the oxen would be kept near the farmstead in pastures which were enclosed ('several' was the term then used) for, as Sir Anthony Fitzherbert wrote in his *Book of Husbandry*, if an ox 'be in a good pasture all night, he will labour all day daily'. Moreover, 'Oxen will plough in tough clay, and upon hilly ground where horses of indifferent goodness will stand still.' Oxen were cheaper to harness, to shoe and to keep, and they were healthier than horses.

Harrison described English horses as smallish but easy paced. (Frederick, Duke of Württemberg, surprised by the smallness and hardness of English saddles, took one home with him as a painful souvenir.) Five or six cart-horses would be strong enough to draw a ton and a half, and a pack-horse would carry four hundredweight. Country people used both two-wheeled and four-wheeled carts to transport their goods. Noblemen's luggage went by cart, and – according to Harrison – during the Queen's progresses 2,400 horses drew her movables in 400 carts.

Travel on horseback was beloved of Englishmen 'seeking their ease in every corner where it is to be had', and the rider who travelled at a leisurely pace twenty or thirty miles in a day, before putting up at an inn for the night, found the clip-clop of hoofs 'very pleasant, and delectable in his ears'. However, not only had mounts – which were 'commonly gelded' – become very expensive, 'especially if they be well coloured, justly limbed and have thereto an easy ambling pace', but everywhere crooks battened on innocent horse-users. There was, said Harrison,

'. . . no greater deceit used anywhere than among our horse-keepers, horse-corsers and ostlers, for such is the subtle knavery of a great sort of them . . . that an honest meaning man shall have very good luck among them if he be not deceived by some false trick or other.'

The colour of horses was rated highly. Best of all was a bay horse with a white star on its forehead and Smithfield horse-dealers specialized in faking such stars. Horse-racing, which began in Scotland before England, was boosted by James I on his accession and it offered fresh scope for sharp practice. Horses pastured on commons or tethered on 'champaign' were an obvious prey to thieves.

Wool was so profitable in early Tudor times that landlords converted arable land to pasture wherever they could. The Elizabethans were painfully aware that because sheep-farming and grazing employed few people, the increase of pasture land over arable led to unemployment and swelled the crowds of beggars roaming the highway. Far more sweeping developments were to follow later, but Elizabeth's reign was a time of great change.

Wheat became costlier, wool cheaper. Sheep, valued for fleece and leather rather than for meat, lost their popularity, and farm-workers found their labour needed again. A variety of animals had kept their places on the land. 'Goats', wrote Harrison, 'we have plenty and of sundry colours in the west parts of England, especially in and towards Wales and amongst the rocky hills, by whom the owners do reap no small advantage'. Goats' milk and cheese are good for 'sundry maladies', though Harrison finds the milk unpalatable. Pigs abound in England. In 'champaign' country, writes Harrison, 'they are kept by herds' and a 'hogherd . . . gathereth them together by his noise and cry and leadeth them forth to feed abroad in the fields.' Tame boars, specially fattened 'with oats and peas' are made into an English speciality, brawn, from November till the end of February and chiefly at Christmas.

Harrison enthuses over brawn and pig-meat generally, but he is scornful about the eating of boars' testicles. They used to be thrown away with the bowels 'till a foolish fantasy got hold of late amongst some delicate dames, who have now found the means to dress them with great cost for a dainty dish' for ladies who desire 'the provocation of

fleshly lust'. The Elizabethans were very interested in aphrodisiacs, which were believed to include sweet potatoes and the candied roots of eringo, the sea holly. Foods which could 'increase man's seed' had special appeal when death struck so many children. Because couples wished to make sure before marriage that their union would produce a family, the pregnancy of some Elizabethan brides may be ascribed to social prudence rather than sensual rashness.

Hogs contributed to the laundry, but this nauseated Harrison:

'In some places . . . women do scour and wet their clothes with their dung, as other do with hemlocks and nettles: but such is the savour of the clothes touched withal that I cannot abide to wear them on my body.'

Pigs then were lanky, with longer legs and snouts than modern breeds. To limit the damage they could do in wandering about they were yoked – generally in pairs – and each pig had a ring in its nose: this prevented the uprooting of turf from the common. In the oak-woods of autumn and winter, however, the pigs were temporarily unyoked to feed on acorns, which the hogherd shook from the

Detail of the Bradford Carpet, late sixteenth century. In Elizabethan homes, finely worked carpets of canvas embroidery were used to cover tables and cupboards. This delightful carpet (about 400 stitches per square inch, from a professional workshop) shows an Elizabethan manor house, fashionably dressed people, village, villagers, country pursuits, animals and birds.

branches with a long pole. Unyoked and unringed pigs were forbidden in Stratford. In October 1560 Richard Shakespeare was fined eightpence at Snitterfield for not yoking and ringing his pigs.

His poultry would have included not only chickens but – to make good use of his rivulet – ducks and geese too. Ducks were not allowed to go free in the streets of Stratford. Where geese abounded in the country they were 'driven to the field, like herds of cattle, by a gooseherd'. He carried a paper rattle with him in the morning 'to gather his goslings together, the noise whereof cometh no sooner to their ears', writes Harrison, 'than they fall to gaggling and hasten to go with him'.

Honey was the commonest sweetener in the time of Richard Shakespeare, when all sugar had to be imported, so he – like nearly all country householders – would have kept bees. Hives were made of wicker, coated with clay and thatched with straw. They and the swarms that they housed were sufficiently prized to be willed as legacies. The Archbishop of Canterbury in *Henry V* (1.2.187) begins a detailed account of the habits of bees – 'so work the honey-bees' – as an example of social order depending on obedience to the monarch, which was the prime duty of Elizabethans and a central theme in Shakespeare's plays.

According to Gervase Markham, a versatile writer of Shakespeare's time who excelled in country topics, bees are gentle, provided that their keeper:

'... come sweet and cleanly amongst them; otherwise, if he have strong and ill-smelling savours about him they are curst and malicious, and will sting spitefully. They are exceeding industrious and much given to labour. They have a kind of government amongst themselves, as it were a well-ordered commonwealth, every one obeying and following their king or commander, whose voice (if you lay your ear to the hive) you shall distinguish from the rest, being louder and greater, and beating with a more solemn measure.'

A garden where hives are placed should be well fenced to prevent swine and other cattle overthrowing them and 'offending them with their ill savours'. Church towers were sometimes considered suitable for hives.

The country landscape did not provide the bees with flower-filled hedgerows: large, open fields were undivided, not split up into a patchwork by fences, hedges or walls. The medieval, common-field system of farming – 'champaign' – persisted. Beside the river, at Stratford as in other towns and villages, grass for the hay-harvest grew in meadows that the people's cattle and sheep grazed in autumn and winter. The meadow was divided into strips, for which people drew lots. Between meadow and woodland there would be three vast fields, each of them, too, divided into strips of an acre or half an acre. Narrow, grassy paths ran between the strips. One of the fields would be under wheat or rye; another under oats, barley, peas, beans or vetch; and the third would be lying fallow to regain its strength. All this open, arable land was held in common. After the crops had been cleared it was open for all cattle to graze until seed-time.

Every year, the strips of arable land were redistributed in an attempt to give everybody a fair deal. A share of average size consisted of eighteen acres of arable and two acres of meadow. Each man's holding of arable was divided between the three fields: about six acres in each. The six were not united in one labour-saving plot, but scattered over the field in strips of an acre, or half an acre, so that every man had the same amount of good, mediocre and bad land as his fellow. Democratic farming like this needed efficiency as well as good will: a lazy, selfish or incompetent man could cause a lot of friction.

The wasteful and unprofitable aspects of the system had long been recognized, and some parts of the country had turned to farming in small fields bounded by fences or hedges. Enclosures were only just beginning, however, compared with developments still to come. As yet only the central triangle of England was affected by this more intensive, economic and controllable way of using land in 'several', which was pronounced by the Queen's map-maker, John Norden, to be one and a half times as profitable as 'champaign'. However, the change-over from 'champaign' to 'several' was manipulated by unscrupulous men of substance: they grabbed acres for themselves, encroached on common land, fenced the arable and turned it into pasture. Cottagers, bereft of their strips, were forced to seek work as day-labourers or as servants, but could find none. Unemployed through no fault of their own, many of these poor people were reduced to beggary and took to the highways. After 1566 the law required every new cottage to be provided with four acres of land.

Shakespeare may have felt at home with his country grandparents in the village life of Wilmcote and Snitterfield, but he was born and bred a town boy. John Shakespeare's neighbours in Henley Street included a glover and a whittawer (two men of his own trade), a tailor, a smith who forged chains 'to make fast ... prisoners', and a miller; a woollendraper with beehives in his garden and 'wax, honey and other things in the apple chamber'; a haberdasher who was also a mercer; a baker with seven children including twins, and a mercer with fourteen children including two sets of twins. There were plenty of children in the street for young William to play with: but children were treated as

small-scale adults and were expected to mature fast.

William's father, progressing from constable, was elected one of the fourteen principal burgesses, which entitled his children to free education at the King's New School – Edward VI's grammar school – in Stratford. From 1561 to 1563 he was one of the two chamberlains. They administered the borough property and revenues, and John Shakespeare did this so well that he continued as acting-chamberlain. Then, in 1565, he was elected one of the fourteen aldermen, entitling him to be called respectfully 'Master Shakespeare' and to wear a black gown. One more promotion awaited him. In 1568 he was chosen to be bailiff. Red-gowned, chief magistrate, he was holder of the highest office in Stratford, decreeing the weekly price of corn, sitting in the front pew in church – to which he was ceremoniously escorted – and occupying the best seat at plays in the Guildhall.

The first professional players known to have acted in Stratford came when he was bailiff. These two companies were the Queen's Men and the Earl of Worcester's Men. Shakespeare was not yet six

Halesworth, Suffolk: murder-victims of a land-hungry 'Papist': four children of widow Leeson. Top left, eldest son, falsely imprisoned to die c1612. Second son being clubbed to death; below, youngest son and daughter, slain. Right: their skeletons, found by farmer clearing muddy pond, are re-assembled by surgeon, bottom right.

when they came. A year or two earlier he would have started going to the petty school, attached to the grammar school, to work from his hornbook: a wooden bat framing a printed sheet of the alphabet and the Lord's Prayer, with a thin layer of transparent horn for protection. At school, he would learn by heart the catechism and some psalms and other religious pieces, and learn to read and write. (His mother – like many Elizabethans – was probably illiterate.) Some petty schools started their pupils on arithmetic. Girls were taught sewing by the elementary teacher's wife, while boys studied the hornbook.

After two years, Shakespeare would have moved up to the grammar school, where Latin was the subject to be mastered. The textbook was Lily's *Short Introduction to Grammar*, on which the school-

River Avon: a 'rank of osiers by the murmuring stream' (*As You Like It* 4.3.80) near the site of Luddington chapel where Shakespeare's marriage may have taken place. Elizabethan records are presumed burnt. The chapel was demolished before 1800. The Avon rises at Naseby, Northamptonshire; it joins the Severn at Tewkesbury.

boy William in *The Merry Wives of Windsor* is tested by his Welsh schoolmaster – 'What is the focative case, William?' (4.1.45). Lily's book led on to the syllabus of the second form: moral sentences from Latin authors, followed by Erasmus's *Cato* and Aesop in Latin culminating in Latin comedies by Terence and – sometimes – Plautus. There was a weekly session, in some schools, of acting out a scene: practical drama tethered to the script. Amateur theatricals sometimes took place in the town at Whitsun and young Shakespeare could have taken part in those, or perhaps in a Christmas mumming play, but at school there was no provision for any sort of English drama.

In the third form, Latin moral poems and eclogues entered the syllabus. Next, the boys studied Latin dialogues and colloquies, and learnt to speak Latin. All the boys of both Lower and Upper School worked in one room throughout the eight or nine hours of class each day. Shakespeare would have moved into the Upper School at the age of ten or eleven, leaving behind the usher (an assistant teacher) and coming into the master's class for rhetoric and some logic – with Cicero and Quintilian as two of the authors to be studied – and for poetry as written by Virgil and Horace, and by Ovid whose *Metamorphoses* he absorbed. He studied history from Sallust and Caesar and he learnt some Greek from the Greek New Testament. The very learned Ben Jonson claimed that Shakespeare only acquired 'small Latin and less Greek'. The most learned and witty people at Court, including some of the highest ladies in England who had been taught by private tutors in rich homes, knew Greek: but the teaching of it was very unusual in ordinary grammar schools. Shakespeare was fortunate in going to a good one. However, Harrison notes that 'there are great number of grammar schools throughout the realm, and those very liberally endowed for the better relief of poor scholars, so that there are not many corporate towns now under the Queen's dominion that have not one grammar school at the least, with a sufficient living for a master and usher appointed to the same'.

Most country grammar schools were inferior to Stratford's, where the master was well paid and held a university degree. When Shakespeare entered the Upper School his master was probably Simon Hunt, who may have later become a Jesuit priest. Hunt was succeeded in 1577 by Thomas Jenkins, a Londoner who had been to St John's College, Oxford, and had become a cleric. He had taught at Warwick, was married, seems to have had Catholic sympathies and may have been Shakespeare's principal schoolmaster at a time when the boy's family was having to adjust to new circumstances. John Shakespeare's prosperous days were over. In 1576 he stopped going to council meetings and he seems to have got into financial difficulties. These increased during the next few years, at a time when other Stratford families, too, felt the pinch of economic recession in the area. At Shakespeare's school, Jenkins found a master to take his place and resigned in 1579. John Cottom of Brasenose, Oxford, took over. Two years later he retired to Lancashire, a county where the old Roman Catholic religion, which was banned throughout England, was still devoutly – though unofficially – followed. Elizabethans were required by law to go to their parish churches and receive the bread and wine of Holy Communion in the Anglican rite; those who refused to do so were known as recusants. Cottom became a Catholic recusant.

How many years Shakespeare spent at school, and what he did as soon as he left, are not known. At the age of fifteen or so he would have needed to earn his own living. Possibly he became an apprentice, to learn a trade such as his father's of glover and whittawer. Apprenticeship was considered good training, appropriate to the sons of gentlemen and of 'persons of good quality'. The government and local authorities controlled prentices' wages, conditions of employment, hours of work, clothes and amusements. Twenty-one days in prison awaited the prentice who accepted too high a wage; ten days in prison and a fine of £5 awaited his master who had over-paid him.

The families that the Shakespeares knew included the Hathaways, and in November 1582 when Shakespeare was eighteen (Elizabethans did not come of age until they were twenty-one) he married Anne Hathaway, who was about eight years his senior. She came of yeoman stock. Her father, Richard Hathaway, who died before her wedding, farmed fifty to ninety acres and their home was a well-built farmhouse, now inaccurately called her 'cottage', about a mile west of Stratford church, at Hewlands Farm in Shottery. The Hathaways' house was built on stone foundations. Its walls were of timber frame, filled in with wattle and daub. Shottery is in the parish of Stratford, and in Anne's day the Forest of Arden (which is still indicated on modern road-signs) extended almost to the house, not far from the River Avon.

At the time of her wedding, Anne, who was three months pregnant, may have been living in the manor of Temple Grafton, on a ridgeway three and a half miles west of Shottery. Old thatched cottages remain in the straggling village, but the church of Temple Grafton, where the wedding perhaps took place, has been rebuilt. John Frith, the vicar who may have conducted the service, was intriguingly described, in a Puritan survey, as:

'. . . an old priest and unsound in religion, he can neither preach nor read well. His chiefest trade is to cure hawks that are hurt or diseased, for which purpose many do usually repair to him.'

It was not only in the stage forest setting of *As You Like It* – a setting that is both French Ardennes and English Arden – that a country vicar like Sir Oliver Martext might be found, but also in real Warwickshire.

Other buildings where the wedding may have been held were the chapel at Bishopton, a mere quarter of a mile north of Shottery, or the chapel at Luddington. Neither chapel remains.

When Anne's father made his will in 1581 seven of his children were living. He left them substantial legacies. Richard Hathaway seems to have married twice, and Anne may have been a child of his earlier marriage. His widow continued to live in Shottery for almost twenty years until her death in 1599. One of Anne's brothers continued to farm at Shottery: he outlived Shakespeare.

After William and Anne were married, they may have lived in Henley Street with his parents. Until 1597, when Shakespeare bought New Place, there is

The Holy Bible

THE HISTORY
of the
REFORMATION
of the
Church of England
The Second Part

Bp Ridley.   Bp Latimer.   Arch Bp Cranmer.

no evidence that he and Anne had a house of their own. When he came of age in 1585 he was the father of three children: Susanna, christened on 26 May 1583, and Hamnet and Judith – twins – named after the Shakespeares' lifelong friends, the Sadlers, and christened on 2 February 1584/5. The name Hamnet, otherwise spelt Hamlet, Amblet and Hamolet, was not uncommon in Stratford.

There has been much speculation about the next years of Shakespeare's life; but no irrefutable evidence has come to light as to where he was or what he was doing. Theorists have sent him off to spend those lost years of his early manhood as a heavy drinker in villages and hamlets around Stratford; or as a poacher of Sir Thomas Lucy's deer in the park of Charlecote, the grand Elizabethan manor house which is still to be seen four miles from Stratford, up the Avon; as an apprentice butcher, chafing against his commitment to seven

Opposite
Burnet's title-page (1679) glorifies the Church of Elizabeth I (top, with cornucopia) and attacks (right) Queen Mary's monk-abetted burning of Protestants, including Cranmer who also appears (left) at a table set according to the Second (1552) Prayer Book of Edward VI, kneeling. Elizabeth based her settlement largely on that Prayer Book.

Schoolboys and master at work, most of them writing. Equipment on the table includes rule, dividers, pointer, scroll, inkpots (one standing on a 'penner' or pen-case) and penknives. 'We write with goose quills. Cut off the feathers with a penknife, scrape away that which is rough.' (C Hollyband, schoolmaster.)

years of meat-cutting; as a holder of horses outside London theatres while the shows went on; as a country lawyer's assistant; as a soldier in the Low Countries; as a sailor, a barber-surgeon, a physician, a scrivener copying other men's documents . . . but the likeliest suggestion comes from John Aubrey, whose informant was the son of a fellow-actor of Shakespeare, that Shakespeare 'had been in his younger years a schoolmaster in the country'. To work as an usher a man did not need a degree, so Shakespeare would have qualified: and scholars have suggested a post for him in Lancashire, with a wealthy Catholic landowner as his employer and connections to help him to his career in the playhouse.

However, perhaps he found his own way in. By the time he was seventeen there had been at least nine visits to Stratford by players on tour, the troupes including the Earl of Leicester's, the Earl of

A performing 'green man' of the woods showers fireworks from his club. Concluding a bear-baiting in Southwark (1584), 'rockets and other fireworks came flying out of all corners' (von Wedel). And for Princess Elizabeth's wedding (1613), Whitehall fireworks showed St George delivering the Amazon Queen from Mango the Necromancer.

Warwick's, the Countess of Essex's and the Earl of Derby's. Outside Stratford, he could have seen medieval drama at its greatest, performed in Coventry. There, during his boyhood, the craft guilds were giving the last performances of their Mystery play cycle. He may, at the age of eleven, have joined the crowds at Kenilworth, a few miles north of Warwick and twelve miles from Stratford, to enjoy a wealth of pageants, shows, theatrical happenings and fireworks. These 'princely pleasures' of great splendour were presented before the Queen by the Earl of Leicester in 1575, when she stayed at his castle for nineteen July days. In 1587, when Shakespeare was twenty-three, at least five companies of players visited Stratford, more than in any other year. He may have taken his chance to join one of them and launch out on his theatrical career, perhaps going off with Leicester's or Warwick's troupe, or with the best of all in England at that time, and one in which there was a sudden vacancy, the Queen's Men. The corporation paid twenty shillings, its highest sum ever, to the Queen's Men for playing at Stratford in 1587. (A bench, probably broken by a crowded audience, had to be repaired.) Either before or after that performance, William

Knell, a player with the company, was killed on the night of 13 June at Thame in Oxfordshire by a sword-thrust in the throat. He had been a good actor, so his roles may have been a challenge to a novice. A year or so after Knell's death, his widow married John Heminges, who was to be a colleague and close friend of Shakespeare in London.

Travel for the Elizabethans was a rough, slow and dangerous business. Roads were unmetalled and only those built by the Romans were constructed on adequate foundations. The country was crossed by highways going in all directions and the chief centre on which they converged was London. The four biggest and busiest roads came from Berwick-on-Tweed, Chester, Bristol and Dover. Next in importance to London as road-centres were Coventry, Gloucester, Worcester, Chester and – to a lesser degree – Shrewsbury, Salisbury, Bristol and Exeter. Stratford was on the important London–Holyhead route where it crossed the Gloucester–Coventry road. Small towns were connected by mere tracks.

Because roads were inadequately built, the local terrain and the type of rock they were made on generally determined their condition. When Will

Opposite
Robert Dudley, Earl of Leicester (artist unknown, *c*1575), Elizabeth I's favourite to whom she granted the royal residence of Kenilworth in 1562. He deputized for her in the Great Hall at Charlecote in 1565, and dubbed Thomas Lucy a knight. James Burbage, a player among Leicester's Men in 1572, later built the Theatre.

Kemps nine daies vvonder.

Performed in a daunce from London to Norwich.

Containing the pleasure, paines and kinde entertainment
of *William Kemp* betweene *London* and that Citty
in his late Morrice.

Wherein is somewhat set downe worth note; to reprooue
the slaunders spred of him: many things merry,
nothing hurtfull.

Written by himselfe to satisfie his friends.

LONDON
Printed by *E. A.* for *Nicholas Ling*, **and are to be**
solde at his shop at the west doore of Saint
Paules Church. 1 6 o o.

Will Kemp morris dancing (bells on legs) 125 miles in nine days, with taborer/piper, from London to Norwich. To keep up, people had to dance or run: '. . . my pace was not for footmen'. At Norwich, the Mayor presented £5 and granted Kemp a life pension: forty shillings a year.

Kemp, after five years as the comedian of Shakespeare's troupe, danced from London to Norwich, his route took him across clay, gravel, chalk and sand. Monday 17 February 1600 was the fourth of his nine dancing days, and the stretch of road between Chelmsford and Braintree consisted of London clay with small gravelly patches: a recipe for ruts, stickiness and waterlogged holes. This stretch was the worst of his entire journey.

'This foul way I could find no ease in, thick woods being on either side of the lane: the lane likewise being full of deep holes, sometimes I skipped up to the waist. But . . . I had some mirth by an unlooked-for accident.

It was the custom of honest country fellows, my unknown friends, upon hearing of my pipe (which might well be heard in a still morning or evening a mile) to get up and bear me company a little way. In this foul way, two pretty plain youths watched me, and with their kindness somewhat hindered me. One, a fine light fellow, would still be before me, the other ever at my heels. At length, coming to a broad plash of water and mud, which could not be avoided, I fetched a rise, yet fell in over the ankles at the further end. My youth that followed me took his jump – and stuck fast in the midst, crying out to his companion:

"Come George, call ye this dancing! I'll go no further."

For indeed, he *could* go no further, till his fellow was fain to wade and help him out! I could not choose but laugh to see how like two frogs they laboured.'

That 'dirty way' should have been kept in good repair by local amateurs. A statute of 1555 had made every parish in England responsible for maintaining part of the highway, under the direction of two local men, Surveyors of Highways, elected annually. Their unpopular task was to muster a workforce and equip it. Rich people were to provide horses and workmen, and poor men were to labour on four consecutive eight-hour days, all in a national effort to improve roads that were in summer bone-shakingly rutted and rough and in winter often quagmires. Town roads, unpaved, were generally worse than modern farm-tracks. To mend a pothole or fill in a rut men used faggots and brushwood. Under a horse and rider these soon collapsed, endangering life and limb. Lacking drains and solid

Opposite
The White Tower; centre of the Tower of London, legendary founder Julius Caesar. In *Richard II* 5.1.2 the Queen laments the 'flint bosom' of 'Julius Caesar's ill-erected Tower'. One of the doomed boy princes, Edward, in *Richard III* 3.1.69 asks if Caesar built it. 'He did,' replies Buckingham, 'begin that place'.

Overleaf
Holy Trinity Church, Stratford-upon-Avon. In Shakespeare's day William Camden described Stratford as 'a handsome small market town'. Its parish church, on the bank of the River Avon, had been developed during many centuries. An avenue of lime trees leads to this handsome, spacious building.

Kenilworth Castle. Here in 1575 gentry, players, country folk combined in shows for Elizabeth I. 'Arion', tearing off his costume headpiece, declared himself 'no Arion, but honest Harry Goldingham, come to bid her Majestry welcome to Kenilworth'. Similarly, Shakespeare's 'Lion' (*A Midsummer Night's Dream* 5.1.221) announces he is Snug the joiner.

? G Gower: Lettice Knollys, Countess of Essex, whom the Earl of Leicester married at Kenilworth, 1578, when he had despaired of marrying the Queen. Elizabeth, appalled by news of his marriage, imprisoned him at Greenwich. In 1597, Lettice – widowed – sought reconciliation with Elizabeth, in vain. Lettice lived to be ninety-four.

foundations, roads were so decayed that, more than fifty years after the statute, frustrated travellers used to avoid the highways, break fences down, ride on the corn and cause great damage.

Travellers needed to beware of highwaymen, who might be lurking in woods or forests or waiting to strike in lonely country. Shooter's Hill near Blackheath, Gadshill near Rochester, Salisbury Plain and Newmarket Heath were notorious danger spots. Hanging was the punishment for highway robbery, and thieves knowingly risked it: not only in jest, like Falstaff, but in earnest, like Gamaliel Ratsey, from Lincolnshire, partner of Snell and Shorthose. That trio once robbed a group of no less than nine travellers. Ratsey used to wear a repulsive mask for his exploits, but to the poor he was endearingly generous. Snell and Shorthose betrayed him: he was hanged at Bedford in 1605.

By then fact had grown into fiction, and his imaginary exploits in a publication of that year, *Ratsey's Ghost*, include his meeting a troupe of players at a country inn and advising them, Hamlet-like, against 'striving to overdo and go beyond' themselves. 'Your poets', he says, 'take great pains to make your parts fit your mouths, though you gape never so wide.' Later, the players give a 'private play' before Ratsey and he pays them forty shillings, which delights them, 'for they scarce had twenty shillings audience at any time for a play in the country'. Next day on the highway he meets them with their wagon, robs them, and advises the country players to go to London: 'and when thou feelest thy purse well lined' after 'penny-sparing and long practice of playing', then 'buy thee some place in the country' for retirement, after 'growing weary of playing'. Eight years before *Ratsey's Ghost* was published, Shakespeare had prepared for a comparable retirement from theatrical work in London by buying Stratford's eminent house, New Place.

Travellers need to be vigilant, notes Harrison, especially at Christmas time. Then robbers abound because 'serving men and unthrifty gentlemen want money to play at the dice and cards'. But:

'. . . seldom shall you see any of my countrymen above eighteen or twenty years old to go without a dagger, at the least, at his back or by his side, although they be aged burgesses or magistrates . . . our nobility wear commonly swords or

rapiers with their daggers, as doth every common serving man also that followeth his lord and master. Some desperate cutters we have in like sort, which carry two daggers or two rapiers in a sheath always about them, wherewith in every drunken fray they are known to work much mischief.'

Such weapons are 'of great length' and their owners are 'commonly suspected . . . to be thieves and robbers', so 'the honest traveller' needs to ride with a case of pistols 'at his saddle-bow' to defend himself at a distance.

'Finally, no man travelleth by the way without his sword, or some such weapon . . . except the minister, who commonly weareth none at all, unless it be a hanger or dagger at his side.'

The traveller frequently met vagrants. Crowds of them, unemployed and wretchedly poor, were kept on the move, rejected by townsfolk and villagers scared of having to maintain them and of catching plague from them. Even the Queen could not avoid them. In 1581, when she rode out of London one evening towards the country town 'commonly called Islington', she found herself surrounded by a crowd of beggars. This frightening encounter with the riff-raff of her kingdom 'gave the Queen much disturbance'.

London was about 120 miles from Stratford, a journey of three days on horseback, whether by Banbury and Aylesbury or by the route that Shakespeare seems to have preferred: Shipston-on-Stour, Long Compton, Woodstock, Oxford, High Wycombe, Beaconsfield and Uxbridge, with the alternative of the Henley-on-Thames road between Oxford and Uxbridge. As for accommodation, according to the international traveller, Fynes Moryson:

'. . . the world affords not such inns as England hath, either for good and cheap entertainment . . . or for humble attendance . . . even in very poor villages. . . . For as soon as a passenger comes to an inn, the servants run to him, and one takes his horse and walks him till he be cold, then rubs him and gives him meat: yet I must say they are not much to be trusted in this last point, without the

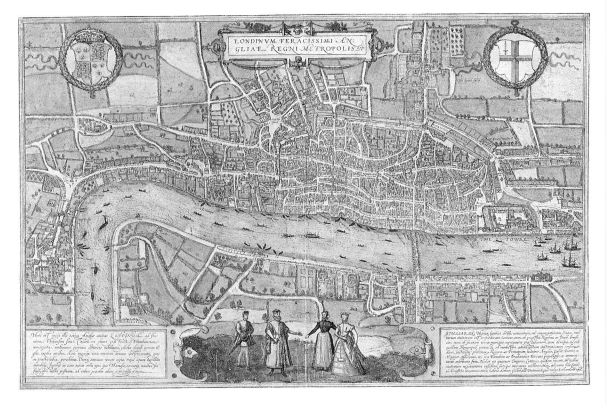

G Braun and F Hogenberg: a map of London in *Civitates Orbis Terrarum* (Cologne, 1572), probably from an anonymous map engraved on copper. St Paul's Cathedral is shown with its spire – destroyed in 1561. Structures for bear-baiting and bull-baiting appear in Southwark, but no playhouse was built there until the Rose in 1587.

eye of the master or his servant to oversee them. Another servant gives the passenger his private chamber and kindles his fire; the third pulls off his boots and makes them clean.

Then the host or hostess visits him: and if he will eat with the host, or at a common table with others, his meal will cost him sixpence, or in some places but fourpence (yet this course is ... not used by gentlemen). But if he will eat in his chamber, he commands what meat he will ... dressed as he best likes. ... While he eats, if he have company especially, he shall be offered music ... and if he be solitary the musicians will give him the good day with music in the morning. It is the custom, and no way disgraceful, to set up part of supper for his breakfast. ...

Lastly, a man cannot more freely command at home in his own house than he may do in his inn: and at parting, if he give some few pence to the chamberlain and ostler, they wish him a happy journey.'

Harrison gives other details of inn-life. Not only is table-linen 'commonly washed daily', but every guest:

'. . . is sure to lie in clean sheets, wherein no man hath been lodged since they came from the laundress, or out of the water in which they were last washed. If the traveller hath a horse, his bed doth cost him nothing, but if he go on foot he is sure to pay a penny for the same: but whether he be horseman or footman, if his chamber be once appointed he may carry the key with him. . . . If he lose ought whilst he abideth in the inn, the host is bound by a general custom to restore the damage, so that there is no greater security anywhere for travellers than in the greatest inns of England.'

However, Harrison reveals some of the tricks used

by crooked ostlers, chamberlains and tapsters in league with highwaymen. When a traveller dismounts at the inn, the ostler busily lowers his baggage from the saddle-bow and weighs it in his hand. If he fails to do that, then:

'... when the guest has taken up his chamber, the chamberlain that looketh to the making of the beds will be sure to remove it from the place where the owner hath set it, as if ... to set it more conveniently somewhere else, whereby he getteth an inkling whether it be money or other short wares, and thereof giveth warning to such odd guests as haunt the house and are of his confederacy, to the utter undoing of many an honest yeoman as he journeyeth.... The tapster ... doth mark his behaviour and what plenty of money he draweth when he payeth the shot, to

the like end: so that it shall be a hard matter to escape all their subtle practices. ...

In all our inns we have plenty of ale, beer and sundry kinds of wine; and ... some of them ... are able to lodge 200 or 300 persons and their horses at ease, and thereto with a very short warning make such provision of their diet as ... may seem to be incredible. Howbeit, of all in England there are no worse inns than in London, and yet many are there far better than the best that I have heard of in any foreign country. ...'

Harrison goes on to say that in some of our towns most used by travellers, twelve or sixteen inns are to be found. Each owner competes with the others in quality of entertainment, linen, bedding, 'service at the table', plate, 'strengths of drink, variety of wines, or well using of horses'. Gorgeous inn-signs, some costing as much as £30 or £40, are intended to attract 'good guests'.

Postboy riding with news.

2 LONDON: THE CITY AND ITS LIFE

The River Thames . . .

. . . on by London leads, which like a crescent lies,
Whose windows seem to mock the star-befreckled skies;
Besides her rising spires, so thick themselves that show,
As do the bristling reeds, within his banks that grow.
There sees his crowded wharfs and people-pestered shores,
His bosom overspread with shoals of labouring oars,
With that most costly bridge. . . .

MICHAEL DRAYTON: *Polyolbion*

At some date before 1592 Shakespeare came to London (perhaps on foot) leaving behind in Stratford his wife, his three children and his ageing parents. London was the thriving, growing, cultural centre of the kingdom. Men of ambition who were eager to make their fortune flocked to the capital city where the population was increasing to 100,000 or more. Here Shakespeare established himself as an actor and a playwright and here his poetry was published. Through London flowed the Thames, an essential highway for local boats and for ships sailing to and from the river mouth, about fifty miles distant. Hundreds of swans floated on the Thames at London and all sorts of fish abounded, many varieties nourished by refuse and sewage.

The Romans had built their city on the north bank. The wall which surrounded it was bow-shaped, curving north-west from above the Tower of London and then turning west and south, an arc of more than two miles down to a point on the Thames near the present Blackfriars Bridge; then the wall ran straight back again along the river-side. The landward section of the wall remained in Shakespeare's day, but the river-wall had disappeared, leaving Billingsgate, Dowgate and Queenhythe to show where entrance was gained from the river, which had no regular embankment. On the landward side, the gates were the Tower Postern, Aldgate, Bishopsgate, Moorgate, Cripplegate, Aldersgate, Newgate and Ludgate. In Tudor times the gate-houses were used as homes and prisons. The main highways into London were Oxford Road, from the west; the Great North Road, from the north; and the Old Kent Road, or Pilgrims' Road, from the south, bringing travellers from Kent and the Continent. To the east beside the river stood the forbidding, mighty Tower, on guard: 'a citadel' wrote Shakespeare's contemporary, John Stow:

'... to defend or command the city: a royal place for assemblies and treaties. A prison of estate, for the most dangerous offenders; the only place of coinage for all England at this time; the armoury for war-like provision; the treasury of the ornaments and jewels of the crown, and general conserver of the most records of the King's courts of justice at Westminster.'

To the west, at the far end of London, the establishment of the Inns of Court had led to the extension of the city westward along Fleet Street and Holborn. Temple Bar marked its new western limit, so the whole town was said to extend 'from Tower to Temple'. On the south side of the Strand – as its name implies, near the river's edge – stood the houses of the great nobles. Westminster was a separate city, and King Street (now called Parliament Street and Whitehall) led down to it from Charing Cross.

Outside the wall of the City of London there had been some building to the east and north, but most of London was ringed by separate villages: Bromley, Bow, Hackney, Islington and Kensington; and beyond them lay others: Barking, Tottenham, Highgate, Hornsey, Hampstead and Hammersmith. The Thames was spanned by one bridge only, London Bridge, connecting the city with the Surrey bank near the church of St Mary Overy (now Southwark Cathedral), the dwellings of the Bankside, the playhouses and Paris Garden.

Within the City, the old lines of many of the streets that Shakespeare knew remain even now, but almost all the buildings that he saw have been destroyed by the Great Fire, the Blitz or redevelopment. The streets in his time were lined with gabled and timber-framed buildings, distinguished by painted signs hung outside. Shopkeepers with their families and apprentices lived at their shops, and merchants lived in city mansions. In almost every important street, water was available from a conduit, or water-standard. Drainage was into individual cesspools; and street channels, strictly for rain and other excess water, ran into the Fleet Ditch or the Thames. Ninety-seven parish churches stood within the City area, the sound of their bells recalling life's brevity and seriousness.

At the heart of the City was one of England's largest cathedrals, St Paul's: to many Elizabethans, a worldly meeting place rather than a centre of worship. It stood where Wren's cathedral now

Opposite
The Great Hall, Gray's Inn, heart of this Inn of Court; burnt in World War II; restored. In Shakespeare's day, scene of students' meals, teaching sessions, oral exercises and mock trials; and of revels, dances, masques. Shallow fought 'with one Samson Stockfish, a fruiterer, behind Gray's Inn' (*Henry IV Pt ii*, 3.2.31).

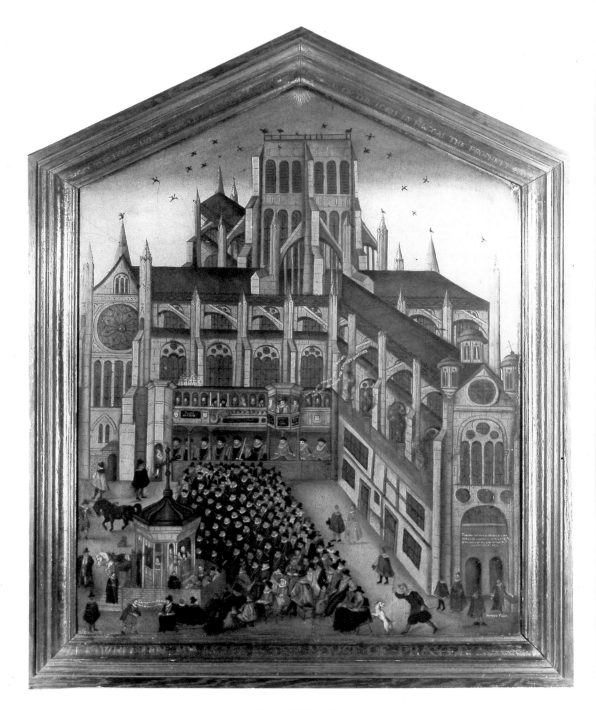

J Gipkym, 1616: dream of Henry Farley, who yearned
obsessively for swift repairs to St Paul's. Here, a bishop
preaches from Paul's Cross. Up in a two-storey building James I,
Queen Anne and Prince Charles listen. 'I have seen the Globe
burnt,' wrote Farley, envying its quick restoration.

stands, at the east end of Ludgate Hill and the west end of Cheapside. The cathedral in Shakespeare's time was a Gothic building, chiefly in the early English style, almost three hundred yards long and thirty-five yards wide. It had a central tower, but the steeple, built of wood covered by lead, had been destroyed in 1561 during a terrific storm – interpreted as God's vengeance on a sinful city – when the steeple caught fire from a lightning-flash. Molten lead flowed down in sheets of flame, the fire burned for four hours and the cathedral roof fell in. Restoration was partly funded by collections in every diocese. The Queen, the City and the Clergy contributed and St Paul's was re-roofed with timber and lead (in which soft metal Elizabethan sightseers and foreign tourists enjoyed carving their names or making their marks); but, much to the Queen's annoyance, the steeple remained in ruins for lack of cash. The City authorities promised to rebuild it, but they never did.

Earlier, the Roman Catholic Queen Mary, in an attempt to stop people degrading the house of God, had forbidden them to carry through St Paul's 'great vessels of ale or beer, great baskets full of bread, fish, flesh and fruit, fardels [bundles] of stuff and other gross wares' or to lead through the cathedral 'mules, horses and other beasts'. Elizabeth, too, tried to impose a reverent atmosphere; but in vain.

Almost as soon as the roof was repaired a man caused an affray in the cathedral: to punish him a pillory was set up in the churchyard and his ears were nailed to the post and then cut off. The Queen threatened to imprison anyone who, in the cathedral, even put out a hand to draw any weapon 'or shoot any hand-gun or dag [heavy pistol]'. No-one was to make any business deal there or carry any burden through the cathedral. Such threats had no effect. The cathedral thrived as a centre for all kinds of business, however low. Idlers, thieves, hungry paupers, cheats, pimps and every sort of crook lounged in the nave and the aisles. Advertisements – some of them disreputable – covered the walls. Robberies were plotted and sexual liaisons arranged. Anything could be bought, sold or hired. 'I bought him in Paul's', says Falstaff about his rascally man Bardolph in *Henry IV Pt ii* (1.2.51).

The noise, according to the seventeenth-century Bishop of Salisbury, John Earle, 'is a kind of still roar or a loud whisper', a mixture of 'walking, tongues and feet'. This crowded 'thieves' sanctuary ... is the ears' brothel, and satisfies their lust and itch ... for news'. And here, too, in this 'general mint of all famous lies' could be heard lessons read from the Bible, the voice of a great organ and an anthem of the singing boys.

St Paul's churchyard was surrounded by shops and open stalls, most of them booksellers', although trunk-makers were also found here. This was the centre of England's book trade. Apart from Oxford and Cambridge, London was the only place where printing was allowed, and the crowds which flocked in from the provinces four times a year for the law-terms included many book-buyers. 'What lack you, gentleman?' cries the apprentice in a tract by Samuel Rowlands: 'See a new book come forth, sir! Buy a new book, sir!' The sound was familiar in the churchyard, for this was the place to come not only to inspect large, handsome volumes, such as Raphael Holinshed's *Chronicles* (a popular history book in which Shakespeare found material for *Macbeth*, as well as for his plays about English history) but also to thumb through trivial, little, unbound books which cost only a few pence: almanacs, pamphlets, collections of jokes and individual plays. It was in this trashy format – in size a quarter of a sheet and so called 'quarto' – that *Romeo and Juliet*, *Hamlet* and *King Lear* were first available to readers. The establishment did not think that plays had literary worth, but admired poetry. Ben Jonson wrote to the Earl of Salisbury in 1605, after objections to lines which insulted the Scots in the comedy *Eastward Ho!* had landed its authors in jail:

'I am here (my most honoured Lord) unexamined and unheard, committed to a vile prison, and (with me) a gentleman (whose name may perhaps have come to your Lordship) one Mr George Chapman, a learned and honest man. The cause (would I could name some worthier) though I wish we had known none worthy our imprisonment, is a (the word irks me that our fortunes hath necessitated us to so despised a course) a play, my Lord.'

The first collected edition of works by an English dramatist was not published until 1616, the year of Shakespeare's death, when Jonson's own collected

After A van Blyenberch: Ben Jonson, who wrote after Shakespeare's death: 'I loved the man, and do honour his memory (on this side idolatry) as much as any. He . . . had an excellent fancy; brave notions, and gentle expressions' but, Jonson regretted, lacked control, especially over 'his wit'.

Cheapside, the broadest street in the City of London, was the most convenient for processions. Gabled buildings from Shakespeare's day appear in this later view of West Cheap seen from the south-west, when Marie de Medici, Charles I's mother-in-law, visited London. Right: Eleanor Cross and – beyond that – the Standard.

works appeared. Such a book of sheets of full-size paper folded only once is known as a 'folio' volume. It is large and impressive. Plays, which the establishment still regarded as trivial, ephemeral, inferior pieces of writing (although their authors could earn a lot of money from them), were not expected to be so grandly conveyed to the public. Jonson valued drama, and his Folio was revolutionary. It paved the way for Shakespeare's collected plays: 'the First Folio', as it is called, published seven years later. Publisher-booksellers were members of the Stationers' Company. In the kitchen of Stationers' Hall, to the west of the Cathedral, were burnt those books that the Bishop of London declared illegal.

A little gate led from St Paul's churchyard to Cheapside, the old market place of London, scene of jousts, executions and city pageants, for all of which the stalls were cleared away. Cheapside was the broadest street in London and it was used as a promenade by fashionable people. Off it ran streets with names that showed what was for sale: on the south side, Bread Street and Friday Street (for fish); on the north side, Wood Street, Milk Street, Honey Lane and Ironmonger Lane. There were four structures down the centre of Cheapside. At the west end stood the little or pissing conduit. Next, opposite Wood Street, was the elaborate Eleanor Cross adorned with statues, a famous landmark often restored and regilded in Tudor times. Here proclamations were usually made. The statues were repeatedly mutilated: vandalism in keeping with Puritan dislike of images of the Virgin and Saints. The Resurrection group on the Cross was replaced by Diana, with Thames water 'purling from her naked breast', writes Stow, antiquary and chronicler of London. A little further east, opposite the end of Milk Street, was the Standard. Often the scene of executions, it was a square pillar with a conduit and

The vpright man
Nicolas Blunt.

The counterfet Cranke.
Nicolas Geninges.

These two pictures, liuely set out,
One bodie and soule, God send him more grace:
This monsterous dissembler, a Cranke all about.
Vncomly coueting, of each to imbrace,
Money or wares, as he made his race,
And sometyme a Mariner, and a seruingman:
Or els an artificer, as he would faine that.
Such shyftes he vsed, being well tryed,
Abandoning labour, till he was espied:
Conding punishment, for his dissimulation,
He surely receaued with much exclamation.

Nicholas Jennings, versatile beggar. Right: disguised as an epileptic, a filthy cloth on his head, his beard trussed up. (Compare Edgar in *King Lear* Quarto Sc 11.) Sometimes Jennings dressed to beg as a sailor, servant or – left – gentleman, beard showing. He was pilloried, both in degrading and handsome clothes, in Cheapside.

statues, and, above, an image of Fame. At the east end of Cheapside, adjoining the Poultry, was the Great Conduit, its water supplied by lead pipes from Paddington. In civic pageantry, the conduits were used as platforms to speak from and as a basis for spectacle.

Other sights here were grim: soldiers, conscripted to fight in the Low Countries, were punished for mutiny by being tied to carts and flogged through Cheapside. Here a student was whipped for libel and had his ears cut off; and another soldier, on his way to life imprisonment, was branded in the face. London was a city of contrasts. Away from the wealth of Cheapside, in the Middlesex suburbs (according to the Privy Council in 1596) 'great number of dissolute, loose and insolent people' lived in 'base tenements' and noisome 'poor cottages and habitations of beggars and people without trade: stables, inns, alehouses, taverns, garden-houses converted to dwellings, ordinaries [eating places], dicing-houses, bowling-alleys and brothel-houses'. Wisely, as Fynes Moryson notes, 'in great cities it is forbidden to kill kites and ravens, because they devour the filth of the streets: England hath very great plenty of sea and river filth' too.

When Shakespeare walked along the south side of Cheapside from the west end he would first pass Old Change, where bullion was received for coining; then the Nag's Head Inn; the Mermaid, at the west corner of Bread Street; and Goldsmiths' Row, described by Stow as:

'... the most beautiful frame of fair houses and shops that be within the walls of London or elsewhere in England.... It containeth ... ten fair dwelling houses and fourteen shops, all in one frame uniformly builded four storeys high, beautified towards the street with the Goldsmiths' Arms and the likeness of woodmen ... riding on monstrous beasts: all ... cast in lead, richly painted over and gilt.'

Then Shakespeare would have come to Bow Church, forty feet back from the street, with a stone house in front of it. When Bow-bell rang the curfew the apprentices' day's work ended. Beyond the church were shops, mostly drapers' and mercers' shining with coloured silks. On the north side of Cheapside, opposite the Great Conduit, stood the Mercers' Chapel and Hall. All sorts of provisions were for sale in the enormous street-market of Cheapside. There were smelts on the fish-stalls, doves, custards, apricots, pies: and, busy among the crowds that thronged round the trestle-tables, pickpockets abounded. The City lock-ups were in Wood Street and in Poultry, close to this likely source of trouble. Potential rioters were all around: but when the rallying cry of 'Clubs!' gave the alarm, prentices would rush from the shops and gather, armed, to attack troublemakers.

London, dominated by the Tower, is of great importance in Shakespeare's history plays. Part of each of them is set in London. In his other plays, apart from *The Merry Wives of Windsor*, he does not even mention London, although there are references to features that might belong there, such as 'the bells of St Bennet' (a form of the name 'Benedick') mentioned by Feste in *Twelfth Night* (5.1.35). (Several London churches were dedicated to St Bennet; perhaps this was the one on the north side of Thames Street, above Paul's Wharf.) Other dramatists of Shakespeare's day, such as Jonson,

Massinger, Beaumont and Fletcher, Middleton, Dekker and Nashe, not only set many of their comic scenes in London, but introduced a wealth of detail: streets, churches and taverns are named and they create a realistic map of the city. Of Shakespeare's comedies, *The Merry Wives of Windsor* is the only one with a detailed English setting.

The importance of London to the kingdom is analysed by Stow, most devoted of Londoners. The City provides a centre for foreign trade, thanks to the Thames, which is also 'the chief maker of mariners and nurse of our navy: and ships (as men know) be the wooden walls for defence of our realm'. The counties of Norfolk, Suffolk, Essex, Kent and Sussex 'as they lie in the face of our most puissant neighbour' (France) depended for their greatest strength and richness on 'the nearness which they have to London'. The poor 'from each quarter of the realm' flocked to London to be relieved, because 'scarcely any other town or shire looks after those who are in want'. (No-one was to prevent the poverty of Stow's own old age in London, where he lived for eighty years.) The beauty of London, he continues, 'is an ornament to the realm', and the city's great wealth and the multitude of her citizens terrified other countries. London was the one place in the kingdom that could swiftly raise a strong army and provide the monarch with ready money. Not only did Londoners pay a kind of capital levy known as 'subsidy' at a higher rate than other Englishmen, but many Londoners, for the sake of their reputations, 'refuse not to be rated above their ability'. (More often, Londoners were rated *below* their ability.)

Stow's enthusiasm for foreign trade was not shared by those who believed, as did the author of a pamphlet published in 1581, that England should rely on its own products and not pay 'inestimable treasure' for foreign trifles that it did not need or could make for itself:

'I mean as well looking-glasses as drinking, and also to glaze windows; dials, tables, cards, balls, puppets, penners [pen-cases] ink-horns, toothpicks, gloves, knives, daggers, ouches [ornaments or jewels], brooches ... buttons of silk and silver, earthen pots, pins and points [tagged laces, worn instead of buttons], hawks' bells, paper both white and brown....'

Drawing by (?) H Peacham (?) 1595: Shakespeare's *Titus Andronicus* 1.1. Tamora pleads with Titus for the life of her (off-stage) son, Alarbus. Her two other sons kneel with her. Aaron the Moor stands, sword in hand. This drawing does not accurately show any one moment in the play. Costumes vary in style.

The pamphlet reveals that men would only buy gloves made in France or Spain, even if England did export the skins that they were made of; and would only buy the rough cloth called 'kersey' if it was dyed in Flanders, although it was made of England's own wool; and only buy a dagger, sword or knife if it was 'of Spanish making'. Less than forty years before, there were not a dozen haberdashers in all London selling 'French or Milan caps, glasses, knives, daggers, swords, girdles and such things' but 'now from the town to Westminster along, every street is full of them and their shops glitters and shines of glasses as well drinking as looking' with 'gay daggers, knives, swords and girdles . . . able to make any temperate man to gaze on them, and to buy somewhat, though it serve to no purpose necessary'.

Young people responded to the enticing imports. London prentices, although they were kept hard at work from morning till night, became so luxurious in their dress and so sophisticated in their recreations, that in 1582 the Common Council clamped down. Apprentices' doublets were only to be 'made of canvas, fustian [a coarse cloth], sack-cloth, English leather or woollen cloth . . . without being enriched with any manner of gold, silver or silk'. Apprentices should wear 'little breeches of the same stuff as the doublets' and 'hose or stockings . . . white, blue or russet' but 'no sword, dagger or other weapon, but a knife'. Four years earlier this disarmament would have exposed London prentices to extreme violence, because the fashion was for men to fight with a rapier in one hand and a dagger in the other, a combination of weapons so deadly that it came to be a deterrent to large-scale brawls. These were common

> '. . . until the fight of rapier and dagger took place . . . it was usual to have frays, fights and quarrels, upon the Sundays and holidays: sometimes twenty, thirty and forty swords and bucklers, half against half, as well by quarrels of appointment as by chance.'

Laertes used rapier and dagger, as Osric says in *Hamlet* (5.2.110). The prentice was also forbidden, by the new order, to wear 'a ring, jewel of gold, nor silver, nor silk in any part of his apparel', or to go to any dancing, fencing or 'musical schools'.

It was taken for granted that he should not be at any theatre. Plays were acted in the afternoons and to attend them he would need to miss his work. Nevertheless, apprentices did slip along with other theatre-goers. All sorts of people, including courtiers, lawyers, tinkers, carters, waiting-women, captains, students, man-servants and foreign visitors, went to the open-air playhouses on weekdays. By mid-1593 London audiences may already have sampled Shakespeare's earliest history, comedy and tragedy. Perhaps there had been performances of all three parts of *Henry VI*, *Two Gentlemen of Verona* and *The Taming of the Shrew*, as well as plays more obviously appropriate to a schoolmaster: *The Comedy of Errors*, derived from Plautus, and *Titus Andronicus*, influenced by Ovid and Seneca. Which of the acting companies then performed Shakespeare's early plays is not known.

19

The picture here set down
within this letter. T:
A right doth shew the forme
of Tharlton vnto the shap

When hee in pleasaunt wise
the Counterset expreste
of Clowne w cote of russet :
and sturtups w y reste; hew.

Whoe merry many made
when he appeard in sight
The graue and wise as well as
at him did take delight; (rud.

The partie nowe is gone,
and closlie clad in claye,
Of all the Iesters in the land,
he bare the praise awaie.

Now hath he plaid his pte
and sure he is of this
If he in Christe did die to liue
with him in lasting blis.

J Scottowe: Richard Tarlton (? 1588, when this famous jester died). Wearing his russet suit and buttoned cap, Tarlton blows his pipe, taps his tabor. In the provinces, 'people began exceedingly to laugh when Tarlton' – playing with the Queen's Men – 'first peeped out his head' (Nashe). Taverns were named after him.

In the northern suburbs of London stood James Burbage's purpose-built playhouse, the first in England. It was built in the Middlesex parish of St Leonard's, Shoreditch. Called 'the Theatre', it had opened in 1576; and in the following year a building for physical sports – a game-house – opened in the Curtain Close, only about 200 yards to the south of the Theatre. This newer building, called 'the Curtain' because of its location, was later used as a theatre. A multitude of playgoers flocked to the 'sumptuous theatre houses, a continual monument to London's prodigality and folly', as the outraged preacher Thomas White described them in a sermon at Paul's Cross, the open-air pulpit beside the Cathedral. Such fiery sermons were well attended, but family life had its gentler pieties. Sons of the house received their father's blessing before going off to school and, later in the day, said grace at the family table.

Two spheres of influence met in the creation of the 'theatre houses': the design of the auditorium developed from the arena-like game-houses, used for bear-baiting and bull-baiting, and the design of the stage developed from arrangements in Tudor banqueting halls, where players were used to acting indoors. Plays were also acted at London inns. Particular companies had specific inns assigned to them as official winter quarters. There is no evidence that the inn-yards were roofed, so presumably halls or galleries inside the inns were used as theatres. The Queen's Men were linked with the Bull, Bishopsgate Street; the Earl of Worcester's Men with the Boar's Head in Whitechapel; and the Lord Chamberlain's Men with the Cross Keys in Gracechurch Street. Performances were also given at the Bel Savage on Ludgate Hill, the Bell in Gracechurch Street, and the Red Lion in Whitechapel.

South of the river, where roads from Camberwell and Clapham merged towards Southwark, stood a playhouse known as Newington Butts. Plays were acted there in 1580, but this theatre was too far out, takings were poor, and it did not thrive. In contrast, the Rose playhouse, built in Southwark on the site of a former rose garden, drew crowds of theatre-goers and flourished. It was in the area of the brothels – 'stews' – and it stood at the corner of Rose Alley and Maiden Lane. Lord Strange's Men, led by Edward Alleyn, the great tragic actor of the age, opened in 1592 at the Rose, of which Philip Henslowe was the landlord. Sussex's Men acted *Titus Andronicus* there during a short season in 1594. Further west on the Bankside, near the moorings of the royal barge, Francis Langley built the Swan in the Manor of Paris Garden, nearly 150 yards south of the stairs where water taxis – the boats called 'wherries' – could be hired. The Earl of Pembroke's Men played at the Swan. Johannes de Witt, a Dutch

Copy of J de Witt's sketch of the new, multi-purpose Swan playhouse, Bankside, c1596. In this galleried, circular theatre – a 'wooden O' (*Henry V* Prologue 13) – suitable for sporting shows, a thrust stage is erected: spectators above, trumpeter aloft, flag on top: no inner stage. Audience omitted: but perhaps players are rehearsing.

visitor, was there – probably in 1597 – and he drew the inside of the playhouse and wrote notes:

'There are four amphitheatres in London of notable beauty.... In each of them a different play is daily exhibited to the populace. The two more magnificent ... are called the Rose and Swan. The two others are outside the city towards the north on the highway ... called ... Bishopsgate. There is also a fifth, but of dissimilar structure, devoted to the baiting of beasts.... Of all the theatres, however, the largest and the most magnificent is ... the Swan theatre: for it accommodates in its seats three thousand persons, and is ... supported by wooden columns painted in such excellent imitation of marble that it is able to deceive even the most cunning.'

The playhouses that de Witt mentions were all built before the Globe, where much of Shakespeare's drama was performed. Shakespeare would have been familiar with those earlier theatres and their work.

A peep into a playhouse is provided by Thomas Dekker (who wrote more than fifty plays) in his satirical primer for a simpleton – a dupe or 'gull' – who wants to seem a man of the world: *The Gull's Hornbook*. The gull arrives at the playhouse in the afternoon, walks straight onto the stage and pays the maximum price to be allowed to sit there, on a hired stool, among the fashionable spectators who want to show off. Like them he puffs a pipe, utters loud critical remarks and makes 'the dear acquaintance of the boys' who are acting. By sitting on the stage you may – Dekker assures the gull – 'at any

Lambeth Palace, London residence of the Archbishop of Canterbury: the Great Hall, restored in the seventeenth century, with oak hammer-beam roof. Wycliffe's followers are said to have been imprisoned in Lollards' Tower beside the quay. In Shakespeare's time, Lambeth Marsh nearby was notorious for its thieves and prostitutes.

time know what particular part any of the infants present, get your match lighted, examine the play-suit's lace, and perhaps win wagers upon laying ''tis copper' and not real gold. But make sure that there are plenty of people to see you. At the Swan there might be De Witt's full house of 3,000 seated spectators, plus the 'groundlings' who stood in front of them. (Today, London's Barbican Theatre seats 1,162, and the National Theatre's Olivier auditorium seats 1,170.)

Do not arrive 'on stage (especially at a new play)

until the quaking' speaker of the 'prologue hath (by rubbing) got colour into his cheeks and is ready to give the trumpets their cue, that he's upon point to enter'. Then you should mount the stage with your 'three-footed stool in one hand', your sixpence for hiring it in the other and place yourself 'on the very rushes where the comedy is to dance' so that everyone can see what fashionable clothes you are wearing. Then 'fall to cards', but at the 'third sound' of the trumpet 'throw the cards (having first torn four or five of them) round about the stage'. Stay put, even though the groundlings, who have paid only one penny to stand in the open yard between the stage and the galleries, 'hoot at you, hiss at you, spit at you, yea, throw dirt even in your teeth'.

But if the playwright 'hath either epigrammed you' in his script or mocked 'your feather, or your red beard, or your little legs, etc. on the stage' you must 'rise with a screwed and discontented face from your stool to be gone'.

Outrage, not mockery, is however the tone of a letter about plays from the Lord Mayor to the Archbishop of Canterbury, written in the winter of 1591. Secular as well as spiritual reasons prompt the Lord Mayor to ask for the Archbishop's 'help for the reforming and banishing of so great evil' because:

'... by the daily and disorderly exercise of ... players and playing houses erected within this city, the youth thereof is greatly corrupted and their manners infected ... by reason of the wanton and profane devices represented on the stages ... apprentices and servants withdrawn from their works ... to the great hindrance of the trades and traders. ... To which places also do usually resort great numbers of light and lewd-disposed persons as harlots, cutpurses, cozeners, pilferers and suchlike.'

Some members of the ill-reputed acting profession re-grouped in June 1594, after performing at the unsuccessful Newington Butts. One of the companies involved was the Lord Admiral's. The other, of which Shakespeare was a member, was the Lord Chamberlain's. Shakespeare was to stay with it for the rest of his career both as an actor and as a dramatist.

A family meal.

Opposite Above
Deer at Charlecote Park. Shakespeare shows, from experience of hunting (Jonson learnt from books) how deer behave. The herd expels a wounded deer: so Lavinia, mutilated, is described

'straying in the park,
Seeking to hide herself, as doth the deer
That hath received some unrecuring [incurable] wound'.
(*Titus Andronicus* 3.1.88)

Below

William Smith: London viewed from the south, 1588. A lively, decorative drawing, inaccurate in its presentation of Bankside, where the Rose playhouse already stood. Smith, a herald, included the arms of Queen Elizabeth and of the City of London. Later, he was appointed one of the four pursuivants, Rouge Dragon.

In Shakespeare's boyhood, his father applied for a grant of arms, did not pursue it, but renewed his application in 1596. Shakespeare saw it through. A herald's note, 1602, derides 'Shakespeare ye player'. Smith scorned Shakespeare's fellow-actors, Augustine Phillips and Thomas Pope, for falsely claiming heraldic badges of gentility.

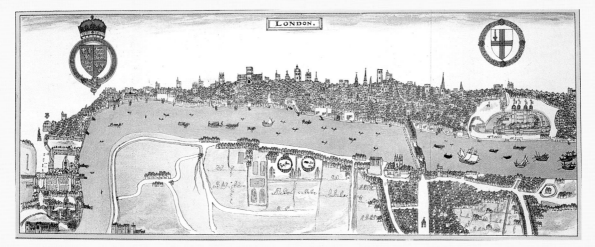

Previous page
The difficulty of Cotswold travel is stressed in *Richard II* 2.3.1:

'Bolingbroke:
    How far is it, my lord, to Berkeley now?
Northumberland:
    Believe me, noble lord,
    I am a stranger here in Gloucestershire,
    These high wild hills and rough uneven ways
    Draws out our miles and makes them wearisome. . . .'

A fête at Bermondsey, south of the Thames, *c*1570, by Hoefnagel. Top left: a maypole, the river, the Tower and Wapping. Right: aristocrats in black – the lady might be Elizabeth I or possibly a bride – move from church to feast. People carrying large cakes precede them, with fiddlers and a festive gentleman. Villagers dance.

A prospect of London and the Thames from above Greenwich (oil, Flemish School *c*1620–30). The easiest Kent-London route was via Greenwich. Lower right: Placentia, where Elizabeth I signed Mary Queen of Scots's death warrant. Bonfires in the park celebrated her execution. In *Henry VIII* 1.2.189, treason at Greenwich is reported to the king.

3 THE LORD CHAMBERLAIN'S MEN ON TOUR

MARLBOROUGH

Alas, 'tis true, I have gone here and there
And made myself a motley to the view . . .

Sonnet 110

The River Kennet, Marlborough. Shakespeare, knowledgeable about birds, describes the swan
saving its 'downy cygnets' by 'Keeping them prisoner underneath his wings' (*Henry VI Pt i*,
5.5.12). Shakespeare makes poignant use of the legend that swans die singing, in Emilia's
declaration: 'I will play the swan, And die in music' (*Othello* 5.2.254–5)

Shakespeare was thirty when the newly constituted troupe of actors of which he was a member went on tour in the west country. They were known as the Lord Chamberlain's Men because of the post of their patron, old Henry Carey, first Baron Hunsdon. As Lord Chamberlain of the royal household he was a most important public figure. His duties brought him close to the Queen and included responsibility for all entertainments at court. Sometimes he put his white staff of office to practical use in controlling throngs of courtiers at plays and masques. The Queen's first cousin, and much favoured by her, he had championed the players in their conflicts with civic authorities. In 1594, aged about seventy, he was living in Somerset House, which the Queen owned, beside the Thames. On that site the present Somerset House has replaced Elizabeth I's Tudor palace, and the National Theatre has been built opposite it, on the South Bank: so theatrical history spans the Thames.

On tour in the west country, about September 1594, the Lord Chamberlain's Men played in the Wiltshire market town of Marlborough, where nearly fifty visits in forty years, from fifteen companies of players, are recorded. Evidence for this, like most of the evidence for theatrical tours in Elizabethan and Jacobean times, is to be found in local chamberlains' accounts, statements of public money paid out by town mayors. Musicians, jugglers, tumblers, bear-wards, swordplayers and wrestlers, as well as actors, appear among the recipients. Theatrical entries usually record nothing more than a date, the name of the troupe, the cash paid to them, and sometimes refreshments such as wine and sugar. The dates are generally difficult to interpret. Account books rarely mention play titles or actors' names: so it is not surprising that the Marlborough records fail to do so.

The sum paid to the Chamberlain's Men on this occasion was two shillings and eightpence. Marlborough payments to players in the 1590s vary between that sum and twenty shillings, but in addition to civic payment players were able to collect from the public and to give more than the single show that features in account books. The number of performances given is not known. Despite the low civic fee recorded in 1594, the Chamberlain's Men evidently thought that Marlborough was a town worth playing in and they returned in December 1597, when they were paid six shillings and fourpence. After the death of Queen Elizabeth in 1603, her successor, King James I, brought the best acting companies directly under royal patronage: so the Chamberlain's Men had been re-named the King's Men by the time they played in Marlborough again in 1606 (for twenty-three shillings and fourpence) and in 1608 (for twenty shillings).

In the chamberlains' accounts at Marlborough and elsewhere, payment is only recorded for the one official performance, before the mayor and aldermen, generally in the Guildhall, financed by the local council. On the following days or nights, if further performances were given by the visiting company, no players – unless they had to – would undertake the upheaval of moving their stage, costumes and equipment out of the Guildhall to another venue, such as an inn or a church in the same town. Takings at any performance after the official one would be the troupe's own responsibility: an admission charge, with or without a collection.

Some fifty-five years before the Chamberlain's Men first played in Marlborough, Leland came to the town from Ramsbury 'by hilly ground', noting 'good corn and wood' as he came. Marlborough, he writes, 'standeth on an hill from east down to a vale by west', the Kennet Valley, with 'St Mary's parish church by the market place' at the east end of the High Street, another church, 'St Peter's at the bottom of the town by west', and beyond that a remnant of the castle where King John had held court: 'The dungeon half standeth'. It has all gone now.

The Guildhall, on the north side of the High Street, where the Chamberlain's Men first performed in Marlborough, has vanished too. The Castle and Ball Hotel now stands near the site of it. In 1601, during a visit by a company of players not named in the records, but perhaps the Queen's, the Guildhall windows and a table were broken. All the windows had to be reglazed (ten shillings and

Opposite
May-game figures or morris dancers, Betley Window
*c*1620. Possibly, top left: Jester, Spaniard, Moor; second row: Gentleman, maypole, Minstrel; third: Peasant, King of May (juggler's dagger in cheeks; hobby-horse holds gourd for collection), Lover; bottom: Fool, Queen of May (she and King appear in *Two Noble Kinsmen*, 3.5.138), Friar.

A MERY MAY

twopence) and the table repaired (ten shillings), the players – who were paid twenty shillings for their performance – duly contributing three shillings. Considering the rowdiness of audiences at that time and the exciting political and social themes, such as regicide, war and rebellion, presented in Elizabethan drama, it is not surprising that windows and furniture were sometimes broken. At Marlborough, which the Lord Chamberlain himself visited in 1602, the borough, perhaps in response to the damage done in the previous year, put a stop to all 'plays and interludes' in the Guildhall.

When players came to Marlborough after the passing of that bylaw, they almost certainly performed next door to the Guildhall at the White Hart, a large inn on the site now partly occupied by the Tudor Tearooms. There were three or four storeys and at least sixteen chambers, including the Great Chamber, the King's Chamber, the Queen's Chamber and the Chapel Chamber. Indoor performances would presumably have been staged in the hall. Out of doors there was a yard in the shape of a horseshoe, and beyond that a garden with three arbours. So there was scope for open-air performances at a little distance from the noisy High Street and the stables, though the coming and going of horses must have been distracting. The area is now called Russell Square.

Shows with music would have appealed to at least one Marlborough family, that of William Richards. In 1591, he left to his son, by will, 'my best treble violin and the case of the same and the bass viol next to the best', and to his son-in-law 'my best bass viol and my new treble violin'. To his elder son, Richards left his cross-bow. With Savernake Forest just beyond the River Kennet and only a twenty-minute walk from the town, the temptation to poach must have been strong. Many Elizabethans, if they had the chance, would have delighted in being – as the Earl of Leicester put it – 'altogether hunters, doing nothing but ride about from bush to bush with a cross-bow about their necks' in pursuit of deer. In 1621 the Archbishop of Canterbury, George Abbot, when shooting his cross-bow at a buck, accidentally killed a gamekeeper. Arrows for the cross-bow were stout and short, and they were used not only by men but by women too, as can be seen in *Love's Labour's Lost* (4.1.1–29), in which a forester advises the Princess where to stand during

the hunt so that she can 'make the fairest shoot' (line 10). Queen Elizabeth herself was a notable huntress who even in her last years was 'excellently disposed to hunting, for every second day' at Oatlands, her palace in Surrey, she was on horseback and continued 'the sport long'.

In Savernake Forest there is still a deer-park. However, patriotism rather than hunting may have made archery important to Marlborough men like William Richards. In his day, despite the superiority of fire-arms, the bow was still an official weapon for the country's defence and Henry VIII and Elizabeth encouraged archery by statute. The need for this is shown when French troops (according to Harrison) during a pause in an open skirmish, 'turn up their tails and cry' – sarcastically – 'Shoot, English!' Harrison comments on this insult:

'But if some of our Englishmen now lived that served King Edward III in his wars with France, the breech of such a varlet should have been nailed to his bum with one arrow, and another feathered in his bowels, before he should have turned about to see who shot the first.'

However, Englishmen now 'wax skilful in sundry other points, as in shooting ... the caliver and handling of the pike'.

Shakespeare's father is associated with Marlborough through a law-suit in the Court of Common Pleas. In 1599 John Shakespeare, two years before his death, sued John Walford (who had already served Marlborough twice as Chamberlain and twice as Mayor) for £21. This was an alleged debt for twenty-one tods of wool, bought more than thirty years earlier. Walford denied any debt to John Shakespeare and declared that he could prove his case in court. The outcome is unknown, nor is there any documentary proof that either John or William Shakespeare ever visited Marlborough.

In Elizabethan times there were no local journalists to review plays or write gossip about 'showbiz' people from London; no provincial diarists jotting down their impressions of important actors; no stage-struck clerks making sure that, whenever Shakespeare acted, he got a mention in the margin of notes recording payment to the company he performed with. His name simply does not feature – or, if it does, no-one has found it – in any document

Elizabeth receiving a huntsman's report, to help her decide which hart to hunt. The huntsman presents fewmets (droppings), details of which reveal the hart's condition.
'From out my horn, my fewmets first I draw
And these present on leaves, by hunter's law . . .
The moistness shows what venison he bears.'
(G Turberville)

about players in the provinces. So we can only speculate as to whether he went on tour with his company.

There are strong arguments for his having done so. He was a supporting actor whose presence

Richard Burbage (*c*1567–1619) of Shoreditch: star player of Chamberlain's/King's Men.

'He's gone, and . . . what a world are dead. . . .
No more young Hamlet, old Hieronymo:
King Lear, the grievèd Moor, and more beside,
That lived in him, have now for ever died'.
                                                                (? J. Fletcher)

An epitaph tersely says: 'Exit Burbage'.

would improve performances and whose absence would inconvenience and disappoint his colleagues. He depended on the company for his livelihood: and money interested him. There were long periods when no-one could act in London, and although provincial dates were less lucrative than playing to the London public, and far less lucrative than playing at Court, they did bring in some income. Perhaps he would want to increase it by doing his share of the arduous work. His company was closely knit: important members of the troupe, such as he was, would value the enhancement of fellowship through experiences shared in varied places among different people.

On the other hand, it can be argued that if Shakespeare was, as Aubrey tells us, 'wont to go to his native country once a year', some useful opportunities for solo trips to Stratford may have occurred when the company went elsewhere on tour. Provincial audiences were less important than London ones. So, while his colleagues loaded their wagon with costumes, properties and stage-cloths and trundled off into the provinces, Shakespeare might, without letting the troupe down disastrously, head for home. Back in Stratford he could enjoy being with his wife and children again and catch up on family business. He might also use the time to write a play. His large output of roughly two plays each year is proof, so the argument runs, that he got away from London, and escaped the exacting demands of the playhouse, for uninterrupted spells of creative writing at regular intervals. Aubrey's 'once a year' would provide the opportunity.

Company tours were not, however, a regular annual event. In some years they did not occur. But might the company have taken a holiday every year anyway? This seems very likely. Henslowe's company, the Lord Admiral's Men, took a number of weeks' holiday during Lent and in the summer, as Henslowe's diary for 1594 to 1597 shows. Whether the Lord Chamberlain's men were similarly enlightened in their arrangements we do not know; but the company, like Henslowe's, worked so hard that regular holidays must have been essential.

Touring was certainly not a holiday. It was a relentless grind, even for players better provided than those whom Ben Jonson – himself an actor in the 1590s – portrayed as men trudging along with their shoes 'full of gravel . . . after a blind jade and a hamper' in order to 'stalk upon boards and barrel heads, to an old cracked trumpet'. If Shakespeare was spared the drudgery of touring, his fellow

Rat-catcher with flag, ensign of his trade.

Plague. Woodcut, printed above a 'lamentable list of Death's triumphs in the weekly burials of the City of London' and adjacent parishes. Shakespeare's Timon tells Alcibiades:
> 'Be as a planetary plague when Jove
> Will o'er some high-viced city hang his poison
> In the sick air.'
> *(Timon of Athens* 4.3.109)

players in the company were not: Richard Burbage, John Heminges and Henry Condell would have had plenty to say, back in London, about their experiences on tour. So, at second-hand if not at first-hand, Shakespeare must have known a lot about the roads, towns and villages, guildhalls, inns and churches which the Chamberlain's Men experienced on tour: background material and atmosphere for such plays as *The Taming of the Shrew*, *A Midsummer Night's Dream*, both parts of *Henry IV*, *Henry V*, *As You Like It* and *Twelfth Night*.

Whether a company went on tour or continued to play in London was often determined by the incidence of bubonic plague. Most summers there were few cases: the terrible disease smouldered. Some years, such as 1593 and 1603, it broke out in horrific epidemics. The Privy Council, to prevent the spreading of plague which was wrongly thought to be contagious, forbade public gatherings 'at plays, bear-baitings, bowlings and other like assemblies for sports'. Such measures gratified those religious people who believed, with a preacher at Paul's Cross, that 'the cause of plagues is sin, if you look to it well: and the cause of sin are plays: therefore the cause of plagues are plays'. Especially dangerous were plays acted on Sundays and holy days, when audiences might be drawn from church congregations. Elizabethans, armed with faith, did not consider crowds gathered in church to be prey to infection.

Any individual wishing to protect himself from plague might well use a preventive herb such as elecampane: a yellow-flowered plant whose bitter, aromatic root when powdered, mixed with sugar and taken was recommended for a windy stomach, lung troubles and the prevention not only of fevers but the plague itself. Gervase Markham, in *The English Hus-wife*, prescribed a daily dose of five pre-breakfast spoonfuls of old ale with celandine, powdered ivory and other ingredients boiled in it.

After this drink, his readers were advised to chew dried angelica or to 'smell, as on a nosegay, to the tasselled end of a ship's rope, and they will surely preserve you from infection' by the plague. If, however, you did catch it, orthodox treatment was available, as prescribed by the dramatist and doctor, Thomas Lodge: take a fowl, whose tail feathers have been plucked, and apply it to the plague carbuncle.

In Marlborough during 1593, the year before the first visit of the Chamberlain's Men, plague had broken out violently and killed one or two hundred people in a single month. Ten years later it returned on a frightening scale and during 1604 and 1605 no players acted in the town. Three houses were taken over for the infected poor, St Peter's Fair was cancelled and frankincense was burnt to fumigate the Guildhall when the justices met. Lesser outbreaks followed in the next few years. Public funds were used to tend the sick, provide beer for them, buy many shrouds, dig six communal graves and launch on their grim journey to London a man and his family 'being new here' and therefore soon expelled as a possible source of infection. Wandering rogues and vagabonds were a recurring nuisance. The beadles' regular pay of twopence a time for whipping beggars was increased to fivepence in 1607, when a load of sick beggars was carted from Marlborough.

As for those who stayed, John Knight and his wife and their seven children all died within one month, six of the children in under a week. Patients who survived continued to drain the public purse during their sickness for bread, butter, cheese, oysters, wine, malt, sugar, vinegar, nutmegs, soap, candles, and hay for bedding. Fynes Moryson, the Elizabethan traveller, asserts that the bereaved resort to drama: 'in order to pass over grief, the Italians sleep, the French sing, the Germans drink, the English go to plays'.

A death bed.

4 INNS, PALACES AND INNS OF COURT

THE CROSS KEYS INN, GREENWICH, WHITEHALL, RICHMOND, WINDSOR, HAMPTON COURT, GRAY'S INN AND THEOBALDS

Thou stately stream that with the swelling tide
'Gainst London walls incessantly dost beat,
Thou Thames, I say, where barge and boat doth ride,
And snow-white swans do fish for needful meat!

GEORGE TURBERVILLE: *The Lover to the*
Thames of London, to Favour his Lady Passing Thereon

THE CROSS KEYS INN

On 8 October 1594 the Lord Chamberlain's Men were playing at their official winter quarters in London, the Cross Keys Inn on the west side of Gracechurch Street. Presumably the performances were given indoors, in a hall or a gallery, unless the yard was roofed. Plays were also acted in winter at two other inns nearby: the Bell in Gracechurch Street and the Bull, Bishopsgate Street. All three inns were adapted for stage use in Elizabeth's reign, although keen playgoers, like today's football supporters, might have willingly spent a winter's afternoon standing outside.

Gracechurch Street was a section of the important main road between London Bridge and Bishopsgate, the section between New Fish Street to the south and Bishopsgate Street to the north. It had been narrowed by encroachments, as more and more buildings were being squeezed into the swiftly growing city to be let as tenements at high rents. In a vain attempt to limit development, the authorities imposed fines: but country people kept on flocking to London and were eager to live near the Thames, in this overflowing city of 100,000 people crammed into little more than one square mile. 'In New Fish Street', wrote Stow 'be fishmongers and fair taverns on Fish Street Hill and Gracechurch Street, men of divers trades, grocers and haberdashers.' Poulterers had recently moved in from the Poultry and were conveniently close to Leadenhall Market (at the corner of Gracechurch Street and Cornhill) where all poultry brought to London was first sold.

There was, in Gracechurch Street, a herb market, and – set up within the previous eighty years – 'a boiling house' for making soap, to compete with hard, white soap from abroad and 'grey soap, speckled with white, very sweet and good from Bristol' and black soap, less than half the price and cheapest of all, 'for a halfpenny the pound'.

GREENWICH AND WHITEHALL

At the end of 1594, on 26 and 27 December, the Chamberlain's Men acted at Greenwich Palace.

Opposite

Windsor Forest, haunted at winter midnights by the ghost of Herne the Hunter, a keeper. With great ragged horns he walks round an oak, blasts it, steals cattle, makes cows yield blood instead of milk, 'and shakes a chain In a most hideous and dreadful manner' (*The Merry Wives of Windsor* 4.4.32).

Christmas, New Year and Shrovetide were the festive times when players were most in demand at Court to entertain Queen Elizabeth or King James and their guests. The Court moved from palace to palace; those on the Thames included Richmond, Hampton Court, Windsor and Greenwich. The players appeared wherever they were commanded on a temporary stage set up for the occasion in a lofty hall roughly one hundred feet long and about thirty-five to forty-five feet wide. (A company hall or a provincial guildhall was only about half that size.) There was no permanent theatre in any of the palaces, and a play was only one of many activities that took place in such rooms as the Great Hall and the Great Chamber. Even bear-baitings and joustings occurred indoors, as well as out: for instance, at Whitehall in 1608 both those activities were held in the old Banquet House (Inigo Jones's Banqueting Hall was not yet built).

Protocol dictated the choice of room for each entertainment and the Office of Works set up tiered seating, partitions, doors and trestles as needed. In 1604 arrangements were made at Whitehall so that the King's Men could act *Othello* in the Banquet House on Hallowmas (All Saints' Day, 1 November), *The Merry Wives of Windsor* in the Great Chamber on the following Sunday, and *Measure for Measure* in the Great Hall on St Stephen's Night, 26 December; these three consecutive Whitehall performances by this troupe were each in a different room.

Whitehall was Henry VIII's chief London palace. Wolsey had lived in the buildings before him and enhanced their splendour. When Wolsey fell from grace the King added lavishly to them. His enthusiasm for sport left its mark: at least four tennis courts, a tiltyard, a cockpit and a bowling alley existed there in the sixteenth century, besides a 'ballhouse' for a game that sounds like badminton: 'featherballs'.

Whitehall Palace was burnt down eighty-two years after Shakespeare's death. Of the buildings as they were in his time, there remain only a part of Wolsey's wine-cellar, portions of two tennis courts and most of Cockpit Passage. Similarly, Greenwich, the most easterly of the palaces on the Thames, was completely altered in the seventeenth century. The 'manor of Pleasaunce', called 'Placentia', a rambling complex of buildings, which formed the Tudor

Unknown artist, *c*1581: Elizabeth I lifted, in her favourite dance, *la volta*, by a partner holding the busk of her dress: it may have had metal in it to facilitate hold. She holds her dress down to conceal her knees. The painting is at Penshurst, Kent, but may show Placentia, Greenwich.

Greenwich Palace, no longer exists. This was the residence where monarchs received important foreigners arriving by sea. Ceremony was impressive. The traveller Paul Hentzner, on a Sunday in 1598, waited in the hall with foreign ministers, councillors of state, the Archbishop of Canterbury, Court officials and ladies and gentlemen, for the sixty-five-year-old Queen Elizabeth to pass through in procession on her way to prayers. She entered wearing a dress of white silk bordered with pearls as large as beans. When she turned to either side, everyone knelt. She 'spoke graciously first to one, then to another, whether foreign ministers or those who attended for different reasons, in English, French and Italian'. The ladies of the Court, very

handsome and shapely, most of them dressed in white, followed her, and she was guarded by fifty gentlemen pensioners with gilt battleaxes.

In the ante-chapel, next to the hall, she received petitions. There was a cry of 'Long live Queen Elizabeth!' to which she replied: 'I thank you, my good people,' and then she moved on to the service. Enriched by good music, it only lasted half an hour; then she returned in procession, as she had come, preceded by the Lord Chancellor who walked between officers bearing the royal sceptre and the sword of state. A table had been prepared 'with great solemnity' in the banqueting room, but the Queen dined in her inner and private chamber. 'The Queen dines and sups alone with very few attendants: it is very seldom that anybody, foreign or native, is admitted at that time.'

She spent most of her summers at Placentia where elaborate ceremonials, disguisings and tournaments had been particularly lavish in the reign of her father, Henry VIII. The tiltyard and the great park for hunting were important amenities. Elizabeth relished walking in the park; she liked the buildings; and the players came to Greenwich, bringing their costumes and properties by water, to please her. At Christmas in 1594, Kemp, Burbage and Shakespeare performed two comedies at Placentia, and it was probably on the next night that their troupe played *The Comedy of Errors* at Gray's Inn.

Elizabeth enjoyed the Thames. From Greenwich she visited the royal shipyards nearby at Deptford and Woolwich. Her interest in ships was not shared by James I, a passionate hunter bored by naval affairs. 'The King took so little notice of his fleet at Chatham', reported the French Ambassador in 1604, 'that not only the seamen, but likewise persons of all ranks were much offended, and said that he loved stags better than ships, and the sound of hunting-horns more than that of cannon.' Visitors coming up and down the river must have been impressed by the long façade of Greenwich Palace, topped by the great tower built in Henry VII's time. Among the many famous sights along the Thames, Hentzner noted the *Golden Hind*, the little ship of merely 120 tons in which 'that noble pirate', Francis Drake, had sailed round the world. Laid up at Deptford near the Mast Dock, the *Golden Hind* was a tourist attraction, with refreshments available in the cabin converted to a 'banqueting house'. Visitors, especially sailors, carried off parts of the ship as souvenirs: a year after Shakespeare's death only the broken ribs remained on the shore.

It was at Deptford that the 800-ton *Barque Raleigh* had been built, in a dockyard about a mile up-river from Greenwich. (A muddy entrance to Placentia was the reputed setting for young Walter Raleigh's gallant sacrifice of his cloak, as a carpet over the filth for Queen Elizabeth.) *Barque Raleigh*, renamed *Ark Royal*, became the flagship of Lord Howard of Effingham, High Admiral of the Fleet, at the defeat of the Armada, that 'tyrannical, proud and brainsick attempt', as Elizabeth described it to James VI of Scotland.

RICHMOND AND WINDSOR

Of the Thames-side palaces to the west of London, Richmond – where Queen Elizabeth died – has vanished, leaving only one gateway. Windsor Castle, however, retains some features that Shakespeare would have known. Queen Elizabeth delighted in the place. From 1563 she visited the castle every year in late summer, either on a Progress or to avoid the plague in London. At first, repairs and renovations were badly needed: she had them put in hand. She also 'clean altered' the chapel in the royal apartments. Hentzner, in 1598, found golden roses and fleurs-de-lys painted on the ceiling. He visited the royal bedchamber, noted 'two bathing rooms, ceiled and wainscoted with looking-glass' and was impressed by 'the horn of a unicorn' over seven feet long and worth £10,000. Unicorn's horn was believed to be an infallible antidote to any poison. (The horn was probably that of a narwhal.)

The Great Terrace, first made in wood by Henry VIII but lavishly repaired by Elizabeth who built a retaining wall of masonry, was described by Hentzner as 'a walk of incredible beauty, 380 paces in length ... from whence persons of distinction' could watch hunting and hawking. 'For the fields and meadows, clad with ... plants and flowers, swell gradually ... up to the castle', while the plain below 'strikes the beholder with delight'. Elizabeth used to walk on this terrace (now called the North Terrace) every day for an hour before dinner, unless high winds prevented her. The figures of the Windsor landscape came to life for Hentzner in their ancient, yearly ritual:

'As we were returning to our inn, we happened to meet some country people celebrating their Harvest-home: their last load of corn they crown with flowers, having besides an image richly dressed, by which perhaps they would signify Ceres. This they keep moving about, while men and women, men and maid servants, riding through the streets in the cart, shout as loud as they can till they arrive at the barn.'

A mixture of rye and wheat or of barley and wheat was generally used for bread-making: but bad harvests pushed prices up and then peas, beans, lentils or – at worst – acorns would be ground in with the flour. So a good harvest was well worth celebrating.

In August 1592 another visitor, Frederick, Count of Mompelgard (who next year became the Duke of Württemberg), was graciously received by the Queen at Reading. Then he moved on to Windsor,

The Thames at Richmond, with ferry: the Palace, left, where the Bishop of St David's preached offensively to old Queen Elizabeth I that 'age had furrowed her face and besprinkled her hair with its meal'. James I's son Prince Henry repaired and embellished the Palace. Bottom left: morris dancers with a hobby-horse.

shooting and hunting red deer in parks as he came. He arrived at St George's Chapel, where he found both the organ music and the treble singing of a little boy exquisite. The Castle he considered 'right royal and splendid', being built entirely of freestone which is unusual 'in this country and cannot be procured without enormous and incalculable expense; ... all the roofs are covered entirely with lead'. His Highness 'cut his name in the lead upon the highest tower'.

He was convinced that he had been promised the Order of the Garter by Queen Elizabeth: she kept him waiting – despite his pestering – five years for his election. Shakespeare, who had written in *Henry VI Pt i* (4.1.33–44) a glowing speech about the original Knights of the Garter, in *The Merry Wives of Windsor* (4.5) seems to be mocking the Count of

Opposite
Sir Walter Raleigh with his son (artist unknown, 1602). Raleigh wrote of life as theatre:

'Our graves that hide us from the searching sun
Are like drawn curtains when the play is done;
Thus march we playing to our latest rest,
Only we die in earnest: that's no jest.'

Mompelgard and playfully reversing in the obscure word 'Garmombles' (line 72, Quarto, but not Folio) the syllables of his name.

How much time Shakespeare spent at Windsor before he wrote *The Merry Wives* is not known. Perhaps he could have picked up all the local knowledge he needed in one brief visit to the neighbourhood and supper with mine host of the Garter Inn, where Falstaff lodged and much of the play is set. (No trace remains of the inn, which was in Thames Street near the Peascod Street crossing.) The play suggests familiarity with the Windsor area and with the installation of the Knights of the Garter in St George's Chapel. But Shakespeare was a dramatist who quickly seized whatever ideas and facts he needed. He would not have had time for much research, especially if the Queen and her new Lord Chamberlain (George Carey, Lord Hunsdon, who had succeeded his father, Henry, and had also recently become a Knight of the Garter) wanted this play in a hurry. Perhaps, though, with one of John Norden's Maps of the Parks and Forest to help him, he did find, near Frogmore, 'Heron's Wood' or 'Herne's Wood', named after a heronry close by. This is speculation; it is a fact, however, that Windsor Castle and Hampton Court, alone of the 'gorgeous palaces' in which Shakespeare and his fellow players acted for their monarch, still possess important features that Elizabethans and Jacobeans knew.

63

Datchet Mead, fields on the River Thames opposite Datchet, a village near Windsor. In *The Merry Wives of Windsor* 3.3.13, Mistress Ford arranges for her servants to carry the buck-basket of foul linen – and Falstaff! – to 'Datchet Mead, and there empty it in the muddy ditch close by the Thames' side'.

In the Tower of London: Tower Green, with the Queen's House beyond. From a window here, in 1554, Lady Jane Grey watched her husband taken to execution and the scaffold being set up for her own beheading on the green. Here Anne Boleyn, Catherine Howard and Essex were also executed.

At the Tower of London, the White Tower – a Norman keep developed into a fortress – contains the chapel of St John. Here the body of Henry VI lay in state, stabbed in *Henry VI Pt iii* by cynical Richard of Gloster: 'See how my sword weeps for the poor King's death' (5.6.63).

Above

? R Peak, *c*1600: procession of Elizabeth I. The
spectacle, normal towards the end of her reign, is shown
against a composite background. Garter Knights
accompany her litter. Second from left, Lord Howard of
Effingham, who commanded the fleet against the
Armada. Gentlemen pensioners, with halberds, line the
route. Ladies follow.

Right

Hawking at heron (Turberville's *Book of Hawking*),
probably with peregrines and/or gerfalcons, a sport needing
open country. Modern authorities deny the heron defends itself
in the air, as shown: it climbs for height, then dives to safety in
trees. On the ground, it defends itself with its rapier-like bill.
Hounds shown: possibly greyhounds.

Opposite

William Shakespeare: Chandos Portrait, probably by
John Taylor. Shakespeare was described by
contemporaries as 'no less civil than . . . exellent in the
quality [skill] he professes' (Chettle); 'gentle
Shakespeare' and 'indeed honest, and of an open and
free nature' (Jonson); 'so worthy a friend, and fellow . . .
our Shakespeare' (Heminges and Condell).

Pages 66/67

Holmedon, Northumberland: battlefield in 1402.
   'On Holy-rood day the gallant Hotspur there –
   Young Harry Percy – and brave Archibald,
   That ever valiant and approvèd Scot,
   At Holmedon met . . .
   Ten thousand bold Scots, two-and-twenty knights,
   Balked in their own blood did Sir Walter see
   On Holmedon's plains. . . .'
               (*Henry IV Pt i*, 1.1.52, 68)

HAMPTON COURT

Hampton Court in Middlesex was the lavish creation of Wolsey. He wanted to build a palace worthy of himself in the dual roles of Lord Chancellor and Cardinal. Physicians advised him to choose for his site the manor of Hampton, from which the Thames provided swift access to London. He built landing stages for royal barges, an elaborate conduit for water from Surrey, and – to house a retinue which sometimes exceeded five hundred people – courts, halls, chambers, kitchens and stables. Most noblemen built their houses of stone, but Wolsey used bricks, locally made and of different colours, decorative in effect.

Wolsey's flaunting of power contributed to his downfall. Henry VIII seized Hampton Court and immediately set about developing it on an even grander scale. He demolished and rebuilt the hall and added new courts, a tiltyard and a new tennis court, and he built an ornamental path with heraldic beasts from the landing stage to the house, glorifying the river approach. On the west wall of Clock Court, the astronomical clock shows not only the time and the phases of the moon but also – of help to river travellers, rowing or sailing – the time of high water at London Bridge.

Henry VIII's Hampton Court was the largest house in England. Now, the remaining Tudor areas are smaller than his original palace, but overall today's Hampton Court is slightly larger than the old palace was. Sir Christopher Wren's additions have joined the formal grandeur of a later age to the more homely splendours of the Tudors: but some of Wolsey's small rooms and a little knot garden remain, besides Henry VIII's Watching Chamber and his Great Hall, with its majestic ceiling and Flemish tapestries. In Queen Elizabeth's time, Hampton Court moved Frederick, Duke of Württemberg, to rapture:

L Knyff: Hampton Court, with the third quadrangle by Wren. In older parts, James I conferred many knighthoods and peerages for fees in 1603, celebrating with receptions for ambassadors, tennis matches, banquets, balls, plays and a grand running at the tilt in which even he, despite his nervousness, took part.

'Now this is the most splendid and most magnificent royal palace of any that may be found in England – or, indeed, in any other kingdom. It comprises ten different large courts, and as many separate royal or princely residences, but all connected; together with many beautiful gardens both for pleasure and ornament – some planted with nothing but rosemary; others laid out with various other plants, which are trained, intertwined, and trimmed in ... extraordinary shapes. ...

All the apartments and rooms ... are hung with rich tapestry, of pure gold and fine silk. ... In particular, there is one apartment belonging to the Queen, in which she is accustomed to sit in state, costly beyond everything; the tapestries are garnished with gold, pearls and precious stones ... not to mention the royal throne, which is studded with very large diamonds, rubies, sapphires, and the like, that glitter among other precious stones and pearls as the sun among the stars.

Many of the splendid large rooms are embellished with masterly paintings, writing tables inlaid with mother-of-pearl, organs, and musical instruments which her Majesty is particularly fond of.'

The Duke noticed 'life-like portraits of the wild man and woman whom Martin Frobisher ... took in his voyage to the New World, and brought alive to England'. (They died in Bristol and their child, shortly after, died in London.) More frivolously, the Duke was intrigued by 'a splendid, high and massy fountain' in the middle of a courtyard, 'with an ingenious waterwork, by which you can, if you like, make the water play upon the ladies and others who are standing by, and give them a thorough wetting'.

GRAY'S INN AND THEOBALDS

Ladies were in great danger on the night of 28 December 1594, when rowdy behaviour disturbed the Christmas revels of the high-spirited 'gallant gentlemen' – as they described themselves – of Gray's Inn, the largest of the Inns of Court: others included the Inner and Middle Temples, and Lincoln's Inn. These centres of legal training, in the area of Chancery Lane, tutored nearly 2,000 students during term-time. Gray's Inn was, wrote Stow, 'a goodly house' at Holborn, in a lane 'furnished with fair buildings, and many tenements on both the sides, leading to the fields, towards Highgate and Hampstead'. Its Elizabethan garden, with hedges, vines, cherry trees, roses, eglantine, pinks and violets, was begun by Francis Bacon, a Bencher at the time of these revels and, fifteen years later, Treasurer. Theatricals were a feature of Gray's Inn, with its strong tradition of masques and revels, including indoor jousts ('fighting at barriers') but 'such pastimes had been intermitted by the space of three or four years, by reason of sickness and discontinuances'. The prospect of their resumption had worried Lady Bacon. She wrote to her son, Anthony, brother of Sir Francis: 'I trust they will not mum nor masque nor sinfully revel at Gray's Inn.'

The Queen, however, enjoyed theatricals presented by Gray's Inn at Court and she used 'most gracious words' to thank the Inn 'for that it did always study for some sports to present unto her'. Fortunately she was not present on this 'Innocents' Day at night' to which 'a great presence of lords, ladies and worshipful personages' – most notably from the Inner Temple – had been invited.

They arrived in force about nine o'clock expecting 'some notable performance', a home-made show by their talented hosts. Far too many spectators had crowded in, however: 'there was no convenient room for those that were actors'. The stage was crammed, a disordered tumult arose, and even the sex of gentlewomen did not 'privilege them from violence'. Guests, 'discontented and displeased', left. The uproar abated but there was still too much disorder for the show to go on. Instead, after some dancing and revelling with gentlewomen by the lawyers – Justices and Serjeants, besides Benchers, used to dance – the Chamberlain's Men acted *The Comedy of Errors*, which they had performed the night before at Court in Whitehall. 'So that night was begun, and continued to the end, in nothing but confusion and errors; whereupon it was ever afterwards called "The Night of Errors".' This account, not printed until 1688, dismisses the professional players as a 'company of base and common fellows'.

The hall where they performed, Gray's Inn Hall, still contains its noble Elizabethan screen of Spanish

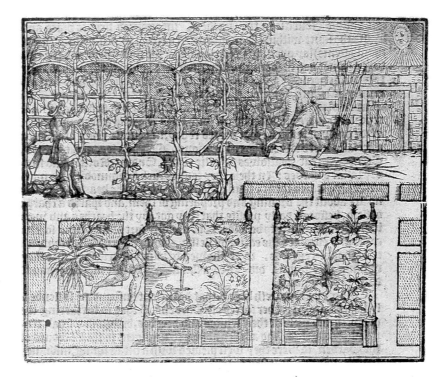

chestnut, damaged in World War II but since restored. There may well be truth in the suggestion that timber from the flag-ship of the Andalusian Squadron of the Spanish Armada was made into this screen. On it are carved wreaths of victory, branches of palms, and nymphs. The English Lord High Admiral at the time of the Armada, Lord Howard of Effingham, was a member of Gray's Inn.

The background of the Gray's Inn audience is indicated by Stow. Although Elizabethan England contained only two universities, Oxford and Cambridge, crowds of lawyers were needed for the ceaseless torrent of cases, many of them trivial, so 'there is, in and about this city, a whole university, as it were, of students, practisers or pleaders and judges of the laws of this realm.' Many law-suits were about land and boundaries, but law would not be the profession of all the students. Some had come on from Oxford or Cambridge to spend a year or two on the way to public life: 'the younger sort are either gentlemen, or sons of gentlemen, or of other most wealthy persons'.

The chaos of their 'Night of Errors' was less squalid than that at a masque, twelve years later, for James I and Christian IV of Denmark in Theobalds,

T Hill: *The Gardener's Labryinth* (1586): training roses over a wooden trellis for an arbour; (below) planting flowers with a 'dibble'. Perdita refuses to 'put The dibble in earth' to plant bastardized flowers (*The Winter's Tale* 4.4.99). Garden paths were kept dry with gravel, sand, shells, brickdust, ashes and sawdust.

the magnificent palace in Hertfordshire. Sir John Harington wrote, of *Solomon and the Queen of Sheba*:

'The lady who did play the Queen's part did carry most precious gifts to both their Majesties; but, forgetting the steps arising to the canopy, overset her caskets into his Danish Majesty's lap and fell at his feet. ... Much was the hurry and confusion: cloths and napkins were at hand, to make all clean. His Majesty then got up and would dance with the Queen of Sheba; but he fell down ... [another drunken king from Hamlet's Denmark?] and was carried to an inner chamber, and laid on a bed of state: which was not a little defiled with the presents of the Queen ... on his garments: such as wine, cream, jelly, beverage, cakes, spices.... The entertainment and show went forward, and most of the presenters went backward, or fell down: wine did so occupy their upper chambers [of the brain].'

5 EAST ANGLIAN VISITS

IPSWICH AND CAMBRIDGE

Cambridge:

*Sirrah, this is a famous university and those, scholars; these, lofty
buildings and goodly houses, founded by noble patrons.*

THOMAS DEKKER AND JOHN WEBSTER: *Sir Thomas Wyatt*

Trinity College, Cambridge: late-Elizabethan fountain, Great Court. A comedy
occasioned a riot at Trinity Great Gate, February 1610–11, when play-goers from St
John's were refused admission. Weapons included clubs, flaming torches and stones.
Arrests followed. Polonius says that at university he played Julius Caesar: Brutus
killed him (*Hamlet* 3.2.100).

73

IPSWICH

Either towards the end of 1594 or in 1595 the Chamberlain's Men played at Cambridge and at Ipswich. In each place the official fee was forty shillings. Although there is no evidence that these players acted elsewhere in East Anglia in those years, in order to pay their way on tour they must have performed a number of times while they travelled a circuit including Ipswich and Cambridge, or two separate circuits each including one of those places.

William Smith, a herald in Shakespeare's time, described Ipswich as 'the greatest town in Suffolk and one of the most famous towns in England' for trade 'and other respects'. Boys came from as far north as Northumberland, probably travelling in coal ships from Newcastle, to be apprenticed in Ipswich to shipwrights, mariners, fishermen, oatmealmakers, gardeners, painters, apothecaries, drapers, goldsmiths, haberdashers and merchants. A market town and port, Ipswich had always been the county capital. It was built mostly on the northeast side of the navigable River Orwell, in which ships gathered before sailing to the Continent.

In Shakespeare's time the town was growing and developing. The Ancient House in the butter market was enlarged and improved by an occupant who was a London draper and fish-trader. This house had been owned in the fifteenth century by Thomas Fastolf, a descendant of the Sir John Fastolf whose name Shakespeare may have taken over for Prince Hal's companion in *Henry IV Pts i and ii*: Falstaff, the old coward and lecher whose 'staff' would 'fall'. Shakespeare had previously called this character 'Oldcastle'. The real Sir John Oldcastle, denouncer of the Pope as anti-Christ, was a protestant martyr. In Henry V's reign he was hanged and burnt in London at St Giles's Fields. One of his descendants was Sir William Brooke, Lord Cobham, who, as Lord Chamberlain from August 1596 to March 1597, was responsible for the Master of the Revels and was supremely powerful over drama. He objected to his ancestor's name, Oldcastle, being given to the immoral, scurrilous character. After Oldcastle had appeared on stage in *Henry IV Pt i*, the name was censored. Shakespeare changed it to Falstaff and wrote in the Epilogue to *Henry IV Pt ii* (30): 'Oldcastle died a martyr, and this is not the man.'

In Ipswich, merchants whose money came from the export of Suffolk cloth to Turkey, France, Barbary, Muscovy and (despite English embargoes) the Spanish Netherlands, lived in pleasant houses near the quayside, especially in the neighbourhood of the Neptune Inn. Some of them survive, backed by warehouses running down to the quay.

The town's prosperity was based on the shipbuilding trade, stimulated by Elizabeth's grant of five shillings a ton for all vessels of a hundred tons and more. William Wright of Ipswich built twenty-six ships big enough to qualify for the grant, and many smaller vessels too, in about thirty years up to the 1590s. Then Ipswich, well supplied with local timber, became the shipyard of London. Towards the end of Shakespeare's life, Ipswich had far more shipwrights than any other English town. Its cordage, also, was famous, and shortly before the Armada Ipswich was supplying canvas to the Navy.

Glimpses of life on the River Orwell in Shakespeare's day appear in cases brought before the local Admiralty court. People were accused of secretly loading a lighter with a pack of cloth after sundown; casting ballast overboard into the channel; shooting at fowl with small shot that scatters like hail; transporting woad 'in strange bottoms'; unlawfully dredging for oysters; 'fishing with heave nets by one alone'; selling outside 'the liberty' fish caught within it; laying an anchor in the middle of the channel for two tides and longer; and spoiling a boat 'by another boat rowing against it'. More disturbing cases included enticing a 'servant mariner' from his master's service; and the 'extraordinary correction' of twenty blows with a rope's end, given by a master of a hoy to his servant.

A great benefactor of Ipswich was Henry Tooley, a wealthy Tudor merchant of St Mary Quay, who founded almshouses for poor persons lamed in war. Tooley dealt in wines from Gascony and in cloth and canvas. Although some Suffolk cloth was undyed, most of it was dyed blue with woad and

Opposite
Frontispiece to *The Wits* (1662), an anthology of dramatic pieces, including episodes from *Henry IV Pts i* and *ii*. Characters from items in the book act on a deep, rectangular stage with spectators beside it and above the curtained entrance. Lighting comes from candelabra and a row of candles in front. Bottom left: Falstaff drinks.

indigo. There were three varieties of the colour: blues, azures and plunkets (grey or light blue). Canvas for sails was made from hemp, which grew in Suffolk, but French canvas, known as 'milder-nex', was the 'best and profitablest'. It was scarce, however, and Ipswich canvas, which was improving in quality, filled the gap.

Tooley often sent his ship the *Mary Walsingham* 'by the grace of God Icelandward', on voyages that most eastern ports, especially those of Suffolk and Norfolk, took part in. 'To fish for cod and ling in Iceland', Robert Hitchcock wrote in 1580, 'the ships commonly must go forth in March and return loaden in August.' When the fish was caught, it was gutted on board and packed into barrels between layers of salt.

Some of Tooley's wealth was used to help set up Christ's Hospital for the poor, young, old, homeless and sick of Ipswich. The governors were to bring in idle vagabonds and sturdy beggars from the town and put them to work in the main hall. Very young children were set to card and spin wool. An earlier benefactor, Cardinal Wolsey, founded Wolsey's College in Ipswich, his native town, with the rare instruction that 'tender youth be not discouraged by severe blows or threatening faces'. The building was hardly finished when Wolsey fell into disgrace. Henry VIII seized the fabric: white stone, timber, wainscots and lead were shipped to London for use at Westminster. In Ipswich there remains only a red brick gateway surmounted by Henry VIII's arms. The site, intended by Wolsey for a school to honour his greatness, was later occupied by malt-houses.

In religion, Ipswich was a puritan centre in a puritan county, and on Cornhill, a place used for bear-baiting, martyrs had been burnt at the stake.

Elizabeth visited Ipswich in July 1561. Two vessels 'decently furnished' were at her disposal, so that she could tour by water 'so far as the liberty does extend'. The scandal of her visit was the laxness and impudence of the clergy. Public services were disorderly and many clerics refused to wear surplices, popish vestments retained by government policy so as to minimize change when ordinary people would be upset by black Geneva gowns. At Ipswich, many clergy were married, and the Queen particularly disliked marriage of clergy. One result of her experiences at Ipswich was an order forbidding women to enter cathedral lodgings or collegiate churches.

Puritan doctrine, much of it at variance with the tenets of the Church of England, was spread by long sermons. These were a feature of Ipswich life, where the Borough Assembly provided able, learned divines to preach not only on Sundays but also on Wednesdays and Fridays. During the sermon, all business stopped. 'Silver-tongued' Samuel Ward was town preacher for about thirty years.

In keeping with Ipswich piety, 'A Proved Medicine for the Plague', written by a local schoolmaster, was to 'take a pound of good hard penance and wash it well with water of your eyes, and let it lie a good while in your heart'.

At Elizabeth's accession, legislation imposed a fine of twelvepence on all absentees from parish churches on Sundays and holy days. In 1581 the fine was grossly increased to £20 a month on all recusants, with imprisonment for those who did not pay within three months. In the last nine years of Elizabeth's reign the crown received over £120,000 for absences from church. In default of payment, two-thirds of the offender's lands and all his goods became liable to seizure by the Crown. Although in Suffolk, as elsewhere, this measure was sometimes rigidly enforced, remission was occasionally possible to avoid beggary. William Yaxlee, from an estimated annual income of £220, offered £40; Walter Norton from £100 offered £20; John Bedingfield from £40 offered £10. In Suffolk, there were far fewer recusants than in some counties.

As a social centre, Ipswich offered plays by various touring companies in the Moot Hall and possibly in private houses. Attractions during Shakespeare's lifetime included 'the Masters of Defence' competing for 'their prize'; the man who 'brought the serpent to the town'; Martin the minstrel and his company of fools; the Children of the Chapel; the Turkish tumblers; the town waits, in blue uniforms; and a blind minstrel. Shakespeare's troupe returned to Ipswich some time in 1602–3 and in 1609 (twenty-six shillings and

Opposite
Thomas Candish (Cavendish), navigator/privateer, sailed round the globe, 1586–8, setting out with 122 men. One was Thomas Eldred of Ipswich, tallow chandler: he and forty-nine others returned alive. In Chile, Peru, California, Cavendish was ruthless: 'all the villages and towns that ever I landed at, I burnt and spoiled'.

eightpence was the official fee each time). Perhaps in 1601 and more certainly during the years 1605–7 the troupe returned to Cambridge; and both there and in Oxford they had, by 1603, acted *Hamlet*.

CAMBRIDGE

Cambridge, according to Harrison:

'... is somewhat low and near unto the fens, whereby the wholesomeness of the air there is not a little corrupted. It is excellently well served with all kinds of provision, but especially of fresh-water fish and wildfowl.'

Its chief lack was fuel but wood, charcoal and sea-coal were all brought in. Camden describes its situation:

'... on the river Cam; which, after it has made several pleasant little islands on the west side of it, turns to the east, and divides the town into two parts; so that it is joined by a bridge. ... Beyond

the bridge are a large old castle (almost destroyed by age) and Magdalene College. On this side the bridge (where lies the far greatest part of the town) there is a pleasant prospect of well-contrived streets, of a good number of churches, and of ... fair colleges ... where the studies of arts and languages do exceedingly flourish.'

Harrison, a graduate of Oxford, went on to post-graduate studies at Cambridge. He loved both places, but he could not help comparing them:

'The colleges of Oxford, for curious workmanship and private commodities, are much more stately, magnificent and commodious than those of Cambridge: and thereunto the streets of the town for the most part more large and comely.

D Loggan: Cambridge, across fields. John Chamberlain wrote of a Russian connection (1602): 'We have here four youths from Muscovy to learn our language and Latin, and are to be dispersed to divers schools at Winchester, Eton, Cambridge and Oxford.' In 1600, 'uncouth ambassadors' from Russia were at Elizabeth I's Court.

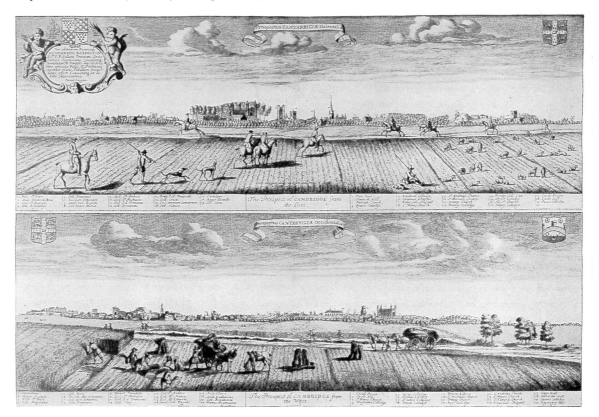

But for uniformity of building, orderly compaction and politic regiment, the town of Cambridge, as the newer workmanship, exceedeth that of Oxford.... The townsmen of both are glad when they may match and annoy the students, by encroaching upon their liberties, and [by charging high prices] keep them bare.'

The students of both universities, who numbered 3,000, lived in colleges (fifteen at Cambridge, eighteen at Oxford) which varied in capacity from 200 students downwards: and 'in these our colleges' wrote Harrison 'we live in . . . exact order and under . . . precise rules of government'. Students were maintained by the colleges or by rich friends. Founders intended their colleges to accept and maintain poor students 'whose parents were not able to bring them up into learning'. (Harrison might have instanced Corpus Christi College, Cambridge, which accepted Marlowe, whose father was a shoemaker) but wealthy students were ousting poor ones. Harrison notes that rich men's sons trifle their time away; they gamble, dice, 'ruffle and roist it out, exceeding in apparel' and 'oft bring the universities into much slander'. In June, students went down to harvest the hay, and returned in October when they had harvested the corn.

If authority had been obeyed, the Chamberlain's Men would not have acted in Cambridge. Only a year or two had passed since the Privy Council renewed its ban, first imposed in 1575, on all performances by 'common players . . . either in the University or in any place within the compass of five miles'. The Mayor of Cambridge, who had previously allowed touring companies in, continued to do so. A similar ban at Oxford was similarly disregarded. The Privy Council's intention in 1575 was to prevent students – who were not supposed to enter university under the age of fifteen, though some did enter as young as ten or even less – from being 'enticed from their places of learning, to be beholders, learners, and practisers of lewdness and unlawful acts'; and the Council intended 'also (which in this special time of . . . plague is to be regarded)' to avoid 'great assemblies of vulgar people'.

The university had lately suffered 'very grievously' from plague. At Oxford, university authorities endorsed the ban, reiterated the reasons for it and mentioned the need to prevent 'the younger sort from extraordinary spending, more than their small Exhibitions will bear'. In early Tudor times, before hostility to professional players developed, actors and musicians had been welcomed by the colleges.

Cambridge students, living in their colleges throughout the year, made their own amusements. In the 1590s, Latin plays based on Italian comedies were in vogue; created within colleges, they were acted in college halls for the academic audience that belonged there. Sharp comedy in English, satirizing officials of the city, also flourished. Civic authorities, including the individuals being ridiculed, were invited to these college plays and the feasts that followed.

For the Queen's only visit to Cambridge, in 1564, the play chosen for her to see first was a Roman comedy by Plautus, *Aulularia*, acted in Latin at King's College by 'certain selected' members from various other colleges. A 'great stage', specially erected in the hall of King's, 'was judged by divers to be too little . . . and also too far from her lodging' so it 'was taken down' and the Chapel was made ready as a playhouse.

This choice of a religious building for a Sunday performance of a pagan comedy caused no concern. At the Queen's cost, her surveyor built 'a great stage' which filled the nave of King's College Chapel; and, instead of scenic 'houses' being built 'of canvas, framed, fashioned and painted' for the show, side-chapels were put to use. Stands were erected for the audience, which was to exclude undergraduates.

At the Queen's arrival in Cambridge, students were to kneel and welcome her with cries of 'Vivat Regina' and then 'quietly and orderly to depart home to their colleges'. Such peace was not always achieved; windows were quite often deliberately smashed while plays were being acted, so protective netting was sometimes put up or glass removed beforehand. Some time in 1606–7, students who were excluded from a performance at King's broke the Hall windows 'with loud outcries and shoutings for the space of two hours together', to ruin other people's pleasure. During Elizabeth's visit of nearly five days, if the young scholars could not avoid going into the town, 'then they should go two and two', or risk severe punishment.

In general, students were provided with few recreations. Fashionable pastimes, such as archery, tennis and bowls did not appeal to all. Other amusements could lead to trouble, as they did later in Elizabeth's reign at Chesterton. For a football match, the students arrived peaceably without any weapons, though the townsmen of Chesterton were secretly spoiling for a fight and in playing 'did pick quarrels against the scholars and did bring out' staves which they had hidden in the church porch before the match and 'did so beat the scholars that divers had their heads broken'. Other students, 'greatly beaten, were driven to run through the river'. One of the Chesterton players was the Chief Constable, Thomas Parish. Students shouted to him to keep the Queen's peace: instead, he brazenly cheered on his team 'to beat the scholars down'. For this incitement to violence he was eventually tried and imprisoned. A ban was imposed by the university on scholars playing football outside college precincts and with anyone, anywhere, who was not a member of the university.

Other pastimes at Chesterton were unacceptable too. On Sunday 22 April 1581 university officers tried to stop bear-baiting in sermon-time (1–2 pm). They were resisted by Richard Parish, brother of Thomas, whom he had succeeded as Chief Constable since the football affray, in which both brothers had done battle. On this Sunday, Richard Parish pushed himself between the Beadle and the

'The country swains at football here are seen,
Which each gapes after for to get a blow,
The while some one away runs with it clean
It meets another, at the goal below,
Who never stirred; one catcheth here a fall
And there one's maimed who never saw the ball.'
(Henry Peacham)

bear-ward and 'thrust the Beadle upon the bear in such sort that he could hardly keep himself from hurt'. Chesterton men, who denied that the university had any authority over them, 'began to shout and laugh at the Proctor'.

Students were banned from many ordinary pastimes and pleasures, such as swimming or washing in rivers, pools or other water, day or night: but they were not exempt from the obligation of all men to help mend roads, giving their labour for four days per year alongside the townsfolk.

It is not surprising if students' feelings about drama sometimes exploded: but while the Queen was in Cambridge, they did not. On the Sunday, after supper, she appeared on the stage by torchlight in King's College Chapel at 9 pm and sat there in state, the focus of attention, throughout the comedy, members of her Court watching from the rood-loft.

She saw a good deal of university life during her days in Cambridge, but the town was allowed to play only a very minor role. Every inhabitant had to provide sand for covering the streets, all of which had been specially paved, and for her arrival 'the bells both of the colleges and also of the town were rung most part of the afternoon. And such churches as were negligent herein were afterwards called upon and were fined, some eight shillings and fourpence, some more, some less'.

Near Newnham she was greeted by the Mayor, aldermen and burgesses with a gift of a double-gilt cup of coins and an oration. So, on to Queen's College, where 'a solemn blast' by the trumpeters announced her coming and some chosen scholars presented written orations to her. All her retinue had dismounted, but she:

'... remained on horseback. She was dressed in a gown of black velvet pinked: a caul upon her head, set with pearls and precious stones; a hat that was spangled with gold, and a bush of feathers.'

The Mayor, bareheaded, obeyed instructions to wait outside King's College, which the Queen approached to be met by the beadles, whose task was to keep order. They were kneeling and, as a prelude to a brief ceremony, kissing their staves. After evensong she was given by the University 'four pair of Cambridge double gloves, edged and trimmed with two laces of fine gold, and six boxes of fine comfits'.

On Monday morning at 8 am 'the University bell did sound unto ordinary lectures' in 'physic, dialect [logical disputation] and rhetoric, as of divinity and law', and many 'lords and gentlemen' went to hear them. At 1 pm the Queen attended a disputation in St Mary's Church, for six hours. She was critical – as she had been the day before – of some of the postgraduates' clothing: 'their habits and hoods were torn and too much soiled'. She enthused about the orators' speeches, but alas 'their voices were small and not audible'.

However, she liked Cambridge so much that she would gladly have stayed an extra day 'if provision of beer and ale' for her retinue had not run out.

On Wednesday, the climax of her visit, the university was up with the lark. Lectures and disputations had already finished by 6 am when:

'... the Queen's Majesty took her Progress about to the colleges, riding in state royal, all the lords and gentlemen riding before her Grace, and all

the ladies following on horseback. . . . The Mayor that day came not abroad, which was noted of divers and thought some part of his duty.'

The Queen on her seven-hour tour was presented with many books and gloves and 'boxes of comfits'. Orations addressed to her included at least two in Greek. For one 'she rendered thanks in Greek', and as she rode through the streets to the Old Provost's Lodge at King's where she was staying 'she talked very much with divers scholars in Latin', and finally 'at her lighting off her horse, with Latin dismissed them'.

On Thursday morning she left Cambridge with ceremony, escorted along the town by the Mayor 'on horseback and bearing his mace'. At Hinchinbrooke, in Huntingdonshire, where she was to spend the night, a surprise awaited her. Some scholars, who had pursued her from Cambridge, acted a burlesque in which a bishop carried a lamb in his hands and ate it as he walked along, and a dog held the consecrated wafer of the Eucharist in its mouth. This flagrant parody of the Mass so angered the Queen that she 'at once entered her chamber using strong language, and the men who held the torches – it being night' left the players in the dark, like those in *Hamlet* (3.2.257) when Claudius orders 'Give me some light. Away.'

The Queen's visit was smoothly managed to hide animosity between 'town' and 'gown', but ill-feeling between the two was a fact of Cambridge life. A list of complaints against the university shows what particularly irked the town in 1596. The Justices, who governed the university and the town separately, would not co-operate; the university picked on particular tradespeople and forbade students to trade with them; students had physically attacked the Mayor and insulted him, and the university said it could not and would not take any action.

Stourbridge Fair, a cause of recurring conflict, featured in the list of sixteen complaints. This annual international fair, a huge, elaborate market lasting for three weeks in September, from St Bartholomew's Day to St Michael's Day, was described by Camden as 'the most famous fair in all England, whether in respect to the resort of people or the quantity of goods'. It was held to the east of the town, in cornfields between the Cam and the

Women tried by jury, hanged for 'mischief' – including murder – through witchcraft, 1589; Chelmsford, Essex. Illegitimate children gave evidence against their grandmothers, to whom Satanic spirits had spoken through familiars: black frogs, 'Jack' and 'Jill'; a dun-coloured, fiery-eyed ferret, 'Bid'; toads. In *Macbeth* 1.1.9, the Second Witch hears 'Paddock' (a toad) call.

little River Stour: heavy goods came by water. If, by 4 September, the harvest had not been gathered, booth-holders could trample it down and set up their booths.

Merchants came from all over the country 'to buy and provide salt-fish, butter, cheese, honey, salt, flax, hemp, pitch, tar and all other ware and merchandises'. Two shopping lists for the household of Lord North, the Queen's Lieutenant for Cambridgeshire, included cod, sugar, currants, raisins, prunes, 'horse-meat' (provender), soap, kettles, dust-baskets, pails, feather-bed ticking, a frying pan, 'dog couples: twenty pence', fifty-four pounds of gunpowder and fourteen pounds of match to ignite it. Profits from the fair were crucial to Cambridge because they 'maintained the town in its ways, streets, ditches and other burdens'. Elizabeth had made the town responsible for control of booths and the university for weights and measures and the sale of bread, wine and ale.

The financing of the fair led to continuous wrangling between 'town' and 'gown'. There were complaints that the university allowed beer to be overpriced at the fair and that the university proctors exacted gifts from every 'grocer, soaper and such-like', which frightened merchants away altogether. Areas of the fair included the Duddery for woollen goods; Cheapside for mercers and grocers; Goldsmiths' Row; Fish Hill; and Garlic Row for booksellers. The main row was nearly half a mile long. The Mayor and the Chancellor each had a booth for feasting his friends, and there was a court-house where cases of false measure, false dealing, debt and assault were heard.

Early in James I's reign, when a person named Knightley was charged with bewitching two girls, the King's interest in witchcraft led the Privy Council to send the three people to Cambridge for investigation: Knightley by Justices of the Peace, and the girls by 'skilful physicians and learned divines' who were to decide whether the supernatural was indeed involved. Because 'so many young men' might 'out of novelty ... be desirous' to see 'the maidens', those two girls were to be lodged in private houses and visitors restricted. Eventually the girls' disease was pronounced 'natural' though 'somewhat strange and of much difficulty to be cured'. Unfortunately 'the time of year for medicines proper for their disease' had passed; so, as those herbal remedies were unavailable, the girls were sent home to rely on fresh air, exercise and 'orderly government' for their cure.

The King's Men acted Jonson's *Volpone* in Cambridge in 1605, 1606 or 1607, and about this time university discipline was tightened up. Student disorders, 'specially in the night time', included the shooting of guns, cross-bows and stone-bows, 'excessive drinkings, foul drunkenness and taking tobacco in taverns'. Students kept greyhounds and horses, and went coursing and hunting, 'to the destroying of game and the mis-spending of their time'. All this was to stop, and students were no longer to bring tobacco into St Mary's Church, the schools, halls or places 'of comedies ... tragedies, shows and assemblies'. Anyone in the town who kept a greyhound for a student was liable to imprisonment and a fine.

6 LONDON: CITY OF CONTRASTS

BISHOPSGATE AND CLERKENWELL

What life is best?
Courts are but only superficial schools
To dandle fools.
The rural parts are turned into a den
Of savage men.
And where's a city from all vice so free,
But may be termed the worst of all the three?

SIR FRANCIS BACON: *The Life of Man*

St John's Gate, entrance to the twelfth-century Priory of Knights of St John, Cripplegate. Wat Tyler's rebels damaged it, 1381. Henry VIII dissolved the order, stored tents and nets here for hunting and warfare. In Shakespeare's day, as Tilney's residence it included thirteen chambers, parlour, hall, kitchen, stable and garden.

BISHOPSGATE

When the Chamberlain's Men were working at the Theatre in Shoreditch, to the north-east of the City, Shakespeare lived for at least part of the time in the parish of St Helen, Bishopsgate. Which house he lived in is not known, and his being in the parish is only evident from the first of a series of tax documents. This document shows him living there about 1596 and owing the small sum of five shillings, assessed – for a tax subsidy to the Crown – on goods worth £5.

Bishopsgate Ward lay partly inside ('Within') the City Wall and partly outside it ('Without'). Each of the twenty-six wards, or administrative areas, was represented by an alderman. Bishopsgate Ward had seven constables, seven scavengers and a beadle. Shakespeare was living in a neighbourhood that

T Wyck (mid-seventeenth century): London from the South Bank (*c*1600): 'here a palace, there a wood-yard, here a garden, there a brew-house' (Davenant). The Thames, much used for swimming and bathing, seldom froze over but in 1564 and 1608 it did: people 'slid away the time upon the Thames' (W Rowley).

was largely upper-middle class, but not entirely so. Through the centre of the ward ran Bishopsgate Street, a section of the main road to the north-east. This road from London Bridge passed through the City Wall at Bishopsgate (surmounted by impaled heads of traitors) to Shoreditch, and on towards Suffolk, Cambridgeshire and Norfolk. Shakespeare was to write most of his plays later, for the Globe. Meanwhile, at St Helen's, he lived close enough to the Theatre and the Curtain at Shoreditch to be able to walk to work. Traffic was, however, a problem. As more and more carts, coaches and drays crowded into the narrow streets and lanes, danger increased. Drivers were notoriously careless:

'The coachman rides behind the horse-tails, lasheth them, and looketh not behind him. The drayman sitteth and sleepeth on his dray, and letteth his horse lead him home. I know that . . . shod carts are forbidden. . . . Also that the fore-horse of every carriage should be led by hand: but these good orders are not observed.'

So wrote Stow, the meticulous observer gathering material for his detailed *Survey of London*. He wrote about places, landmarks and buildings that Shakespeare, as a resident, must have seen very often. Stow singled out for special comment a 'large and beautiful house with gardens of pleasure, bowling alleys and suchlike' in Bishopsgate Without, on the east side of Bishopsgate Street. This opulent home had been built by Jasper Fisher, Warden of the Goldsmiths' Company but heavily in debt. His house was 'mockingly called "Fisher's Folly"'.

A less savoury part of Bishopsgate Without was Petty France, close to the City Wall, on the west side of Bishopsgate Street. The French residents lived in 'dwelling houses lately built on the bank' of the City Ditch, where a stream flowed into the ditch from the north. The builders were 'citizens of London that more regarded their own private gain than the common good'. The Ditch, almost filled up with 'soilage of houses, with other filthiness' cast into it, was in 'danger of empoisoning the whole city'. In other wards, too, the City Ditch, which used to compass the City Wall as a defence, had recently been neglected and was either reduced to a narrow, 'filthy channel or altogether stopped up for gardens planted, and houses builded thereon, even

An up-market tavern, status shown by cushions and style of table-cloth. A drawer, less harassed than Francis in *Henry IV Pt i*, 2.5.36 serves customers. One, left, holds a chalice of wine. Bread is set on the table. The dark vessel is either a wine-jug or an ale-tankard.

to the very wall'.

Across Bishopsgate Street from Petty France, further out towards Shoreditch than Fisher's Folly, was Tassell Close, which:

'. . . being enclosed with a brick wall, serveth to be an artillery-yard, whereunto the gunners of the Tower do weekly repair, namely every Thursday, and there levelling certain brass pieces of great artillery against a butt of earth, made for that purpose, they discharge them for their exercise.'

Between Fisher's Folly and Tassell Close was 'a continual building of tenements, with alleys of cottages, pestered' (overcrowded), ending at Hog Lane. In Shakespeare's childhood, this lane:

'. . . had on both sides fair hedgerows of elm trees, with bridges and easy stiles to pass over into the pleasant fields, very commodious for citizens

therein to walk, shoot and . . . recreate and refresh their dulled spirits in the sweet and wholesome air, which is now within a few years made a continual building throughout of garden houses and small cottages: and the fields on either side be turned into garden plots, tenter-yards [for stretching cloth], bowling alleys and suchlike, from Houndsditch in the west, so far as White-chapel and further towards the east.'

Beyond Hog Lane, on the way to Shoreditch, were 'many fair houses builded for receipt and lodging of worshipful persons', on the site of a priory and hospital dissolved by Henry VIII. To the east lay Spitalfields, a large open space used for grazing cattle and practising archery. Clay was dug there for brick-making. The warm kilns were used by tramps to sleep in.

Inside the City Wall, on the east side of Bishops-gate Street, were seven almshouses. Poor parish clerks, their wives and their widows used to live there, but recently – Stow grumbles – Queen Elizabeth granted the almshouses to people she favoured, 'such as can make best friends' at Court and 'some of them taking the pension appointed, have let forth their houses for great rent'.

Towards Leadenhall Street, set well back from Bishopsgate Street, the Parish and Priory Church of St Helen still stands, now dwarfed by towering City banks and assaulted by the roar of weekday traffic. Since this was Shakespeare's parish church, presum-ably it was here that he received Easter communion, which was compulsory whether or not he came to worship at other times.

This church, still much used for services and sermons, consists of two aisles separated by a row of arches. Many handsome monuments remain which Shakespeare would have known. That of Sir William Pickering, Elizabeth's Ambassador to Spain, is a magnificent marble tomb surrounded by a wrought-iron rail. Sir Thomas Gresham is com-memorated by his black funeral helmet and by his

tomb: the heraldic carving is topped by a grasshop-per, his crest.

Sir Thomas Gresham was the most successful of Shakespeare's fellow-parishioners. A mercer, the greatest financier of his time, and promulgator of the law that 'bad money drives out good', he saw that Elizabethan London needed an international trading centre like the bourse in Antwerp. At his own expense he built the Royal Exchange between Cornhill and Threadneedle Street, and its large open piazza, flanked by colonnaded covered walks in the Italian style, became the commercial centre of the world. On the first floor, above the loggias, a hundred small shops sold the finest glass, jewellery, books and armour in London. Huge effigies of the Gresham grasshopper crouched on top of this vast public building, the only one put up in Shakespeare's lifetime. As a social centre, the Royal Exchange was almost as popular as St Paul's.

In St Helen's is the tomb of Sir John Crosby, an eminent grocer and woolman, whose mansion, Crosby Place, in Shakespeare's time stood close by, beyond the churchyard and a well. 'This house he builded of stone and timber', wrote Stow, 'very large and beautiful, and the highest at that time in London', but after only four years in 'his large and sumptuous building' Sir John died. One of its last Elizabethan owners, Sir John Spencer, became Lord Mayor, and his monument in the church, with its gorgeous colours, winged skull and hourglass, is very impressive. His home was later moved stone by stone to Chelsea, and there, in Danvers Street, Crosby Hall still stands.

On the other side of Bishopsgate Street, beside the gate itself, was a water conduit and 'divers fair inns large for receipt of travellers, and some houses for men of worship, namely one most spacious of all . . . thereabout, builded of brick and timber, by Sir Thomas Gresham'. Plays had often been acted at the Bull Inn (number 91 on the west side of Bishopsgate Street) by Tarlton and the Queen's Men, and in 1594 Anthony Bacon's mother feared that shows at the Bull would corrupt her son's servants, but whether theatricals were still held there when Shakespeare lived in St Helen's is uncertain.

London's disreputable citizens come and go all day and night in the pages of Dekker's pamphlets exposing the seamy side of life. Early in the morning, before any attorney or solicitor appeared

Opposite
Thomas Gresham in youth. Later, as Elizabeth I's agent in the Low Countries, he imported arms into England; brought gifts of Bologna sausages, salt tongues, paving stones for friends; sent 'rollers' for the Queen's 'headpieces of silk'. In London, he established lectures on divinity, astronomy, geometry, music, law, medicine and rhetoric.

Westminster Palace: Court of Wards and Liveries which supervised feudal revenue and enforced property rights of wardship and marriage. Lord Burghley, between the Chief Justices, presides. A lawyer, standing right, pleads. *All's Well That Ends Well* 2.3.157: the King of France insists 'It is in us' to order his ward Bertram to marry Helena.

Opposite
St Helen's, Bishopsgate, with wooden bell turret. Sir Thomas Gresham was buried here in pomp in 1579: two hundred poor people in black followed his body. In recompense for his splendid tomb's ground-space in church, he had promised the church a steeple. His widow refused to build it.

at Westminster Hall, the pickpockets would arrive, ready to steal nimbly as soon as the lawyers' 'clients begin to come crowding in'. While the lawyer pleaded, his poor client standing beside him 'draws out his purse to pay fees', and if the pickpocket's talons 'can but touch it, it is their own'.

Meanwhile, in the stable of a sick horse that is due to race in Smithfield, the horse-courser disguises the beast's filthy disease – glanders, which clogs the nose with mucus – by blowing sneezing-powder up its nostrils and poking into them 'two long feathers plucked from the wing of a goose, they being dipped in the juice of garlic'. Later in the day 'at the best ordinaries' – eating-houses – you could hear the

Two elegant whores – one, left, a pick-purse – banquet with wealthy customers. An allegorical figure, far left, offers the cup of 'horror' which leads to 'murder' (top left) and the mouth of 'hell' (top right). Thersites, in *Troilus and Cressida* 5.2.197 gibes at mankind's unquenchable thirst for 'wars and lechery'.

A bellman/night-watchman walking the streets, calling the hours with lantern, candle, staff and dog (like Starveling in 'Pyramus and Thisbe', but without the thorn-bush). At midnight before London executions he would ring outside condemned cells: 'the fatal bellman, Which gives the stern'st good-night' (*Macbeth* 2.2.4).

music of dice, 'square rattling bones', for gallants spent their afternoons dicing with wealthy merchants, unaware that the winner was cheating all comers with a false die, of which 'dice-makers that work in corners' can supply fourteen varieties.

At night 'the doors of common brothelries' fly open to receive 'grave and wealthy lechers' with gold jingling in their pockets. These customers 'durst not pass that way' by daylight, 'for fear that noted courtesans should challenge them of acquaintance, or that others should laugh at them to see white heads growing upon green stalks'. At midnight the bellman 'with a lantern and candle in his hand, a long staff on his neck and a dog at his tail', walks up and down ringing his bell and beating on doors to prevent fires and deter thieves. Through the dark streets, 'midwives running till they sweat' are let in at the back doors of houses 'in blind lanes or in by-gardens' and set to work in 'rooms builded for the purpose, where young maids, being big with child by unlawful fathers, or young wives (in their husbands' absence at sea, or in the wars) having wrestled with bachelors or married men, till they caught falls', lie safely till they are delivered. The infants, 'for reasonable sums of money,' are secretly killed or sold. And in the suburbs the doors of notorious bawds 'stand night and day wide open, with a pair of harlots in taffeta gowns (like two painted posts) garnishing out those doors, being better to the house than a double sign ...'. This is laughed at, or ignored, or winked at: although the venereal disease 'that a whore-house lays upon a city is worse' than the plague itself.

Beggars used barns as doss-houses. One such haven, at Harrow-on-the-Hill, was known as 'Draw the pudding out of the fire'. Others were Ketbrook (near Blackheath) and Kingsbarns (near Dartford). Sometimes forty beggars would gather, with their women, and – says Dekker – engender more beggars. 'Adultery is common amongst them, incest but laughed at, sodomy made a jest.' The owners of these barns are so frightened of their houses being burnt down or of themselves being murdered, that they dare not deny the beggars entrance. 'In all shires they have such inns as these.'

CLERKENWELL

A few streets away from the modern Barbican Theatre, the London base of the Royal Shakespeare Company, there still exists part of a building that was the administrative centre of Elizabethan and Jacobean drama: the Revels Office. This remaining part is St John's Gate, large and imposing, just off the south side of Clerkenwell Road towards the Aldersgate Street end. In Shakespeare's day a representative of his company, perhaps the book keeper, must often have come here bringing the scarcely dry script of the latest play. Every new play had to be vetted by the Master of the Revels, who was directly responsible to the Lord Chamberlain for censorship and licensing. And the Master, like Theseus's adviser in *A Midsummer Night's Dream*, had to decide which shows would be best for Court performance.

This dictator of drama, for most of Shakespeare's working life, was Sir Edmund Tilney, a conscientious man. Appointed when Shakespeare was in his teens, Tilney had connections at Court but no experience of theatre: as the years passed, more and more power was given to him, and the censorship of printed plays was put into his hands. He was in office during the 1590s when the Church was eliminated from active control over the stage, a control it had shared with the Crown and the City of London. Next, a precarious balance developed between Crown and City. This dual control of the stage continued until, at James I's accession in 1603, the source of power again altered: despotism, imposed by the Crown alone, ruled over the stage. Tilney administered these changes and from St John's Gate he supervised the flowering of English drama. Playwrights who sent or brought their work to him for approval during his many years in office included Kyd, Marlowe, Jonson, Beaumont and Fletcher, besides Shakespeare.

One of the few surviving manuscripts of plays which bear Tilney's notes as censor is that of *Sir Thomas More*, a play by numerous authors, one of them probably Shakespeare. Tilney began: 'Leave out the insurrection wholly and the cause thereof. ...' He wanted to rid the script of a dispute between Londoners and foreigners which led to a riot, and of More's refusal – later in the script – to sign articles that the king sent him. The changes Tilney required were on behalf of order and civil obedience.

Inflammatory shows did sometimes get staged, however, and dire trouble could result. In 1597 *The*

Isle of Dogs, a play (no longer extant) which criticized the Government, landed Ben Jonson and his fellow actors in jail and evoked an order (which was not carried out) for all playhouses to be demolished.

Shakespeare avoided punishment throughout his career, despite the tendentious revival of his *Richard II*, with its scenes of the King's deposition and murder; a single performance, commissioned to inflame rebellion, was staged at the Globe the afternoon before Essex's uprising. Because Elizabeth I was the last of her line, she was known as 'Richard II', and the deposition scene was impolitic. Nevertheless, the spokesman for the Chamberlain's Men, after the uprising failed, insisted that they had no idea their performance had been commissioned for political ends. They were let off and remained in favour, though Essex and his leading rebels were executed. The printed text of *Richard II* shows the censor's hand.

Tilney's office was housed in a former priory. The buildings were outside the City of London, beyond Smithfield cattle-market, on ten acres of land near the well of the Parish Clerks. Storage, however inadequate, was provided for the splendid costumes and properties used at Court pageants, masques, disguisings, tilts, plays and all sorts of shows. Tilney was responsible for a staff whose work included:

'... repairing, perusing, amending, brushing, sponging, rubbing, wiping, sweeping, making clean, putting in order, and safe bestowing of the garments, vestures, apparel, disguisings, properties and furniture of the same ... in readiness for service, which else would be mouldy, musty, motheaten and rotten by means of the dankness of the house and want of convenient presses and place requisite.'

Summer 'airings' of everything perishable took three weeks.

Those Elizabethans who were not puritanical were likely to be mad about clothes. Some observers, such as Harrison, were amazed and appalled by 'the costliness and the curiosity, the excess and the vanity, the pomp and the bravery, the change and the variety, and finally the fickleness and the folly that is in all degrees [all classes and ranks] insomuch that nothing is more constant in England than inconstancy of attire'. Men, even more gorgeous and extravagant in their dress than women, also indulged in what the Queen called 'superfluous apparelling their wives, children and families'. Instead of indicating the wearer's rank in the traditional way, clothes were chosen in response to the whims of fashion, irrespective of class. Elizabeth tried to check 'this increasing evil' with proclamations. They were ignored.

Women, who seemed to Harrison to be as outrageous as men, confused him by wearing clothes that looked masculine but distorted:

'What should I say of their doublets with pendant codpieces on the breast full of jags and cuts, and sleeves of sundry colours? their galligaskins to bear out their bums and make their attire to fit plum round (as they term it) about them? their farthingales, and diversly coloured nether stocks of silk, jersey and suchlike, whereby their bodies are rather deformed than commended? I have met with some of these trulls in London so disguised that it hath passed my skill to discern whether they were men or women.'

As for fashionable colours, their outlandish names – 'gooseturd green, peas-porridge tawny, popinjay, lusty gallant' – these were beneath Harrison's contempt: 'I pass them over.'

The Queen, however, was roused to enforce statutes about dress, 'confusion of all degrees in all places being great, where the meanest are as richly apparelled as their betters, and the pride that such inferior persons take in their garments, driving many for their maintenance to robbing and stealing by the highway'. She banned specific materials for men's clothing at precise levels in society. For example:

'None shall wear ... velvet in gowns, cloaks, coats or other uppermost garments, embroideries with silk, netherstocks of silk, under the degree of a knight, except ... such as have been employed in ambassage to foreign princes ... Captains in Her Majesty's pay ...'

Opposite
Boy actor as Moll, heroine of *The Roaring Girl* (Middleton and Dekker, 1611). 'Roaring boys' were quarrelsome hooligans. Moll was based on Mary Frith who, dressed as a man, went to the Fortune playhouse *c*1604, where this play was later acted. She was a bawd, cutpurse, swordsperson and smoker.

10 # The Roaring Girle.

OR
Moll Cut-Purse.

As it hath lately beene Acted on the Fortune-stage by
the *Prince his Players*.

Written by *T. Middleton* and *T. Dekkar*.

My case is alter'd, I must worke for my liuing.

Printed at *London* for *Thomas Archer*, and are to be sold at his
shop in Popes head-pallace, neere the Royall
Exchange. 1611.

or men who had more than a stated sum of free income. Satin, damask and taffeta hose and doublet were banned to men 'under the degree of a gentleman bearing arms' and of his equals.

Ruffs, a feminine extravagance in the 1580s, were 'pleated and crested full curiously, God wot', complained Philip Stubbes. When fashionable ladies were caught in the rain 'their great ruffs strike sail and flutter like dish-clouts about their necks'. Such 'great and excessive ruffs' were banned by Elizabeth as a foolish, 'disguised and monstrous manner' of attire. It was from abroad that the English adopted outlandish modes 'for which' wrote Harrison 'I say most nations do – not unjustly – deride us'. As for our greatest extravagance, we Englishmen 'bestow most cost upon our arses', and our 'women do likewise upon their heads and shoulders'.

When clothes were so stimulating and controversial, theatrical costume needed to excel. It was the most important visual feature of any play. Off-stage, the players' own clothes were still officially limited by the statute of apparel in force in Shakespeare's childhood: 'no ... journeyman in handicrafts, taking wages, shall wear in his doublet any other thing than fustian, canvas, leather or woollen cloth'. No doubt every player acquired some theatrical finery, like that included in the bequest of Augustine Phillips (Shakespeare's colleague in the King's Men):

'... to Samual Gilborne, my late apprentice, the sum of forty shillings, and my mouse-coloured velvet hose, and a white taffeta doublet, a black taffeta suit, my purple cloak, sword and dagger, and my bass viol.'

Even to appear on-stage in costume was attacked as presumption by the puritan Stephen Gosson: 'the very hirelings of some of our players ... jet under gentlemen's noses in suits of silk'. A player might indeed be wearing clothes of great value. One costume could cost three or four times as much as a tradesman earned in a year. Companies spent fabulous sums on costumes and materials, far more than on actual plays. Items such as these, from the accounts of Philip Henslowe, landlord of the Rose Playhouse, represent a great deal of money:

'A rich cloak ... £19;'

'To fetch two cloaks out of pawn ... one ... an ash-coloured velvet embroidered with gold, the other a long black velvet cloak laid with silk lace ... £12–10s;'

'Taffeta for two women's gowns for *Two Angry Women of Abingdon* ... £9;'

'A doublet and hose of seawater green satin ... £3;'

'A man's gown of branched velvet and a doublet ... £6;'

'Two pieces of changeable taffeta to make a woman's gown and a robe for the play of *Christmas Comes but Once a Year* ... £3–10s.'

Less costly were 'A robe for Time' which – presumably threadbare – cost £2, and 'A gray gown for Griselda' – no doubt, because of her poor background, very threadbare – £1. 'To buy divers things for to make coats for giants in *Brutus*' cost £1–4s; this sounds little in comparison with some items quoted, but it represents about twelve weeks' wages with 'meat and drink' for a 'most skilful' blacksmith receiving statutory London wages in 1598, when the giants' coats were made. Perhaps it is not surprising that foreign visitors to London theatres were impressed by the 'beauteous clothes' (as the Prince of Anhalt called them) worn by English actors, who indicated character or status by putting on more articles of dress, however incongruous. Dekker remarks that actors who play rogues 'wear rags and patched filthy mantles uppermost, when the under garments are handsome and in fashion'.

Sometimes the costumes and props owned by a company of players were supplemented or replaced, for a Court performance, by items from the wardrobe and store at St John's. Tilney's staff included, according to his terms of office, 'as many painters, embroiderers, tailors, cappers, haberdashers, joiners, carders, glaziers, armourers, basketmakers, skinners, saddlers, wagon-makers, plasterers, feathermakers' as he needed. He was expected to buy for them 'at price reasonable ... any kind or kinds of stuff ... wood or coal or other fuel, timber, wainscot, board, lath, nails, brick, tile, lead, iron, wire and all other necessaries'. He was empowered to imprison disobedient workmen. Wherever the Court might be, the Revels Office was responsible for transporting by wagon, boat or barge, the equipment needed for each Court performance. Included for the players' comfort were a brazier and a close-stool. Candlesticks, lanterns and candelabra – some with ninety-six lights each – were needed even in summer, because Court performances generally started about 10 pm and ended about 1 am. These items, like the gloves which actors were required to wear, the Revels Office provided. From St John's, the Office moved in 1608 to premises beside the Whitefriars Theatre, Fleet Street, and in 1612 to St Peter's Hill, between St Paul's and the Thames.

Tilney devoted much of his arduous working life to stage frippery, but his will sounds like a recantation: 'I bequeath all my apparel wherein I have spent much money very vainly that might have been otherwise better employed, to be sold at the best value thereof' and the money given to the poor. Tilney's nephew, Sir George Buck, succeeded him as Master of the Revels and was responsible for censoring, licensing and setting up Court performances of Shakespeare's most mature plays, such as *The Tempest* and *The Winter's Tale*.

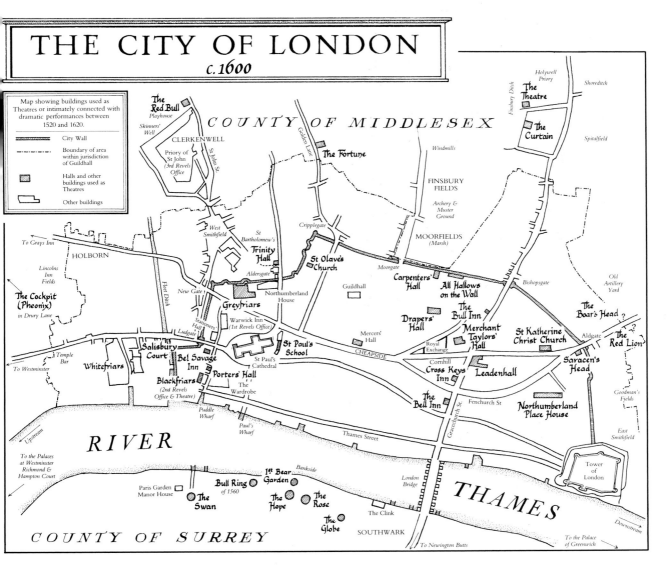

THE CITY OF LONDON c.1600

Map showing buildings used as Theatres or intimately connected with dramatic performances between 1520 and 1620.

City Wall

Boundary of area within jurisdiction of Guildhall

Halls and other buildings used as Theatres

Other buildings

7 THREE SEA PORTS

FAVERSHAM, RYE AND DOVER

No foreign banished wight shall anchor in this port;
Our realm brooks not seditious sects, let them elsewhere resort.

QUEEN ELIZABETH I: *The Daughter of Debate*

FAVERSHAM

The old Lord Chamberlain, Henry Carey, Lord Hunsdon, died in 1596, and William Brooke, Lord Cobham, who was rather puritanical, succeeded to the Chamberlainship; but Henry's son, George, took over the patronage of Shakespeare's company. Lord Cobham died a few months later. The Queen then appointed George Carey, the second Lord Hunsdon, to his late father's office of Lord Chamberlain. Before the beginning of August 1596 his players were in Kent, acting (for an official fee of sixteen shillings) at Faversham, a market town and port which shipped great quantities of grain to London. Faversham lies on a navigable branch of the River Swale, opposite the Isle of Harty which is part of the Isle of Sheppey.

Faversham, Camden wrote in his description of Kent, is 'surrounded by the richest part of this county', with 'a bay convenient for importation and exportation, on which account it is now the most flourishing town in this neighbourhood'. The open shore nearby abounds 'with shell-fish and oysters and plenty of oyster-pits'. The Kentish oyster-fisheries were famous, and attracted raiders from Essex and Holland.

Water was the life-blood of Faversham. 'There cometh a creek to the town that beareth vessels of twenty tons', wrote Leland, and to the 'north-east is a great quay called Thorn to discharge big vessels'. Moreover, as William Lambarde observed in his *Perambulation of Kent*, 1570, Faversham 'hath ... the neighbourhood of one of the most fruitful parts of this shire (or rather of the very garden of Kent) adjoining by land'. Hops were introduced in Tudor times, but Kent already excelled all counties in 'orchards of apples and gardens of cherries, and those of the most delicious and exquisite kinds'. And there are pears and plums and chestnuts,

'whereof' says Lambarde 'even delicate persons disdain not to feed, not commonly seen in other parts'. Cattle are bigger in Kent than elsewhere, he claims, and poultry finer, but sheep are excelled by the county's other products. Henry VIII, on an overnight visit, had been presented with local specialities: 'two dozen of capons, two dozen of chickens and a sieve of cherries'.

On marshy land to the west of Faversham, townsfolk specialized in the manufacture of gunpowder, using imported saltpetre and sulphur, and charcoal from local woodland. The larger towns were required to keep gunpowder in stock after the defeat of the Armada: a Spanish invasion was still feared. In 1591 the beacons throughout Kent were again manned because a Spanish fleet was once more in the English Channel. On and off during the next eight years the county was kept in a state of alarm, until Philip of Spain's death ended the danger of invasion. The burden on Kent is described in a letter of 3 August 1595 by Sir Thomas Fludd and William Sedley:

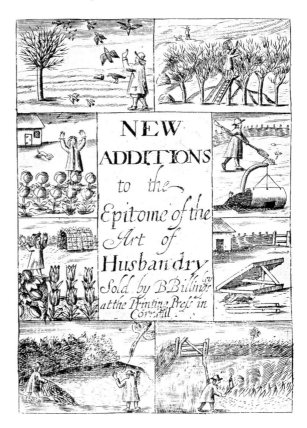

Country activities probably current in Shakespeare's day. Top left, then clock-wise, apparently: 1, bird-scaring; 2, pruning; 3, catching moles and levelling molehills; 4, making garden frames and wattle fences; 5, burning stubble; 6, netting fish – or heron; 7, ornamental gardening; 8, kitchen gardening and bird-scaring.

Opposite
'The main, strong and famous castle of Dover standeth on the top of a hill' (Leland, in Henry VIII's reign). It is to the west of the town, traditionally the key to England. 'All Kent hath yielded,' announces the Bastard (*King John* 5.1.30) 'nothing there holds out But Dover Castle.'

Woodcut (1633) of *Arden of Faversham* 14.120–1. Playing backgammon with Mosby, Arden is attacked by Black Will who planned to: '. . . come behind him cunningly And with a towel pull him to the ground'. Arden is stabbed by his servant, Michael. Two women – Alice Arden and probably her maid – hold daggers.

'It is a maritime county, compelled to watch the beacons, driven to put on arms or keep the field oftener than any other shire of the realm. . . . The shire, being the only high street or way by which all comers and goers into and out of the realm pass, is greatly charged with provisions, horses and carriages. . . . It has lately borne . . . a great burden of the soldiers of other shires, who lie there for wind and shipping, and are often billeted in towns and villages, and many times not paid for. . . .'

Faversham bore a particular responsibility for defence as it was a corporate member of the Cinque Ports. The full title of this confederation of seven towns (not five) is 'The Cinque Ports and The Two Ancient Towns': Hastings, Romney, Hythe, Dover and Sandwich; Winchelsea and Rye. Various limbs, such as Faversham (a 'limb' of Dover), supported them in the naval defence of the vulnerable stretch of coast and of the Channel crossing. Faversham's resources in 1565 consisted of '380 houses, eighteen ships and vessels' and fifty people occupied in merchandise and fishing.

A sensational crime, committed fourteen years before, had caused a great stir. On the evening of 15 February 1551, Thomas Arden, a former mayor of Faversham and one of its chief citizens, was murdered in his own house at the outer gateway of the old abbey by his wife's lover and two accomplices. The real-life drama appeared on stage in a play by an unknown author published in 1592, four years before Shakespeare's company acted in Faversham. *The Lamentable and True Tragedy of Mr Arden of Feversham* (as the town used to be spelt) *in Kent* was described in moral terms as showing Thomas Arden:

'. . . Who was most wickedly murdered, by the means of his disloyal and wanton wife, who for the love she bare to one Mosby, hired two desperate ruffians, Black Will and Shakebag, to kill him. Wherein is showed the great malice and dissimulation of a wicked woman, the unsatiable desire of filthy lust and the shameful end of all murderers.'

Arden's house (80 Abbey Street) still exists, and so does the building (in Preston Street) which used to be the Flower-de-Luce inn, where his death was plotted. Of the criminals, Shakebag seems to have escaped. Alice and Black Will were burnt. Mosby, servants and helpers were hanged.

The passions of Faversham men and women were

intended to be stirred up into loyal fervour by a visit from Queen Elizabeth in 1573. Her first visit, of two nights, cost the town nearly £45, 'including a silver cup presented to her, which cost' just over £27. Two years earlier, the Mayor's salary had been doubled from £5 to £10. The Queen returned in 1581. Faversham responded to her visits. Old military equipment – corselets and pikes – were sold, and replaced by powder and shot. Five years later, the town fitted out a ship of fifty tons at a cost of £400; and one of forty tons, the *Hazard*, was supplied in Armada year, 1588. Faversham's generous contributions continued, with £300 in 1592 for the keep of soldiers going to Portugal; and four years after that the town provided forty tons of shipping, a generous proportion of 160 which was the share of Dover, a far larger town.

After the Chamberlain's Men had played in Faversham, the summer was desolated for Shakespeare by the loss of his only son. Hamnet, twin to Judith, died at the age of eleven and a half and was buried in Stratford on 11 August 1596. Whether Shakespeare was at the graveside with his wife and their two surviving children, Susanna and Judith, is not known.

RYE

A year later the Chamberlain's Men were again in and around the Cinque Ports. In Rye they received official pay of twenty shillings. Even during the

Centre: actors on a railed, angular, jutting stage, whereabouts and date unknown, perhaps in a converted cock-pit. Spectators stand in front, and four watch from a gallery above a curtained inner stage. A vignette from the 1632 title-page of William Alabaster's *Roxana*, a play written for Trinity College, Cambridge, about 1590.

summer, travel was not easy in Kent and Sussex. When the Queen made a Progress there in July and August 1573, Lord Burghley summed up in a letter the start of her journey, saying:

'That the queen had a hard beginning of her Progress in the Weald of Kent; and namely in some part of Sussex; where surely were more dangerous rocks and valleys . . . and much worse ground than was in the Peak. That they were bending to Rye; and so afterwards to Dover, where . . . they should have amends.'

Rye, the largest town in Sussex at the time of the Queen's visit, is just over the Kentish border. It stands a mile or two into East Sussex on a sandstone promontory, which was a headland of the old coastline before the sea gave place to marsh. Three rivers – the Tillingham, Brede and Rother – border the town and meet south of it, where they used to form a wide harbour. This gradually diminished over the years, as the up-channel drift carried beach from headland to headland, forming lagoons and banks. Rivers carried down silt and marshes developed. All

Alleyway off Mermaid Street, Rye, town of many cobbled streets and Tudor and Stuart houses. Queen Elizabeth spent three days in Rye in 1573. To give her a purse of gold angels, the borough had to borrow money from the mayor. Soon after she left, the borough repaid him.

Four years after the Queen's visit to Rye, there was a sudden flood in the Wish, the area of the town outside the walls to the west and north-west. Holinshed records that about midnight water 'was eight or nine feet high in men's houses'. People were 'like to have been drowned' but William White, a boat-man, 'fetched a great company of them out of their windows, and carried them to dry land, as fast as he could fetch them; which were in great danger and fear, and glad to escape with their lives'. Water broke into the marshes, so that where the smallest of boats, 'a cock-boat, could not pass in at low water, now a fisherman, drawing six feet water and more, may come in and have good harbour there'. The marsh used for drying nets on poles was flooded, a loss to fishermen. But 'the same new-opened haven' encouraged 'certain men' of Rye 'to build fair barques to travel the seas' and this, Holinshed prophesies, 'will be a great furtherance to the maintenance of the Queen's navy'.

Sussex, rich in timber and iron ore, was the 'Black Country' of Elizabethan England. There, iron was smelted with charcoal for making fire-backs and cannon.

Although Rye ceased to be a military centre after the Armada, it continued active as a fishing port and trading centre. For the annual fishing off the east coast, boats sailed from Rye to Yarmouth and Scarborough; and Flemings sailed over to buy timber from the forest which covered the land for miles around. Fishermen, sailors and merchants had come from Winchelsea to Rye about seventy years before Shakespeare's birth, and helped the town to flourish. They were followed by troublesome

the coast between Eastbourne and Folkestone has altered since Roman days, notably about Hythe, Romney and Rye. The Elizabethan Lambarde, considering Kent, observed:

'Towns bordering upon the sea ... as the water either floweth or forsaketh them, so must they of necessity either flourish or fall; flowing (as it were) and ebbing with the sea itself.'

Rye's prosperity waned in Elizabethan times, when its harbour silted up, but it continued to be one of the chief ports for travel to and from the Low Countries. Smith called it 'the chiefest'. Unlike Winchelsea, which had room to develop, the walled town of Rye was restricted and crowded, with narrow, hilly streets between houses huddled together.

Overleaf
Windsor Castle, from Henry I's time the chief residence of English sovereigns. In Richard II's day Geoffrey Chaucer was Clerk of Works. Of Elizabeth I's gardens no trace remains. In *The Merry Wives of Windsor* 3.3.206, Page says he would not himself have Ford's jealous ill-humour 'for the wealth of Windsor Castle'.

Opposite
Pontefract (Pomfret) Castle, Yorkshire:

'O Pomfret, Pomfret! O thou bloody prison,
Fatal and ominous to noble peers!
Within the guilty closure of thy walls,
Richard the Second here was hacked to death,
And, for more slander to thy dismal seat,
We give to thee our guiltless blood to drink'.
                                   (*Richard III* 3.3.8)

Richmond Park, Surrey: deer browsing in open woodland, as they have done since long before Shakespeare's day. Many English monarchs loved to hunt here, but Richard II, desolated by his wife's death, pulled down the palace nearby. Rebuilt by Henry VII, it was supremely splendid in Elizabeth I's reign.

Clock Court, in the heart of Wolsey's palace, Hampton Court. This astronomical clock, manufactured in France, was built in 1540, ten years after Wolsey's death.
　'Time's glory is . . .
　　　To ruinate proud buildings with thy hours,
　　　And smear with dust their glittring golden towers . . .'
　　　　　　　　　　　　　　　　　(*The Rape of Lucrece* 939)

refugees, including Scots. The 'strangers' in Rye exceeded fifty in 1523. After the Massacre of St Bartholomew's Day in Paris (1572), hundreds of Huguenot refugees from France took the main cross-channel route used by ambassadors and royal posts and came to Rye, despite orders that 'common passengers or fishermen' should bring in no French or Flemings except 'Merchants, gents, common posts or messengers'. Those Protestants who did arrive from France, 'to the great cry and grief of the inhabitants of Rye and other places' nearby, were 'very poor people, both men, women and children'. In the year before the Queen's visit they numbered over 1,500. Most of those stayed only a short while; but other refugees came, many of them from the Netherlands, and formed a large alien community in Rye. They had almost all disappeared by the late 1590s, when the town was declining fast.

The poor who were given relief at Rye during Elizabeth's reign included sailors bound for Dover or Portsmouth – one party of Frenchmen numbered forty-four – and Irishwomen with many children. A shilling was 'disbursed to a soldier's wife that was left sick behind', and six shillings were paid to Henry Thunder 'for the relief of Anthony Grayson, being sick of the smallpox'.

DOVER

In 1597 the Chamberlain's Men were at Dover, where they were paid an official fee of thirteen shillings and fourpence. Near the end of Elizabeth's reign, Dover failed to impress the German visitor Paul Hentzner by 'its elegance or populousness'; but one feature awed him:

'Upon a ... rock, which on its right side is almost everywhere a precipice, a very extensive castle rises to a surprising height, in size like a little city, extremely well fortified and thick set with towers, and seems to threaten the sea beneath. Matthew Paris calls it the door and key of England. The ordinary people have taken it into their heads that it was built by Julius Caesar.'

Dover was the cross-Channel port most used by passengers in Shakespeare's day: 'with a good wind', according to the herald, William Smith, 'a man may sail in little more than two hours from Dover to Calais, which is thirty miles'. Queen Elizabeth, in the twenty-fifth year of her reign, had set about providing a clear, sheltered harbour. In the bay, a massive wall – 'The Pent' – seventy feet wide at the base and forty at the top, was to be built of cliff-chalk, earth from the fields and harbour-sludge, reinforced and bound together by faggots, thorns and piles.

Operations began on 15 May 1583. According to Reginald Scott (a Kentish gentleman whose book *The Discovery of Witchcraft*, 1584, an attack on superstition, is relevant to *A Midsummer Night's Dream*, *Hamlet* and *Macbeth*):

'There were 542 carts and 1,000 workmen attending them. The carts and horses were so numerous that grazing ground as far out as Shepherdswell was used to turn out the horses to feed on nights and Sundays, for there was no Sunday work in making the Pent .... Every cart was filled overnight, and in the morning at six o'clock they all approached orderly to the place where the wall should be made. The first driver was chosen to be a diligent person, and his cart to have a good gelding, for as he led the dance so must they all follow.'

Generally 200 carts would be unloaded in one place. There were two overseers, the Lieutenant of Dover Castle and Sir Thomas Scott. At 10.30 am:

'... all the drivers entered into a song, whereof the ditty was barbarous; and the note rustical – being delivered by the continual voices of such a multitude – was very strange. The words thereof were these:
"O, Harry, hold up thy flag, 'tis eleven o'clock,
And a little, little, little, little past:
My bow is broke, I would unyoke,
My foot is sore, I can work no more."'

After half-an-hour of this singing, the sergeant of the town on the top of a tower held up a flag. The workers made 'a general shout ... and wheresoever a cart was at that instant, empty or loaded, there it was left till' 1 pm when work resumed. At 5.30 pm the song began again and at 6.0 pm the flag reappeared and the day's work ended.

Tudor ships off Calais, England's main depot for her wool trade and her last Continental possession, besieged and surrendered 1558. At Calais, Nym and Bardolph 'stole a fire shovel' (*Henry V* 3.2.46). Soldier/beggars returning from Elizabethan wars in the Low Countries preyed on the public like 'Calais cormorants' (Marston).

'In almost every action there was imminent danger, particularly in laying the sluice ... also, many times men in digging the chalk stood on the cliff and undermined it so as sometimes a hundred loads fell down at once from under their feet, and sometimes from above their heads; yet all escaped without hurt except two persons upon whom great chalk rocks and much abundance of earth did fall, and yet were recovered without loss of life or limb. ...

A cart laden with earth passed over the stomach of a driver and yet he was not hurt at all thereby. And ... in all this time, and amongst all these people, there was never any tumult, fray or falling out to the disturbance of the works.'

The Pent took three months to build, 'at the small cost of £2,700', and the work was so reliable that three years later the Pent shrank 'not any whit betwixt tide and tide'.

Sluice-gates in the Pent made possible the scouring of a channel, so that ships could pass unhindered. The improvements spurred shipwrights on to build more briskly at Dover. Twenty sea-going ships, sloop-rigged craft of about forty tons, kept 400 sailors employed in regular voyages between Dover and Calais, and Dover and Nieuport near Ostend, with occasional voyages to Boulogne and

Dieppe. English law forbade travellers to carry more money out of the kingdom than expenses of the journey would require. At the end of Shakespeare's life, £20 was the limit.

Travellers to Dover had a choice of inns and victualling houses. Each host was obliged to hang up a painted sign, a foot square, over his hall door and to give a bond of £10 which he would forfeit if there was any disorder in his house. Inns included the Lion (sixteen beds), the Rose (twelve), the Woolsack (ten), the Arms of England – host John Bowles, Mayor – (eight), the Senior (eight), the Maidenhead (seven), the Angel (six), the Ship (six), the Bear (four) and the Spread Eagle (three). All, except the Angel, provided stabling.

Victualling houses were more than twice as numerous: about twenty-six. As to the food provided, according to Fynes Moryson, 'English cooks, in comparison with other nations, are most commended for roasted meats', while Paul Hentzner notes that the English are more polite in eating than the French, consume less bread but more meat and roast it to perfection. A local product was samphire, a fleshy plant from the cliffs of Dover and the nearby coast. 'The leaves kept in pickle and eaten in salads with oil and vinegar is a pleasant sauce for meat,' according to Gerard's herbal. Most of the victualling houses in Dover offered three beds, some more. The Cock topped the list with nine. During Elizabeth's reign, innkeepers and victuallers were not allowed to seek customers by going to the shore and meeting boats on arrival.

Jacob Rathbeg, accompanying Frederick, Duke of Württemberg, found Elizabethan Dover:

'. . . a tolerably large and pleasant place . . . lying . . . right opposite to Calais – which place his Highness likewise saw, for the weather was very fine and clear – at a distance of four hours' sail. Dover is very well fortified; many large cannon were then lying piled up in the harbour, and it could not easily be taken by force: besides which, not far off, several English ships of war ride at anchor to protect it. The mountains in the vicinity are not very high, but quite white like chalk, so that they are seen at a distance.'

An impression of vast, terrifying height is created by Edgar's speech in *King Lear* (Quarto Sc 20,

14–16), when he makes his blind father believe that they are standing on the cliff-edge.

> 'Halfway down
> Hangs one that gathers samphire, dreadful trade!
> Methinks he seems no bigger than his head.'

At Dover, Elizabethan travellers found many churches in ruins. St Martin Le Grande, old and decayed, was being used as a quarry which supplied materials for defensive building, especially on the cliffs and sea front. The chapel of the Maison Dieu still survives as part of the Maison Dieu building.

The old Guildhall, where the players would have been required to appear, was part of St Martin's building near King Street, but it gave place to the Court Hall – sometimes called the Guildhall – built in the Market Place early in James I's reign. George Byng, Mayor when the Chamberlain's Men visited Dover, was again Mayor when the Court Hall was begun and finished and when Shakespeare's company returned as the King's Men in 1610. The Hall was intended 'to be beautified with fair windows fit for such a house, and to have a garret there made'. The craftsman got carried away, however, cutting and carving 'certain escutcheons, letters and marks of particular persons' thus – in the Corporation's opinion – defacing the work rather than beautifying it. So he was ordered to remove all embellishments except the arms of the Cinque Ports.

The Corporation tended to suffer from discord, a feature of the new, more democratic times in which factions struggled for political power and its pickings. Elizabeth sent two commissioners to 'inquire of all manner of griefs, discords and dissensions between the said Mayor, Jurats [municipal officers similar to aldermen] and Commonalty.' The visit produced instant harmony:

'. . . and the said Mayor, Jurats and Commonalty were all in perfect peace, amity and concord, thanks be given unto God, and hath openly promised so to continue by God's grace.'

Within three months, promises were broken: a couple of Jurats disobeyed the Mayor and were fined £4 apiece. And then the Town Clerk was arrested for falsifying the accounts; he broke prison and vanished. The next Mayor, Thames Pepper, introduced a bond of peace which the Jurats signed,

Elizabeth I enthroned in the House of Lords, flanked by her chief ministers. Other lords sit in rows while (foreground) the Speaker, with officials and groups of MPs from the Commons, addresses the Queen. Shakespeare may have envisaged a scene like this when characters in *Richard II* 4.1. 'Enter, as to Parliament'.

to the effect that 'old griefs and slanderous words' would be 'forgotten and forgiven'. The Mayor and Jurats were to be 'lovers and friends, knit in one unity for ever ... for the better government of the town'. Eight days later, a Jurat who had signed the bond was dismissed for breaking it.

At the top of the social scale, the Constable of the Castle, from the last year of Mary's reign, was William Brooke, Lord Cobham, until his death (after a few months as Lord Chamberlain) in the fortieth year of Elizabeth's reign. Sir John Oldcastle's descendant, he was Lord Warden of the Cinque Ports, but by his day they had declined from their height of power. The navy of the Ports was being replaced by a national sea-force: the Armada's defeat owed little to the Cinque Ports' contribution of two large ships and five pinnaces or to Dover's own contribution of twenty-one small ships, each with a crew of twenty men and a boy. Lord Brooke did, however, have much to do with the development of the harbour.

The Queen had visited him in splendour at the Castle for a week, fourteen years before Shakespeare's company is known to have come to the town. When these players came, William Brooke had recently died and been succeeded by his son, Henry, as Constable and – although this appointment had been opposed by Essex – as Lord Warden of the Cinque Ports.

By the time Shakespeare's company returned to Dover as the King's Men in 1610, Henry Brooke, Lord Cobham, had been tried and condemned with Raleigh for plotting against the throne. The Con-

stable and Lord Warden who succeeded Brooke was Henry Howard, Earl of Northampton. Justus Zinzerling, a visitor from Thuringia, noted that at the Castle 'one hundred sheep and twelve cows constantly feed in the grassy court-yard'.

Dover had two seats in Parliament in Elizabeth's reign. The two MPs were often chosen by a recently formed select group, the Common Council, and not – as they should have been – by the general body of Freemen. Parliaments were supposed to be elected annually, but only ten were elected in all the forty-five years of Elizabeth's reign. During that time, ten of Dover's MPs were burgesses and the other ten seem to have been nominees of the Crown. MPs were paid a wage of three shillings a day, plus expenses for riding to Westminster and back. The journey was tedious and often dangerous, especially in the short days of early spring and late autumn, when Parliament was usually convened.

In James I's reign there were five elections, from which six new MPs emerged. One of them, Sir Thomas Waller, Lieutenant of the Castle, gained the Corporation's gratitude for his 'great pains and charges' as MP. He had refused all the expenses he was entitled to, so 'half a tun of wine' was 'forthwith sent to the Castle for his provision, and likewise a great fair sugar loaf' to 'be bestowed on his virtuous lady'. For receiving ambassadors and distinguished foreign visitors to Dover, a Master of Ceremonies was appointed. He provided coaches, carts, horses, barges and supplies to and from London: and the Lord Lieutenant of Kent made available hunting and hawking on the journey.

8 IN THE WEST COUNTRY

BRISTOL AND BATH

The City of Bristol . . .

Well fashioned as the best, and with a double wall,
As brave as any town; but yet excelling all
For easement, that to health is requisite and meet;
Her piled shores, to keep her delicate and sweet:
Hereto, she hath her tides.

MICHAEL DRAYTON: *Polyolbion*

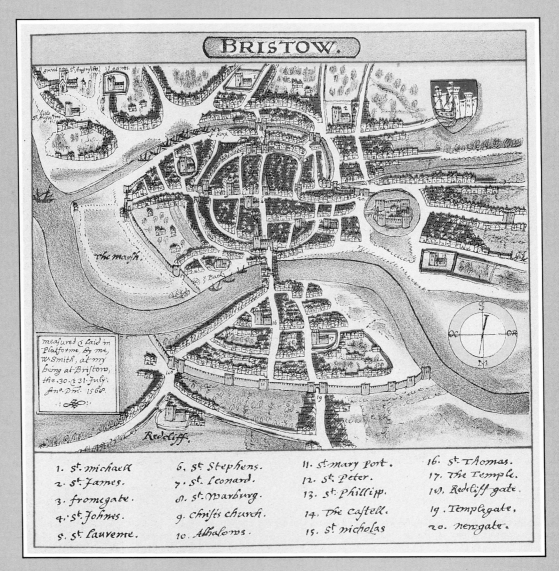

1. S. michaell
2. S. James.
3. fromegate.
4. S. Johns.
5. S. Laurence.
6. S. Stephens.
7. S. Leonard.
8. S. Warburg.
9. Christs church.
10. Alhalows.
11. S. mary port.
12. S. Peter.
13. S. Phillipp.
14. The Castell.
15. S. nicholas.
16. S. Thomas.
17. The Temple.
18. Redcliff gate.
19. Templegate.
20. newgate.

BRISTOL

About mid-September 1597 the Chamberlain's Men acted in Bristol at the Guildhall in Broad Street and received an official fee of thirty shillings. Bristol was at that time second only to London among British seaports. Leland had found 'Bristol upon Avon a great city, well walled, having a fair castle'. Shakespeare placed the first scene of Act 3 of *Richard II* outside this castle: there Bolingbroke condemns the King's favourites to execution. Leland was most taken by Bristol's superb advantages for shipping:

'Avon River, about a quarter of a mile beneath the town, in a meadow casteth up a great arm or gut, by the which the greater vessels, as main-top ships, come up to the town. So that Avon doth peninsulate the town, and vessels may come of both sides of it .... Avon goeth into Severn at King Road, three miles beneath Bristol by land, and six by water.'

The navigable rivers Avon and Severn brought commerce to the port, and the little river Frome fed the city's natural basin, which is now called the 'Floating Harbour'.

Camden, too, wrote enthusiastically about 'the harbour, which receives vessels under sail into the very heart of the city. And the Avon swells so high

Opposite
W Smith: Bristol. The Avon, writes Spenser, is proud of 'Bristol fair' (*Faerie Queene* 4.11.31, 9). But voyages of discovery, such as John Cabot's from Bristol to Newfoundland in Henry VIII's reign, heralded an age more glorious for England than for Bristol, where expectations of growth in trade were unfulfilled.

Above
Berkeley Castle, Gloucestershire (previously the scene of Edward II's murder, dramatized by Marlowe) is important in *Richard II*. York tells loyalists to meet him 'presently at Berkeley Castle' (2.2.119). Rebellious Bolingbroke, too, marches there. When they meet, York feebly opens the castle to him (2.3.159). Richard is doomed.

by the coming of the tide, that ships upon the shallows are borne up eleven or twelve fathoms'. He was impressed by Bristol's handsome buildings and by its efficient sewers, 'so contrived to carry off and wash away the filth that nothing is wanting that can conduce to cleanliness or health. But on account of these sewers no carts are used here, only sledges'. There were no dung heaps to obstruct them.

In the sixteenth century this attractive city, unlike swiftly growing London, did not expand much physically. Its population was about 15,000 when the Chamberlain's Men came. Bristol was the natural outlet for cloth from a wide area, but markets shrank as the years passed. Camden's peace-time declaration that 'citizens derive a rich trade through Europe and make voyages to the remotest parts of America', lost its ring of truth in the fifteen years of war that ended the century. But a port, even with its trade in decline, needed much grain to feed all who kept it working: and when Shakespeare's company visited Bristol in 1597, grain was in short supply.

This was the fourth consecutive year of hunger. Harvests had been disastrous. In those lean years, rye was imported from Danzig (now Gdansk) on the Baltic, the Privy Council in London ordered corn to be sent down the Severn to the famine-stricken city, and the Bristol Corporation commanded each man of substance to give destitute people, two to eight in number, a meat meal every day. Riots and starvation were prevented, but local trade was bad.

When, in February 1596, Elizabeth demanded three ships, fully manned and provisioned, allegedly to defend English commerce in the Channel against privateers and Spanish warships, the Bristol corporation pleaded dire poverty. They blamed London for Bristol's plight. Londoners, they claimed, had monopolized Bristol's former rich commerce with Southern Europe and had also taken over England's internal trade to within ten miles of Bristol. Twenty or thirty tall Spanish ships, laden with wine, raisins and silk, used to bring merchandise and trade to the Avon. Now, that fleet had shrunk to eight or ten small ships. Bristol goods could find no export market, claimed the Corporation. But the Privy Council continued to demand three ships: and it got them, manned by able-bodied Bristol seamen pressed into service. These ships joined the Royal Navy and took part, under Raleigh and Essex, in the sack of Cadiz. John Hopkins, merchant, commanded one of the ships and was elected Mayor of Bristol. His duties included seeing and authorizing performances of plays by visiting companies: but for seven years, from 1600, no payments to players are recorded.

Bristol had a long tradition of civic pageantry and street theatre. In the fifteenth century, at Temple Cross, a mime of St George killing the dragon welcomed King Edward IV soon after his coronation, and Henry VII was greeted by the spectacle of:

'... an elephant, with a castle on his back, curiously wrought: the Resurrection of our Lord in the highest tower of the same, with certain imagery smiting bells; and all went by weights marvellously well done.'

The decay of Bristol's local trade was lamented in a speech by a person representing King Brennus, legendary founder of the city, who asked Henry VII to help remedy the causes of its poverty.

Trade fairs, such as St James's Fair on 25 July and Temple Fair on St Paul's Day, 25 January, had become important events in Bristol's calendar before Elizabeth's accession. Most towns, according to Harrison, had one or two fairs every year during her reign, but some fairs, such as Bristol Fair and Bartholomew Fair in London, are 'not inferior to the greatest marts in Europe'. To such fairs flocked touring players, ballad-mongers like Autolycus in *The Winter's Tale*, jugglers, puppeteers and all sorts of entertainers to amuse the fair-goers and earn a living. In Shakespeare's lifetime, Bristolians could enjoy not only these performers at annual fairs, but also many visiting players throughout the year. One of the stars who came was the great tragic actor, Edward Alleyn, renowned for his portrayals in Marlowe's plays of Tamburlaine, Doctor Faustus

Opposite
Mortimer and Glendower fought in single combat 'on the gentle Severn's sedgy bank'. Three times they drank: 'of swift Severn's flood,
Who, then affrighted with their bloody looks,
Ran fearfully among the trembling reeds,
And hid his crisp head in the hollow bank,
Bloodstainèd with these valiant combatants'.
(*Henry IV Pt i*, 1.3.97, 102)

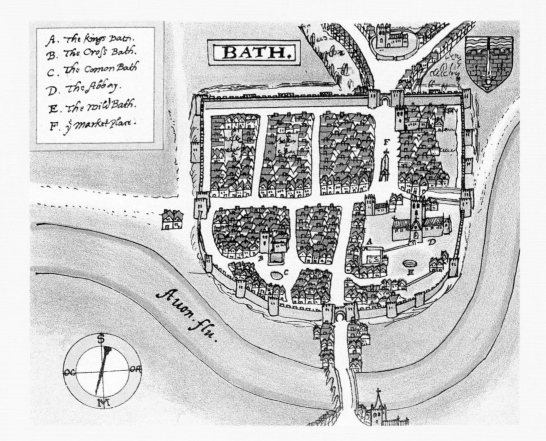

BATH.

Avon flu.

Opposite above
W Smith, 1588: Bath. Elizabeth, on her eleven-week progress,
1574, set out from Greenwich, stayed at Richmond, Windsor,
Reading, Woodstock, Langley, Sudeley, Gloucester, Berkeley,
Bristol, Bath, Longleat, Wilton, Salisbury, Winchester,
Odiham, Farnham, Bagshot, Oatlands and many other places
too, before stopping at Hampton Court. Such travel needed
determination.

Opposite below
Unidentified Flemish artist (? early seventeenth century): the
launch of English fireships at the Armada in 1588, the turning-
point of the campaign. The Spanish fleet (left), anchored off
Calais, fearing – mistakenly – that fireships were floating bombs
('hell-burners'), scattered from anchorage and ran north before
wind. The cresent moon, the Armada's earlier formation, so
eclipsed, proved 'mortal' (Sonnet 107, 5).

Above
Edward Alleyn (1566–1626), the 'Roscius of our age, so acting
to the life that he made any part (especially a majestic one) to
become him' (Fuller). Alleyn, as Genius of the City,
delivered a 'gratulatory speech' during James I's coronation
procession 'with excellent action and a well-tuned, audible
voice'.

and the Jew of Malta. On 1 August 1593 Alleyn wrote from Bristol to his wife in London. He was halfway through a six-month tour with Lord Strange's Men, and he mentions future venues and the play he is about to perform:

'If you send any more letters, send to me by the carriers of Shrewsbury or to West Chester or to York to be kept till my Lord Strange's players come. And thus, sweetheart, with my hearty commendations I cease from Bristol, this Wednesday after St James his day, being ready to begin the play of *Harry of Cornwall* .... We shall not come home again till All Hallows Tide. . . .'

That is, the end of October. Alleyn's wife, Joan, was step-daughter to Philip Henslowe, the theatre-owner, pawnbroker and shrewd financier. He had been worried, at this time of plague, by news that Alleyn was ill, but thirteen days after the letter just quoted he wrote to Alleyn:

'Very glad to hear of your good health which we pray God to continue long to his will and pleasure, for we heard that you were very sick at Bath and that one of your fellows were fain to play your part for you, which was no little grief unto us to hear, ... we had no letter from you when the other wives had letters sent. . . . And I pray you, son, commend me heartily to all the rest of your fellows ... for I grow poor for lack of them.'

The life of companies on tour was precarious. Alleyn asked what had become of the Earl of Pembroke's Men, and Henslowe revealed that they had been unable to pay their bills and so had returned home: 'for they cannot save their charges with travel, as I hear, and were fain to pawn their apparel for their charge'. The plague epidemic was particularly bad that year, 1593, so London's play-houses were closed for a long time, which may account for the unusual length of Alleyn's tour.

Opposite
Henslowe's step-daughter Joan, handsomely dressed wife of Edward Alleyn, wealthy actor. He called her 'my good sweet mouse'; they lived affectionately together for thirty-one years. She died without issue in 1623, aged fifty-two. Five months later he married Constance, daughter of poet John Donne, Dean of St Paul's.

In Elizabethan and Jacobean times at Bristol, the Treasurer paid out money not only to players but to the usual assortment of entertainers. Bear-wards often led their animals to the Marsh, where Queen Square now is, and supervised the baiting. Musicians were supported: a drummer named Audley was provided with board and wages for a fortnight and the waits received a rate subsidy. A tumbler, Edward Fones, was paid for 'feats of vaulting upon a horse and tumbling agility of his body'. Some bills were for repairs after damage. At a play in the Guildhall 'the press of people' bent 'the cramp of iron' which shot the door-bar, and repairs were recorded in August 1576. Some five years later, two benches had to be mended after being broken at a Guildhall play by 'the disorder of the people'.

Law and order, not always easy to enforce in Bristol, were scandalously obstructed shortly before the visit of the Chamberlain's Men. In 1596 Thomas Webb, captain of the Bristol ship *Minion* (one of the three ships which, with a pinnace, made up the city's modest contribution to the English fleet that sailed against the Armada), attacked a Danzig vessel returning from Lisbon. Webb tortured her master and sailors, and stole all her cargo. He stripped her of anchors and cables: she was wrecked and everyone on board was drowned. Webb and his accomplices disposed of their plunder in Southampton and Bristol, but were arrested. Webb seems to have escaped and the Mayor of Bristol flouted justice by releasing three of the *Minion*'s officers, Webb's chief accomplices in piracy. The Mayor was severely rebuked by the Privy Council. His successor was Alderman John Webb: whether John was related to Captain Thomas Webb is not known.

At this time of famine, attempts to keep order were hindered by the arrival in Bristol in the autumn of 1596 of 800 soldiers on their way to Ireland, in the bitter campaign to impose the protestant religion and English rule. The troops, waiting in Bristol for a favourable wind, 'were so unruly that the citizens could not pass the streets in quiet, especially in the night, so that many frays took place, though the soldiers had still the worst'. But they had to be lodged and fed, and the City Corporation claimed subsidies for food and transport from the Privy Council.

Strong measures were taken in this period to

English soldiers destroying Irish cattle-thieves. A: (left) a 'kern' (a 'wild' Irishman) is beheaded; (centre) another is led captive. B: stolen cattle, recovered, are driven away. C: armed soldiers, led by a silent drummer, march after three 'glibbed' (shaggy-haired) heads borne in triumph, D.

forbid non-residents – 'foreigners' – to settle in Bristol. Merchants and traders who lived outside the city boundaries were forbidden to become burgesses: so they were denied full municipal rights in the city. Every craftsman who employed a 'foreign' workman accompanied by a wife or child was liable to a weekly fine of six shillings and eightpence. A fine twice as large was imposed on any citizen who sent linen or woollen yarn out of the city to be woven. At fair-time, visitors with merchandise poured into Bristol. In January 1597 a London mercer claimed that his servants were robbed on their way home of £1,700 and also of promissory notes.

Bristol seems to have been the limit of Queen Elizabeth's journeys to the west. She gave God thanks on her safe arrival in August, 1574, for 'preserving me in this long and dangerous journey'. Each place where she stayed became the Court until she moved on; her souvenirs included a rich haul of jewels, valuable gifts that she expected from her hosts. At Bristol, her host John Young gave her 'a phoenix and a salamander of agate' in a setting of rubies and diamonds.

Often a stone's odd shape suggested to the Elizabethan jeweller a creature he might turn it into, with the help of gold and small gems. Fashion decreed that every gentleman should wear a gold chain. Watches were very costly, so only the rich wore them in Shakespeare's time. Rings, however, were worn by all classes and design varied much: precious stones, cameos and tiny carved skulls – reminders of death and God's judgement – featured as decoration. In his will Shakespeare left seven bequests for the purchase of rings. 'Some lusty courtiers also and gentlemen of courage' wrote Harrison, 'do wear either rings of gold, stones or pearl in their ears.' In the Chandos portrait (page 68), the only supposed portrait of Shakespeare with a claim to have been painted in his lifetime, the sitter wears an earring. This painting later belonged to the Chandos family.

At Bristol, riverside streets were called 'backs'. John Young's house was in St Augustine's Back, now the Parade, at the centre of the city where the Hippodrome (Bristol's largest theatre, used by touring companies) now stands. Shipping came very close up to his house which was near to the

The Earl of Hertford's water-show for Elizabeth I: Elvetham, Hampshire, 1591. Artificial, moon-shaped lake for sea fight and fireworks. Central features: A, Queen's presence-seat; B, Nereus and his followers; C, Neaera's pinnace with her attendant boat; E, musicians in both vessels; F, Fort-mount; G, Snail-mount; I, Queen's Court; K, Queen's Wardrobe.

Gunner in action. The linstock in his right hand holds a piece of slow-burning match. This ignites powder in the gun's vent, which lights the main charge of powder in the barrel. His left hand grasps another linstock, a sort of gunner's badge of office: dragon-shaped heads at each side hold the match.

quay, the marsh and 'the fairest, goodliest and most famous parish church in the kingdom', as his guest, the Queen, described the Church of St Mary Redcliffe. Her very full week's programme in Bristol gave her much pleasure and she expressed her gratitude to her host, John Young, by knighting him. As befitted a great sea-port, her entertainment included pageantry by water. A float is easier to move along a river than along a street, and this type of display, which had developed on the Thames between London and Elizabeth's palaces up and down stream, reflected England's growing sea-power, of which Harrison proudly wrote before the Armada: 'Certes there is no prince in Europe that hath a more beautiful or gallant sort of ships than the Queen's Majesty of England at this present.'

Thomas Churchyard, a minor poet and ex-soldier dogged by poverty and disappointments, devised and wrote this pageant. The Queen was greeted at High Cross by a speech from Fame, played by 'an excellent boy' who 'flung up a great garland, to the rejoicing of the beholders'. Later, 300 soldiers escorted her to John Young's and 'shot off their pieces in passing good order'. At this cue, 300 pieces of artillery 'went off' and the Queen retired for the night.

Englishmen's 'vast' fondness for 'great noises that fill the ear, such as the firing of cannons, drums and the ringing of bells' – change-ringing – was noted by Paul Hentzner. He observed that 'it is common for a number of them, that have got a glass in their heads, to go up into some belfry and ring the bells, for hours together, for the sake of exercise'.

Two artificial forts, built of wood and canvas, featured in the rest of the three-day pageant. The main fort 'made beyond the water' represented Peace and the City. Speeches 'passing between War and Peace . . . could not be said in the hearing' of the Queen – to discuss foreign policy was *her* prerogative – so they were printed, bound and presented to her. Churchyard ascribes some cutting of speeches to the envy of a local schoolmaster, perhaps director of the boys in the show. Churchyard's second fort, small and insecurely built, represented Feeble Policy. Soldiers captured it, then besieged the Peace fort and skirmished until dusk. Fireworks followed.

Next day, the battle continued, with audience participation: 'to the aid of the fort came divers gentlemen of good calling from the Court, which made the show very gallant . . . . Now served the tide, and up the water from King Road came three brave galleys, chasing a ship that came with victuals to the fort' whose defenders in 'extremity, . . . sent a gentleman' to the Queen for aid. Bringing her 'a book covered with green velvet, which uttered the whole substance of this device . . . he . . . swam over the water, in some danger, clothes and all', uttered a speech and swam back again. The broil continued 'till the very night approached'.

Three times in the final day of 'bloodsheds, miseries and other hurly-burlies' the attackers were repulsed. A parley followed: the Main Fort, symbol of Bristol city, declared its confidence in 'the courage of good people' and the power of the Queen. Peace was agreed, both sides 'shot off their artillery, in sign of a triumph, and so crying "God save the Queen!" these triumphs and warlike pastimes finished'. Gratified by the show, Elizabeth sent £40 for the soldiers' light refreshments. Then she boarded 'the galleys, and so down to King Road'.

When James I's Queen Anne visited Bristol thirty-nine years later, in June 1613, a water-pageant featuring a merchantman and a pirate ship was put on during her progress. Her visit and her influence helped an acting company based in the city, the Children of the Queen's Chamber of Bristol, to obtain a royal patent. Such official recognition of a group of actors in the provinces was most unusual. Even rarer outside London was an early seventeenth-century private playhouse: but Nicholas Woolf, a cutler, had one in Bristol, in Wine Street at the top of Broad Street, which seems to have been used both by touring players and local companies.

Bristol had seen the royal company of Players of Interludes, longest established of the Court performers, in 1557, the last year of Queen Mary's reign. Those mirthless times had forced the company to travel, but, when Elizabeth came to the throne, fortune smiled again on this undistinguished troupe and brought it back to London. They acted in Bristol again a number of times in the 1560s but then they dwindled away and in 1580 their last member died.

Three years later, the best dozen actors in the various companies were creamed off to form a special troupe for the Queen's entertainment. These 'very skilful and exquisite actors for all matters . . . were sworn the Queen's servants and were allowed wages and liveries as Grooms of the Chamber', as Edmund Howes recorded. This new company, Queen Elizabeth's Men, included the brilliant comedian Richard Tarlton, who 'for a wondrous plentiful, pleasant, extemporal wit' was 'the wonder of his time'. Their venues included Bristol (April 1583), Shrewsbury, Bath, Marlborough, Stratford-upon-Avon, Maidstone, Faversham and Dover. In winter the Queen's Men played at various venues in London, and they seem to have had the privilege of opening the season at Court, but after the death of their great clown, Tarlton, in 1588, the company's splendour was eclipsed by that of the rising Admiral's Men, with Alleyn shining in Marlowe's plays. The Queen's Men, like many troupes, included acrobatics in their repertoire. The company was big enough to split up and play in two places at once. Earlier, other groups of players had deceitfully called themselves Queen's Men and performed under the prestigious name to which they were not entitled. Trickery of this sort was not unusual in an England hungry for drama and swarming with players.

The Queen's Men, their lustre dimmed, continued to tour the provinces during the rest of Elizabeth's reign. Their final performance at Court was in 1594, the year in which Alleyn became leader of the reconstituted Admiral's Men. At the same time the Chamberlain's Men, with Shakespeare among them, embarked on their starry course. It was to lead to the supreme position at Court which the Queen's Men had occupied in the 1580s. By the time the Chamberlain's Men visited Bristol, their repertoire included a number of Shakespeare's plays, such as *Richard II* and *The Merchant of Venice*. Which plays the company brought to Bristol in 1597 – the company's only known visit there – the typically meagre records leave to conjecture.

BATH

The ancient City of Bath, where the Chamberlain's Men played in 1597, had been approached by Leland on his travels in Henry VIII's reign with delight. Bath was then a tiny city, virtually confined within its walls. These formed an almost complete circuit pierced by four gates that were locked at night. Outside the north gate a suburb had developed. The walls, which Leland estimated at 'not a full English mile' were indeed less than 1,300 yards long. They enclosed a mere 25 acres and a population of only 1,200 or so people in about 300 houses.

'I came down' wrote Leland 'by a rocky hill [Holloway] full of fair springs of water' on the way to 'a great gate with a stone arch', the south gate, and 'I marked fair meadows on each hand'. The city, whose Roman images and inscriptions excited Leland the antiquary, 'is set both in a fruitful and pleasant bottom ... environed on every side with great hills, out of which come many springs of pure water that be conveyed by diverse ways to serve the city'. Lead, being a local product, 'many houses in the town have pipes of lead to convey water from place to place'. Piped water was a prized amenity in an age when housewives and watersellers generally relied on conduits, wells, pumps, buckets and carts.

The 'antique works' of the Romans had been 'gathered of the old ruins' Leland rightly surmised 'and since set up in the walls re-edified in testimony of the antiquity of the town'. The medieval baths,

renowned for their healing powers, still attracted men and women in search of cures. Such clients, needing medical care, food, lodgings, and entertainment, brought business to the people of Bath and to touring players and musicians. 'There be two springs of hot water in the south-west part of the town, whereof the bigger is called the Cross Bath, because it hath a cross erected in the middle of it. This bath is much frequented by people diseased with ... pox, scabs and great aches, and is temperate and pleasant.' 'From scabs and aches', Leland asserts that many patients are cured.

The second, smaller bath, 200 feet away, 'is called "The Hot Bath"; for at coming into it men think that it would scald the flesh at first, but after that the flesh is warmed it is more tolerable and pleasant'. St John's Hospital, close to those two baths, founded for the maintenance of six men and six women, exists 'to succour poor people resorting to them'.

The third bath, 'the King's Bath, is very fair and large, standing almost in the middle of the town and at the west end of the cathedral church', which Leland also calls St Peter's Church (now known also as the Abbey). A high stone wall encompasses 'the area that this bath is in. ... The brims of this bath' are surrounded by a low wall with 'thirty-two arches for men and women to stand separately in. To this bath do gentlemen resort'. By the end of Shakespeare's lifetime, however, the Cross Bath had become the most fashionable bath in the city. English spas were increasingly popular, and though Bath attracted many visitors its arrangements were squalid and unhygienic compared with those of Buxton and Matlock Bath.

Harrison, who based his account of Bath closely on Leland's, says that in all the city's baths the water is 'most like to a deep blue' in colour 'and reeketh much after the manner of a seething pot, commonly yielding somewhat a sulphurous taste, and very unpleasant savour'. Undeterred, people coming 'thither do drink oft-times of that medicinable liquor'. Bathers gain health, according to Camden, because the waters 'by virtue of their heat ... cause sweating' and abate the 'dull and heavy humours' of unhealthy people. At noon and midnight, however, the waters, writes Harrison, 'boil very frequently and become so hot that no man is able to endure their heat or ... their force and vehement working'. In this turbulence, the sediment – 'all such filth as the diseased do leave' – is stirred up and then drains away through sluices. If we were there at these times when the waters 'purge themselves' we might contract 'new diseases' and 'depart more grievously affected than we came unto the city'. So the baths are closed, according to Harrison, for an hour and a half each side of noon and midnight.

A medicinal bath, and perhaps the City of Bath itself, features in Shakespeare's 153rd sonnet, derived from an epigram in the Greek Anthology. The poet says that a maiden devoted to Diana, goddess of chastity, found Cupid's torch burning while Cupid was asleep. She tried to quench it in a fountain of cold water in a valley, but the 'holy fire of love' heated the waters, which became for all time a boiling bath with medicinal power. The poet, love-sick, 'the help of bath desired. . . .' Perhaps 'bath' should be printed 'Bath' with a capital letter to signify the city. But, if Shakespeare did come to Bath, whether or not he was 'sad distempered' – grievously diseased in body or mind – he might still have written 'bath' without a capital. The general idea of medicinal baths was familiar, and such baths were used in various places in Shakespeare's day. Not far from Stratford-upon-Avon the spa of King's Newnham, twelve miles east of Coventry, offered cures. Harrison spoke with a number of men of the same trade as Shakespeare's father, glovers, who had been to King's Newnham. They told him about its water, which was popular enough to be 'daily carried into sundry parts of the realm and drunk' by those who needed it. He tasted some.

The spa waters at Bath had long been used for mixed bathing in the nude, a persistent cause of scandal. Despite attempts to segregate men from women, mixed bathing continued to be a problem until after Shakespeare's death. During his time as an actor, the popularity of Bath as a spa increased. This source of revenue was much needed, because the rich years of woollen cloth manufacture, for a long time the principal business of the city, were over. Chaucer's character the Wife of Bath, Dame Alison, the most exuberant of his Canterbury pilgrims, had thrust herself into his poem as a living advertisement for her thriving cloth business. In the 140 years or so between Chaucer and Leland 'making of cloth . . . hath somewhat decayed' and this recession continued, while pilgrimages for the sake of the soul were being replaced by regular trips to Bath for the sake of the body.

In Shakespeare's day there were many eminent visitors to Bath, including Sir Walter and Lady Raleigh; William Herbert, Earl of Pembroke; Henry Brooke, Lord Cobham; and the successive Lords Hunsdon, old Sir Henry Carey and his son Sir George. Queen Elizabeth granted the city a Charter in 1590 which gave various rights to 'The Mayor, Aldermen and Citizens of the City of Bath', but she did not come in person. For her visit sixteen years before, 21–23 August 1574, after her stay in Bristol, the programme of shows is not known, but the city was suitably spruced up. Men cleared away the dung and ashes generally dumped over the city walls; windows were glazed in the Church of St Mary de Stalls, presumably so that the Queen could worship there on Sunday (a day on which she never travelled); choristers were brought to the city from Wells; the bellman was given a new black coat, and green garlands adorned the half-ruined Abbey Church. Bath spent a lot of money on the Queen's visit, but the city lacked sanitation. Even some years after she granted the Charter, there was still no 'common sewer . . . which, for a town so plentifully served of water, in a country so well provided of stone, in a place resorted unto so greatly' every spring and autumn for 'the pilgrimage of health' was – in the opinion of a former 'Steward of that town' – 'an unworthy and dishonourable thing'. It persisted, despite the invention of a type of water-closet by Queen Elizabeth's godson and favourite, Sir John Harington, who lived nearby at Kelston, away from the stink of the city.

In an age of noisome smells, when people seldom washed their bodies, Elizabethans were lavish in their use of perfumes, some of them elaborate and costly. The Queen's nose was famed for its sensitivity. Her special bath, transported when she travelled, was scented monthly with herbs and spices, and 'sweet boxes' impregnated with scent were kept in all the state bedrooms. Pomanders, originally intended to prevent infection, became luxurious little balls of scented paste in exquisite jewellery hung from the

Opposite
Attributed to M Gheeraerts (painted after 1585): William Cecil, first Baron Burghley, Lord Treasurer. For his son's use, he wrote *Certain Precepts or Directions* (printed 1618). If Shakespeare knew them to be circulating in manuscript, he may have satirized Burghley's worldly wisdom in Polonius's 'precepts' for Laertes (*Hamlet* 1.3.58).

neck, belt or purse. Many pomanders were given to Queen Elizabeth as New Year presents. Her shoes were perfumed and she wore gloves embroidered and scented, a luxury introduced from Spain and Italy. Civet, a perfume from the anal pouches of the civet-cat, was widely used but, like all perfumes, it had to be applied with restraint. A character in a play by Massinger found it not a fragrance but a stench:

'Lady, I would descend to kiss thy hand,
But that 'tis gloved, and civet makes me sick.'

So popular was civet generally, however, that perfumers used the civet cat as their emblem, and if a young man rubbed himself with civet 'That's as much as to say' – in Claudio's words from *Much Ado About Nothing* (3.2.48) – 'the sweet youth's in love'.

Bath attracted those who were no longer young. The Queen's favourite, the Earl of Leicester, was on his way to Bath (and death) when he wrote her the letter on which she inscribed the words 'His Last Letter'. Her minister, Lord Burghley, retired there, and so did his son, Robert Cecil, Earl of Salisbury, James I's Lord Treasurer. The gap between rich and poor at Bath dismayed Harrison, who wrote 'rich men may spend what they will, and the poor beg ... for their maintenance and diet so long as they remain there'. Beggars, hounded from place to place and liable to be branded, were unwelcome throughout the realm, but Bath, Harrison thought, controlled them effectively: 'there is good order in that city for all degrees'.

Yet William Cecil, later Lord Burghley, had been warned in 1552: 'You cannot be without peril at Bath, whither there is daily resort from Bristol, and specially of beggars and poor folks.' The corporation, duly concerned, paid 'for sending a mad man to his country; paid to William Doulton for an iron letter to burn Rouges with, twelve pence; paid to William Ford' cash to keep out wanderers. Despite such measures, 'The Beggars of Bath' were notorious and part of the city was crumbling.

When Queen Elizabeth arrived in Bath in August 1574 for her two day visit – the only time she came to Bath – the Abbey, which had promised to be so gorgeous, was a ghastly ruin, stripped of its glass, bells and lead: and its stones were falling. To raise money for repairs, she authorized public collections for seven years from all over the country. A timber roof was built over some parts of the derelict structure, but most of the nave and part of the south transept remained unroofed until her death.

In the ancient church on this site in 959 Edgar had been crowned King of England, reputedly at

Whitsun. To commemorate his coronation, every Whitsun from the tenth century onwards the townspeople of Bath elected a mimic king and there were revels and feasting. In Elizabeth's reign these special Whitsun games were still flourishing. Whitsuntide was a Church feast, but folk-pageants abounded: maypoles set the scene, and May-games included morris dancing, plays about Robin Hood, and ale drinking. Country and Court met in celebration. Even when Queen Elizabeth was an old woman in her final years, she went a-maying at Highgate and Lewisham, although her poor health prevented her intended visit to Bath in 1602.

For recreation, Bath was equipped with a tennis court to the east of the King's Bath and with a bowling green near the Abbey. Over the years tourists and citizens enjoyed acrobats and tumblers, the music of bagpipes, trumpets and singers, the excitements of bear-baiting and cock-fighting, and performances by many dramatic companies. Mystery plays were formerly given in the Church of St Michael-by-Northgate, in the parish where the wool-trade flourished most. Down the hill, near the Abbey stood the Guildhall (very close to its present site) and there the Mystery plays, ejected from St Michael-by-Northgate after the Reformation, continued to be performed. Presumably it was also at the Guildhall that actors on tour gave their official performances in front of the Mayor. He paid the Chamberlain's Men twenty shillings in 1597, the same year as the Mayor of Marlborough paid them six shillings and eightpence for a show. In Bath, a public collection, besides official payment, is known to have been customary.

At the end of Elizabeth's reign, when Bath was so full of inhabitants and visitors that the chief baker had to buy extra grain from Warminster market, local companies were still performing. The chamberlain recorded payment of six shillings and eightpence to 'young men of our city' for playing at Christmas 1600, and of five shillings 'unto the children that played at Candlemas' in February 1601. In chamberlains' accounts, music and drama are both said to be 'played': so perhaps those two performances were not dramatic. However, there is no doubt that when James I was proclaimed 'our Dread and Sovereign King' a fencer gave a show, shots were fired and musicians played. The shooters 'upon the King's holiday' were regaled with two gallons of beer, five gallons of claret, a pound and a half of sugar to sweeten it, and an unspecified quantity of cake. Shakespeare's company, playing in Bath for thirty shillings official payment shortly after Queen Elizabeth's death, was already called by its new name: 'The King's Men'. So far as is known, this was their last visit to Bath.

9 LONDON AT PLAY
THE CLINK, SOUTHWARK, HUNSDON HOUSE
AND THE MIDDLE TEMPLE

Mark but the waterman
attending for his fare . . .
He carrieth bonny lasses
over to the plays
And here and there he gets a bit
and that his stomach stays.

WILLIAM TURNER: *Turner's Dish of Lenten Stuff*

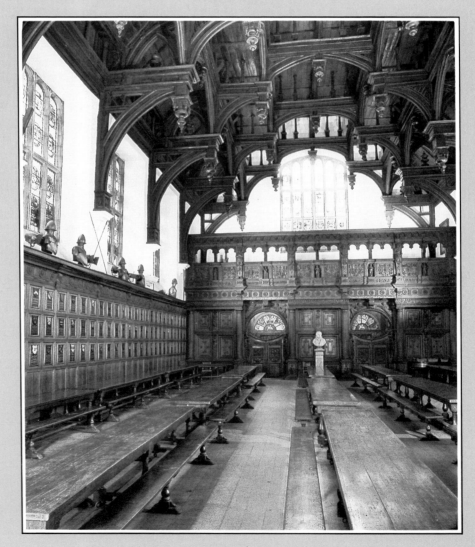

THE CLINK AND SOUTHWARK

In London, further tax records (concerning the unpaid debt of five shillings mentioned on page 84 plus an additional thirteen shillings and four-pence) focus on Shakespeare moving from Bishops-gate by the end of 1597, appearing in an unspecified part of Surrey about the time when the Theatre and the Globe opened, and living in 1600 at the Liberty of the Clink, an area on the Surrey side of the Thames in Southwark. He had evidently followed his job with the Chamberlain's Men to their new base on Bankside, the Globe Playhouse, close to London Bridge.

The Borough of Southwark, south of the Thames, contained a conspicuous parish church. Its old name, St Mary Overy, was changed to St Saviour, and the building, which was then in the diocese of Winchester, is now known as Southwark Cathedral. It is one of the few landmarks that Shakespeare would recognize in this neighbour-hood, now generally called 'the Borough'. Here, in St Saviour's Cathedral, when the Thames was frozen on New Year's Eve 1607, 'with a forenoon knell of the great bell' occurred the funeral of Shakespeare's twenty-eight-year-old brother, Edmund. He, too, was an actor, but achieved no lasting fame in his own right. Theatre men as-sociated with St Saviour's included Philip Hen-slowe and Edward Alleyn: both were vestrymen, and Henslowe was also a warden.

Long Southwark (now called Borough High Street) was the main road from London to the south, and it offered many famous hostelries such as the George, the Bear at the Bridgefoot, the Bell and its neighbour the Tabard – in which Chaucer's pilgrims met before riding on to Canterbury – and the White Hart, headquarters of the rebel, Jack Cade. Indignant with the 'base peasants' in *Henry VI Pt ii* (4.7.177), Cade asks them: 'Hath my sword, therefore, broke through London gates that you should leave me at the White Hart in Southwark?'

In Shakespeare's time, pleasure-seeking Lon-doners flocked to Southwark, a leisure area that offered bear-baiting, bull-baiting and plays. It was also a red-light district, with a long tradition of prostitutes in brothels ('stews') under the jurisdic-tion of the Bishop of Winchester. His connection was mocked in the name for a prostitute: 'Winches-ter goose'. Thomas Nashe provocatively suggested in *Pierce Penniless*: 'Make a privy search in South-wark and tell me how many she-inmates you find.' Stow, however, writes that more than forty years earlier Henry VIII had 'put down' a 'row of stews' consisting of a dozen brothels (with signs such as 'The Gun' and 'The Cardinal's Hat' painted on their Thames-side walls) and had 'proclaimed by sound of trumpet' conversion to 'good and honest rule'.

Next to this dubious part of Southwark was one of the borough's five prisons, the Clink, close to the Thames. Other Southwark jails were the Compter (or Counter, so called because the debtors were jailed there), the King's Bench, the Marshalsea and an inn recently converted to prison use, the White Lion in Long Southwark. Crime abounded in the London streets. There was no regular police force: law and order were left to watchmen, catchpoles, constables and sergeants as inefficient as the con-stable, Dogberry, and the headborough or petty constable, Verges, in *Much Ado About Nothing* (3.3; 3.5; 4.2 and 5.1). Even when arrests were made, justice did not necessarily follow. Jurymen were so corrupt that it was said: 'London juries hang half and save half.' The busiest gallows were at Tyburn (where Marble Arch now stands) and crowds flocked there to enjoy the hangings. Prisons, insani-tary and overcrowded, fostered many diseases, including plague, and imposed hunger. 'Bread and meat, for the tender mercy of God, to the poor prisoners of Newgate!' was the cry. Sometimes prisoners were allowed to live outside a prison but within a limited area, known as a 'liberty': a relief most blessed, after 'lying upon the bare boards', as a prisoners' petition said, 'still languishing in great need, cold and misery, ... almost famished and hunger-starved to death; others very sore sick....' Two liberties in Southwark were those of the Marshalsea and the Clink, where Shakespeare lived.

Nearby was London Bridge, the only bridge that spanned the Thames in London during Shakespeare's lifetime. It was nearly 350 yards long, 'a work very rare' wrote Stow:

Opposite
Middle Temple Hall. In Elizabeth I's reign it took at least ten years to build. Diners at this Inn of Court are still summoned by a horn: in the old days, members hunting hares with hounds across the Thames could not hear a bell. The dramatists Marston and Ford were members.

In Paris Garden: the notorious, moated Elizabethan brothel, formerly a manor-house, later called 'Holland's Leaguer'. George Carey inherited freeholds of brothels from old Lord Hunsdon, let this one to Dame Britannica Holland, an expert bawd. She provided hand-picked whores, comfortable ambience, excellent food, drink and entertainment, and charged high prices.

Part of J C Visscher's engraving: London (Amsterdam, 1625) showing Southwark (foreground) in Shakespeare's day. The Globe should be shown further from the river. For varied entertainment, people visit 'Paris Garden, the Bel Savage [inn/playhouse, Ludgate Hill], or the Theatre, to behold bear-baiting, interludes or fence-play' (Lambarde, 1596).

'... having with the draw-bridge twenty arches made of squared stone, of height sixty foot and in breadth thirty foot, distant from one another twenty foot, compact and joined together with vaults and cellars. Upon both sides be houses builded, so that it seemeth rather a continual street than a bridge.'

There were shops and stalls so crammed together that a passage only twelve feet wide was left for people, cattle and carts to move along. The houses were of great splendour, 'as great and high as those of the firm land' wrote Fynes Moryson, who considered the bridge 'worthily to be numbered among the miracles of the world' although the houses 'combined in the top' made 'the passage somewhat dark'.

Over each gate where the bridge ended was a tower 'on whose top', to deter disloyalty to the Crown, 'heads of such as have been executed for high treason are placed on iron spikes'. Hentzner and his travelling companions 'counted above thirty' of these grisly deterrents.

At the north end of the bridge Pieter Morice, a Dutch servant of Sir Christopher Hatton, set up a water-wheel which pumped river water through lead pipes to houses in the City. Half the river's breadth or more was occupied by the massive piers of the bridge. The tide therefore banked up, causing a difference of as much as four feet in the water levels on the two sides and a torrential flow through the arches. Not only did this sometimes encourage suicide but it also made 'shooting the bridge'

On the south bank of the Thames: Lambeth Palace, residence of John Whitgift, Archbishop of Canterbury when astrologer/physician Simon Forman, hounded by the College of Physicians, took refuge in Lambeth – regarded as sanctuary for felons – after escaping from jail. Forman saw *Macbeth* (1611), *The Winter's Tale* (1611) and *Cymbeline*, and wrote his impressions.

'... omitting to speak of great ships, and other vessels of burden, there pertaineth to the Cities of London, Westminster and Borough of Southwark, above the number, as is supposed, of 2,000 wherries and other small boats, whereby 3,000 poor men at the least be set on work and maintained.'

extremely dangerous. The noise of rushing water was a violent roar. Jonson mentions London Bridge and Paris Garden (with its roaring of baited beasts) as two places 'where the noises are at their height and loudest'. At the Globe, high walls surrounding the audience and the open-air stage would presumably have kept out the sound.

The bridge was (in Overbury's phrase) 'the most terrible eyesore' to watermen – the taxi-drivers of the Thames. Their trade suffered because people crossed by foot instead of paying their penny fare (fixed long ago in Mary's reign) and hiring a boat. Watermen competed fiercely for passengers, with cries of 'Eastward Ho!' and 'Westward Ho!' and Stow wrote that:

Most of the watermen lived in the liberty of the Clink and formed a third of its population. Early in the 1590s, anxious about unemployment, they feared that the Privy Council would close playhouses when disorder among spectators, besides plague, occurred in the summer. Ferrying playgoers was an essential source of watermen's income 'now in this long vacation'. So, led by the Master of the Queen's Barge, they presented a petition (mentioning 'our poor wives and children') for plays to be allowed to continue 'for God's sake and in the way of charity'.

Some twenty years later, when the King's Men opened the Blackfriars Playhouse over the water on the north side of the Thames and the Globe burnt

Savernake Forest, Marlborough, was renowned in
Shakespeare's time for plenteous game and a fern of 'most
pleasant savour'. Puck calls the Athenian wood in *A Midsummer
Night's Dream* a forest. 'Through the forest have I gone'
(2.2.72); Oberon wants the Indian boy 'to trace [range] the
forests wild' (2.1.25).

King's College Chapel, Cambridge; founded by Henry VI,
financed by Edward IV. In Shakespeare's day, theatricals
featured at King's, Queen's, Trinity: and St John's, where
Parnassus plays showed two Cambridge students applying to
Burbage and Kemp for admission to their 'cry of players' and
being tested on Shakespeare's speeches.

down, watermen were even more anxious about unemployment. They looked back on Southwark's richest days, when playhouses flourished there and when, 'hoping that this golden stirring would have lasted ever' (according to the waterman verse-writer, John Taylor, 'water-poet'), the watermen recruited extra men and boys. By 1614 the watermen and their dependants between Windsor and Gravesend had risen in number to 40,000. 'The cause of the greater half of which multitude hath been the players playing on the Bankside' wrote Taylor, 'for I have known three companies besides the bear-baiting at once there, to wit: the Globe, the Rose and the Swan.'

Across the main road (Long Southwark) to the east, on the south bank towards Bermondsey, stood the Bridgehouse, described by Stow as 'a storehouse for stone, timber, or whatsoever, pertaining to the building or repairing of London Bridge ... against the incessant assaults of the river'. A regular staff directed operations. There were also:

> '... divers garners, for laying up of wheat, and ... ovens builded, in number ten ... to bake out the bread corn ... for relief of the poor citizens, when need should require.'

Brewers like to 'remain near to the friendly water of Thames' and there was 'a fair brew-house new builded, for the service of the City with beer'. Maps show Southwark intersected with streams flowing out of the river: they were in effect open sewers. Their filth had been recently increased by the building on walks and gardens of many 'small tenements ... replenished with strangers and other, for the most part poor people'. Southwark kept its six scavengers and sixteen constables busy with squalor and crime.

Further inland, near Long Southwark, a hospital opened its doors to 'poor impotent, lame and diseased people'. Now, Guy's Hospital is close to the site.

The general public, in search of amusement,

Opposite
Queen's College, Cambridge: President's Lodge and Wooden Bridge. For Elizabeth I's Cambridge visit, the lane between King's and Queen's Colleges was strewn with rushes, hung with flags, coverlets, and boughs 'and many verses fixed upon the wall'. Will Kemp, Robert Gough and Richard Robinson, players in Shakespeare's company, were Cambridge graduates.

gathered westward on the other side of Long Southwark, the main road, at Paris (or Parish) Garden. Stairs gave access from the Thames, and the garden contained trees, bushes and fish-ponds. Beside it, in the liberty of the Clink, was the public centre for the baiting of bears and bulls by mastiff dogs, 120 of which were kennelled nearby and 'nourished' wrote Stow 'to bait them'. Sunday was the day for baiting. A thousand spectators could crowd into the wooden amphitheatre or game-house. The demand was so great that another open-air circus for bear-baiting, similar to the first, was later built in a field alongside. The entrance fee was a penny, and a second penny secured a prime place in the galleries.

In September 1598 Hentzner joined the crowd and saw bears and bulls 'fastened behind and then worried by those great English dogs and mastiffs, but not without great risk to the dogs from the teeth of the one and the horns of the other, and it sometimes happens they are killed on the spot; fresh ones are immediately supplied in the places of those that are wounded or tired'. The Queen visited Bankside to enjoy this sport which appealed to all classes, and Sir Walter Raleigh brought the Duc de Biron along to a baiting. During Shakespeare's boyhood, the Earl of Leicester had entertained Elizabeth at Kenilworth Castle with a bear-baiting described by one of the spectators, Robert Laneham, as:

> '... very pleasant ...: to see the bear with his pink eyes leering after his enemies' approach, the nimbleness and wait of the dog to take his advantage, and the force and experience of the bear again to avoid the assaults ... with biting, with clawing, with roaring, tossing and tumbling ... with the blood and the slaver about his physiognomy. ...'

In Southwark, where three Elizabethan play-houses were built – the Rose, the Swan and the Globe – the same form of wooden arena, with galleries, served the same mixed audience for plays as for those 'royal games'. Indeed both types of show were promoted by Philip Henslowe (owner of the Rose) and his son-in-law Edward Alleyn. Mastership of the royal game of bears, bulls and mastiff dogs was an office at Court for which the two

[62]

then two contrary motions at the same time. Wherefore it is a most bitter enemy to the Stomachs of very many men, especially if they use to take it presently after Supper or Dinner. And in this respect it is mischievous to the bodies of all sound men, according to *Hippocrates* his Rule. 2. *Aphorism.37. It is troublesome to purge those that are in good health.* For frequent use of purging Medicaments will soon make a man old; for the forces are broken by the resolving of the solid parts, by an *Hypercatharsis* of all nutrimental juyce.

By these things mentioned, it is easie to collect, that the smoke of Tobacco shortneth mens days. For being that our native heat is like to a flame, which continually feeds, as a Lamp lighted, drinks up the Oyl by its heat; it follows necessarily, that for want of food, life must needs fly away quickly, when the proper subject of life is dissipated and consumed: for with that moisture, the imbred heat fails also, and death succeeds.

You understand therefore (that are Tobacconists) that the sooty fumes of Tobacco, wherein you are wallowing (as it were) in the deepest mire, are of great force to shorten your days. *Galen* speaking of opening Medicaments, asserts, that by the frequent use of them, the solid parts of the body are dried, and that the blood grows grose and clotted, which being burned in the Reins, breed the stone. The same thing may be truly maintained concerning Tobacco, which many use too frequently, and more then any do use those kind of opening Medicaments; for this is more hot and dry then they are, and therefore is more forcible to hurt sound and well-tempered bodies. Take warning therefore you that love Tobacco, that you do not exceed in using too much of it, and enslave your selves to this fuliginous smoke, by hunting after it, and making a god of it. The goods of the body, are beauty, strength, and sound health. The most grave Author *Plutarch*, commending the last as the best of all, affirmed most gravely and learnedly, *That health is the most divine, and the most excellent property of the body, and a most precious thing. There is nothing in this World better; nothing more to be desired, and nothing can be found to be more pleasant. Without this (as Hippocrates saith) there is no pleasure or fruit of any other things. This is it, which in this life fills all perfection:* Without this no man could ever be said to be happy: This far exceeds the greatest Honours, Treasures, and Riches.

Early seventeenth-century pamphlet on the dangers of tobacco. Presumably Shakespeare discussed health with physician son-in-law, John Hall. To cure Drayton (author of *Polyolbion*) of tertian fever Hall mixed 'emetic infusion' with syrup of violets. For Hall's daughter's face-ache, her 'neck was fomented . . . [and] she ate nutmegs often'.

men, well qualified by their professional interest in Paris Garden, jointly applied in Elizabeth's reign: without success. Soon after James I's accession they bought the office from its holder.

Bears and bulls were brought to Court on special occasions for baiting. On 19 August 1604, when the Constable of Castile was entertained in Whitehall at a banquet to celebrate peace, there was a ball followed by a vast assembly 'to see the King's bears fight with greyhounds. This afforded great amusement', Hentzner observed. James also instituted the baiting of lions at the Tower, under the supervision of Edward Alleyn.

The English crowds at animal-baiting and plays 'and everywhere else' according to Hentzner 'are constantly smoking' tobacco:

'. . . they have pipes on purpose made of clay, into the farther end of which they put the herb, so dry that it may be rubbed into powder, and lighting it, they draw the smoke into their mouths, which they puff out again through their nostrils like funnels, along with it plenty of phlegm and defluxion from the head.'

This, with the spittle and filth of the animals, added to the squalor of bear-baiting. The Hope, a combined baiting ring and playhouse on Bankside, was, according to Jonson, 'as dirty as Smithfield and as stinking every whit'. Of refreshments Hentzner wrote: 'In these theatres, fruits, such as apples, pears and nuts, according to the season, are carried about to be sold, as well as wine and ale.'

Puritans objected to bear-baiting, but they were more concerned about Sundays being devoted to it than about its cruelty. When wooden scaffolding collapsed at 4 pm on Sunday 13 January 1583 during a bear-baiting, killing eight people and injuring more, the hand of God was seen at work. Perhaps this episode encouraged the Privy Council some years later to allot Thursdays to bear-baiting and to forbid the acting of plays on that day. But bear-baiting did continue on Sundays.

Cock-fighting was another sport occasionally held at Bankside. 'Cocks of the game are yet cherished by divers men for their pleasures' wrote Stow, 'much money being laid on their heads, when they fight in pits whereof some be costly made for that purpose.' Schools and inns were, however, used – particularly on Shrove Tuesday – throughout the country. Henry VIII had a cock-pit built at Westminster, near the site now occupied by Number 10 Downing Street. During Elizabeth's reign cock-fighting spread widely, although the Queen herself seems not to have been interested in it. James I was, however, an enthusiast who appointed a 'cockmaster' and in Lincoln, on a state visit, 'commanded four cocks to be put in the pit together, which made his Majesty very merry'.

Despite the popularity of the gamehouses on Bankside – drawing the crowds to see animals baited and cocks fight – what Jonson called 'the glory of the Bank' was the Globe playhouse, designed and built entirely for theatrical use as the professional base of the Lord Chamberlain's Men. It had been transported from Shoreditch to Maiden Lane on Bankside and in shape it resembled the gamehouses. It looked like a 'cock-pit' or a 'wooden O' (terms used in *Henry V* (Prol 11 and 13) with reference to another Elizabethan playhouse, the Curtain). The roof of the Globe, before it caught fire in 1613, was thatched, and its ridge was round. There were two narrow doors. It was at the Globe that Thomas Platter of Basle saw *Julius Caesar* in 1599.

'On the 21st of September, after dinner, at about two o'clock, I went with my party across the water; in the straw-thatched house we saw the tragedy of the first Emperor Julius Caesar, very pleasingly performed, with approximately fifteen characters; at the end of the play they danced together admirably and exceedingly gracefully, according to their custom, two in each group dressed in men's and two in women's apparel.'

Platter then refers to a performance at a playhouse which was probably the Curtain. This playhouse, within walking distance of Bishopsgate, was some 200 yards south of the Theatre in Shoreditch, and the two were used in conjunction with one another. The Chamberlain's Men acted at the Curtain after the Theatre closed and before the Globe opened, but Platter is probably remembering a fresh troupe, perhaps with Will Kemp in it:

'On another occasion, also after dinner, I saw a play not far from our inn, in the suburb, at Bishopsgate, as far as I remember. . . . At the end they danced, too, very gracefully, in the English and the Irish mode. Thus every day around two o'clock in the afternoon in the city of London two and sometimes even three plays are performed at different places, in order to make people merry; then those who acquit themselves best have also the largest audience. The places are built in such a way that they act on a raised scaffold, and everyone can well see everything. However, there are separate galleries and places, where one sits more pleasantly and better, therefore also pays more. For he who remains standing below pays only one English penny, but if he wants to sit he is let in at another door, where he gives a further penny; but if he desires to sit on cushions in the pleasantest place, where he not only sees everything well but can also be seen, then he pays at a further door another English penny. . . .'

Dekker's dandy in *The Gull's Hornbook* found fault with stage lace for being copper instead of gold, but not so Platter:

'The play-actors are dressed most exquisitely and elegantly, because of the custom in England that when men of rank or knights die they give and bequeath almost their finest apparel to their servants, who, since it does not befit them, do not wear such garments, but afterwards let the play-actors buy them for a few pence.'

Rushes were strewn on the stage to protect the costumes that actors wore when lying or sitting there. Stage properties also needed looking after: they were stored for use in revivals and future shows. With a swiftly changing repertoire of about twenty plays, this economy was important. Players were used to putting on a new play every fortnight and to acting a different play every day for seven to ten days. Shakespeare wrote, on average, two plays a year for his company. Another troupe's repertoire is conjured up by Henslowe's inventory of properties – some simple, some elaborate – for the Lord Admiral's Men at the Rose on Bankside on 10 March 1598. His list includes properties for a wide range of plays, including some by Marlowe that Alleyn starred in:

'Item, 1 rock, 1 cage, 1 tomb, 1 Hell mouth. . . .
Item, 2 steeples, and 1 chime of bells, and 1 beacon. . . .
Item, 1 globe, and 1 golden sceptre; 3 clubs.
Item, 2 marchpanes [marzipan confections for feasts] and the city of Rome [probably, like other spectacular scenery, painted canvas tacked on to a wooden frame for each performance].
Item, 1 golden fleece, 2 rackets, 1 bay tree. . . .
Item, 1 wooden canopy; old Mahomet's head. . . .
Item, 8 vizards [masks]; *Tamburlaine* bridle; 1 wooden mattock.
Item, Cupid's bow, and quiver; the cloth of the sun and moon. . . .
Item, . . . 2 mossy banks and 1 snake. . . .
Item, 1 copper target [shield] and 17 foils [fencing swords].'

Fifteen more 'Items' follow, including more shields (one 'with 3 lions') and '1 elm bowl. . . . 1 chain of dragons; 1 gilt spear. . . . 2 coffins; 1 bull's head . . . 3 timbrels, 1 dragon in *Faustus* . . . 1 lion; 2 lion's heads; 1 great horse with his legs; 1 sackbut. . . . 1 pope's mitre . . . . 3 imperial crowns; 1 plain crown. . . . 1 ghost's crown; 1 crown with a sun. . . . 1 frame for the beheading in *Black Joan*. . . . 1 black dog' and '1 cauldron for the *Jew*' specified in the stage-direction of Marlowe's *Jew of Malta*. When Ferneze cuts the cord 'the floor of the gallery gives way, and Barabas [the Jew] falls into a cauldron placed in a pit'. Elaborate effects, using stage machinery of that sort, were also available to Shakespeare nearby at the Globe, the rival playhouse to the Rose.

HUNSDON HOUSE AND THE MIDDLE TEMPLE

Private performances given by the Chamberlain's Men in other parts of London included one during the first week of March 1600 in Blackfriars, at Hunsdon House, the residence of their patron. He employed them to entertain an ambassador from the Low Countries, Ludovic Verreyken. 'Upon Thursday my Lord Chamberlain feasted him, and made him very great, and a delicate dinner' according to Sir Robert Sidney's steward, Rowland White, 'and there in the afternoon his players acted, before Verreyken, *Sir John Oldcastle* [the uncensored version of *Henry IV Pt i*] to his great contentment.'

In 1601, when the poor of Stratford-upon-Avon numbered 700, about half the town's population, Shakespeare's father died. He was buried on 8 September.

Pleading a law-suit.

On 2 February 1602, John Manningham, a law student in his fourth or fifth year in the Middle Temple, enjoyed a performance by the Chamberlain's Men in the hall of his Inn of Court. He wrote in his diary: 'At our feast we had a play called *Twelfth Night* ... much like the *Comedy of Errors*. ...' He outlined, with approval, the plot against Malvolio 'by counterfeiting a letter' and its outcome: 'making him believe they took him to be mad'.

The Middle Temple had their own tradition of creating masques and presenting them in their hall during the Christmas season. This hall, about thirty years old when *Twelfth Night* was acted, has been restored after bomb damage in World War II to its full splendour. In this Elizabethan 'great hall' the magnificent oak hammer-beam roof, screen and panelling show the richness of craftsmanship that was achieved in Shakespeare's boyhood. In Elizabeth's reign the four Inns of Court were flourishing and exclusive. Like colleges at Oxford and Cambridge, each was enclosed and had its dining hall, library and garden. *Henry VI Pt i* (2.4), set in the Temple garden, shows the factions of York and Lancaster plucking white and red roses: this quarrel will send 'A thousand souls to death' (line 127) in the Wars of the Roses. The two Temples shared the old church of the Templars, and each of the other Inns had its own chapel.

Legal education was, at its best, practical.

Although, as Stow says, there were lectures and 'mootings' (debates) and 'boltings' (private arguing of cases for practice) 'and other learned exercises', text books were few and all were in Latin. However, the younger students were helped by junior barristers and were able to gain experience in the chambers of counsel and in the courts. At the Inns, chapel attendance was compulsory. So was shaving 'at least once in three weeks'. Gowns had to be worn, even outside; whereas silks, furs, great hose, great ruffs, boots and spurs, swords and bucklers were forbidden. Sanctions ranged from fines to imprisonment. Loose behaviour was discouraged, sometimes by banning temptation. After Christmas 1581, an order was made at Gray's Inn:

'That no Laundresses, nor women called Victuallers, should thenceforth come into the Gentlemen's chambers ... unless they were full forty years of age: and not to send their maidservants, of what age soever, into the said Gentlemen's chambers. ...'

Gentlemen were to be punished for a first offence by exclusion from meals and for the second by expulsion.

The sexual boasting by Justice Shallow, from Clement's Inn, in *Henry IV Pt ii* (3.2.22 and 202), suggests that he pursued the frolicsome girls, 'Bona-Robas', elsewhere in London.

Dicing, widespread and cheat-ridden in Shakespeare's day, is here seen in dubious surroundings. Brothels were often disguised as inns. perhaps a customer, encouraged by a procuress and watched from behind, is using dice in whore selection. *Measure for Measure* and *Pericles* show knowledge of brothel life. Inns lined Bankside.

10 TOWN AND GOWN

OXFORD, SHREWSBURY AND COVENTRY

A maker of Coventry blue thread:

Yet is he undone
By the thread he has spun,
. . . since the wise town
Has let the sports down
Of May-games and Morris . . .
Where their maids and their makes . . .
Had . . . their smocks all bewrought
With his thread which they bought.

BEN JONSON: *The Masque of Owls*

OXFORD

In Oxford, travellers to and from Warwickshire could conveniently refresh themselves in Shakespeare's day at the Tavern on the Cornmarket. The vintner was John Davenant, a reserved and melancholy man who, after Shakespeare's death, became Mayor of Oxford. His wife was handsome, witty and pleasant. Beside the Tavern (renamed the Crown later in the seventeenth century) across a shared courtyard, stood the Cross Inn. This charming courtyard and the buildings that enclose it still retain the general outline that Shakespeare may have known well, and the festive atmosphere too.

He is said by John Aubrey to have generally stayed in the Davenants' house, 'where he was exceedingly respected', on his annual journeys into Warwickshire. The Cross Inn, next door, would have been the obvious place to go for beds and stables: a tavern was usually a drinking-house only. At John Davenant's Tavern wine was available on the ground floor, over his large cellar; but there were other rooms above. One of them, on the second floor, has a big brick fire-place and walls painted with pious texts, Tudor interlace, posies of flowers and bunches of grapes. In the 1590s these charming murals (now again visible) were covered by wainscot, so Shakespeare could not have seen them even if, as a friend of the Davenants, he stayed in this spacious room overlooking Cornmarket.

His intimacy with the family is declared by Aubrey. Robert Davenant, the eldest son, some twenty years younger than Shakespeare's children, became a parson: Aubrey reports having heard him 'say that Mr W Shakespeare has given him a hundred kisses' in childhood. Robert's brother William, who became a dramatist and Poet Laureate, 'would sometimes when he was pleasant over a glass of wine with his most intimate friends' claim to have written with 'the very spirit' of Shakespeare and 'seemed contented enough to be thought his son'.

Perhaps William Davenant, born in 1606, was

claiming Shakespeare as only his poetic father, but Aubrey and the gossips of the late seventeenth century took the claim as one of physical bastardy. Aubrey's quotations from the Davenants, however they are interpreted, place Shakespeare happily in the building which is now Number 3 Cornmarket, and the Painted Room, as it is called, would have been delightful to occupy.

The Chamberlain's Men visited Oxford and acted *Hamlet* there by 1603, possibly in 1601. In James I's reign the troupe, renamed the King's Men, returned six times: for a visit during 1603–4 their official pay was twenty shillings; an entry in the city accounts dated 9 October 1605 (a year in which King James was there) records payment of ten shillings; later entries are: 1605–6, twenty shillings; 7 September 1607, twenty-shillings; 1609–10 ten shillings; and 1612–13 ten shillings.

Entertainment of all sorts flourished during Assize week and the university Act, a ceremony lasting three or four days in July and the climax of the academic year. Plays were acted in the Town Hall and the King's Head, Cornmarket Street or in their courtyards, and from 1607 in the King's Arms, Holywell. Touring actors, while acceptable to the townsfolk, were frowned on by the university. Even enthusiasts for academic drama regarded professional players as vagabonds, whose shows in the city – which occurred chiefly during vacations – should be prevented. Often the university paid troupes to go away without playing; the rate was twenty shillings in 1589–90 and forty in 1603.

Camden notes that the Oxford coutryside 'abounds with all sorts of game both for hunting and hawking, and rivers well stocked with fish'. And:

'... where the Cherwell flows along with the Isis, and meets it; and where their divided streams make several little sweet and pleasant islands, is seated on a rising vale the most famous university of Oxford.... A delicate and most beautiful city, where we respect the neatness of private buildings, the stateliness of public structures, or its healthy and pleasant situation ... walled in ... with hills of wood which, keeping out ... the pestilential south wind and ... the tempestuous west, admit only the purifying east and the north which disperses all unwholesome vapours.'

Opposite
Coventry Cathedral. Shakespeare's contemporary, Drayton from Warwickshire, described Coventry 'Flourishing with ... walls in good repair ... halls in good estate ... cross so richly gilt' (*Polyolbion* 13.321). Shakespeare refers to Mystery plays, a feature of medieval Coventry, in *Hamlet* 3.2.14: Hamlet says that a ranting actor 'out-Herods Herod'.

D Loggan: Trinity College, Oxford, behind the library (B). Trinity students included Thomas Lodge, whose *Rosalynde* is chief source of *As You Like It* and who refers to the Ghost, in a lost 'Hamlet' play not by Shakespeare, crying 'miserably at the Theatre, like an oyster-wife, "Hamlet, revenge!"'.

As for the colleges and halls, these:

'... fairly built and well endowed, together with their excellent and useful libraries, so raise the credit and esteem of Oxford that it may be justly thought to exceed all the universities in the world.'

Comparing the schools of the two universities, however, Harrison writes that those of Cambridge:

'... are far more beautiful than those of Oxford, only the Divinity school at Oxford excepted, which for fine and excellent workmanship cometh next the mould of the King's Chapel in Cambridge. . . .'

Although Oxford was reputed to be healthy, disease – especially plague – was rife there. During

Shakespeare's lifetime twice as many deaths as births were recorded in the parishes of All Saints and St Michael's. Deaths increased in the later summer, the time when fleas are most active. A person bitten by a flea which was carrying the plague bacillus from a rat, would develop a bubo (as mentioned on page 13) in the groin if the bite was on a leg, or in an armpit if the bite was on an arm. Rats were thoroughly at home in Elizabethan houses which were built of clay and plaster on a wooden frame, with dirty rushes on the floor and a muck-heap outside. The Oxford outbreak of plague in

Opposite above
Artist unknown, probably Dutch: the Lord Mayor's water-procession on the Thames, probably 1683. Right, Whitehall Palace: spectators throng the protruding Privy Stairs, the wall where Charles II stands and Whitehall Stairs. Left, distant buildings at Westminster. Livery Companies' standards flying in barges include those of Fishmongers, Goldsmiths, Mercers, Skinners, Vintners and Weavers.

Opposite below
H Eworth: William Brooke, tenth Earl of Cobham, with his wife Frances (left), her sister Jane and the Cobham's fashionably dressed children aged (from left) two, one, six, five (twins), four: with pet animals, birds, bird-perch. Fruit and nuts on silver plates and wine in a gold cup, form a banquet.

Sir Henry Unton (1557?–96), Ambassador in France;
artist unknown. Sir Henry writes, flanked by episodes of
life (right) and death (left). Lower right, as a baby; next
(anti-clockwise) an Oxford student; a tourist in Italy;
officer at war in the Low Countries; Ambassador in
France; there, in bed, ill with fever.

At home, probably in Berkshire, he and his wife banquet
and watch a masque of Mercury and Diana; above, he
reads; to left, plays music; below that, probably
discusses theology. His corpse sails from France, is
mourned by poor tenants and – on the left – buried,
with pomp, in Faringdon Church.

Above
Tewkesbury; Edward IV, before battle:

'Brave followers, yonder stands the thorny wood . . .
Must by the roots be hewn up yet ere night.
I need not add more fuel to your fire,
For well I wot ye blaze to burn them out.
Give signal to the fight, and to it, lords'.

(*Henry VI Pt iii*, 5.4.67)

Right
St Mary Redcliffe, Bristol: with fresh rushes on the floor,
Elizabethan style, as on every Whit Sunday. Rushes preceded
carpets as floor-covering. 'Where's the cook?' asks Grumio (*The
Taming of the Shrew* 4.1.40): 'Is supper ready, the house trimmed,
rushes strewed, cobwebs swept . . . and every officer his
wedding garment on?'

1593 was blamed on the crowd coming to the Act: the Mayor and the Vice-Chancellor united to ban plays and games, limit the lodging of strangers and remove pigs and rubbish from the streets. In the 1603 epidemic, churches were closed and grass grew in the market place.

In Oxford, sport was opposed by the university authorities, who aimed to prevent young people 'consuming the goods of their parents, masters and friends'. Fines were imposed on townsmen who played ball-games or other sports with students. Anyone who wanted to allow the following sports or activities on his property needed the Vice-Chancellor's leave: baiting of bears, bulls or horses; cock-fighting; instruction in fencing or dancing (the same premises were often used for both); plays; dice, cards, backgammon or shovel-groat; bowling-alleys, which were popular with both 'town' and 'gown'. One Elizabethan bowling-alley, next to the house of a doctor of the university, was leased by him. It was near the Bocardo, a house in Cornmarket Street, where a school of fencing and dancing developed and flourished in James I's reign.

Clerics were dismissed from the university if they went to play football, which was specifically banned. A game of it in the High Street at Shrovetide in 1595 degenerated into a brawl. To watch sport was unacceptable, so undergraduates were forbidden to stand around in parks or fields 'gazing idly upon archers, shooters or bowlers, betting or otherwise'. To indulge in sport could lead to worse trouble. In 1586 some students of Magdalen College were convicted and imprisoned for shooting deer in Shotover Forest four miles from Oxford. Lord Norreys, Lord-Lieutenant of Oxfordshire, punished them. Fellow students later flung stones and turfs from the top of the college tower, wounding many of his followers. He escaped with his life by being driven swiftly past in a covered coach.

Tennis courts provided exercise in the city, and two were licensed by the Crown for the use of 'all true subjects' except scholars, vagabonds, apprentices, and those servants whose masters disapproved. Fives was a game increasingly popular among undergraduates, and there was keen support for prize-fights with a basket-hilted stick: the single-stick or back-sword which was favoured in the nearby Vale of the White Horse.

Christ Church and St John's were the two colleges where drama flourished most. At Christ Church there was a decree that two comedies and two tragedies – one of each in Greek, the others in Latin – were to be acted during the Christmas season each year. Whereas Cambridge excelled in comedy, Oxford excelled in tragedy, with Seneca's plays prominent towards the end of Elizabeth's reign.

At the time, Oxford was alarmed at the spreading of Roman Catholicism by Jesuit Priests who had studied at the university and were recruiting followers to be sent to Rome and Douai, and to Rheims (where, in 1583, about twelve students a month from Oxford and Cambridge joined the English seminary). Converts travelled to and fro, despite the Privy Council's system of travel licences. Several Oxford graduates were captured and executed. John Penry, associated with the 'Martin Marprelate' writings, had links with both Oxford and Cambridge. For some time 'an arrant Papist', he became 'a most notorious Anabaptist' and then 'a Brownist' (an Independent, a Separatist). Anthony à Wood called him 'the most bitter enemy to the Church of England ... in the long reign of Elizabeth'. Penry was taken prisoner and tried for sedition, and when dining in prison on 29 May 1593 he was interrupted at dinner and 'suddenly conveyed to the place of execution' at St Thomas-a-Watering, Surrey, 'where he was hastily bereaved of life'.

The Queen visited Oxford twice. She wished to come soon after visiting Cambridge, but at Oxford 'the dregs of a plague' (as Wood wrote) prevented her coming until Saturday 31 August 1566. Her programme followed the Cambridge pattern, and after her reception with its Latin, English and Greek speeches and its gifts, she retired to Christ Church, where her lodging was.

On Monday she heard lectures and disputations, visited New College and at night went to see Richard Edwardes's play (derived from Chaucer) *Palamon and Arcyte Pt i*, in Christ Church Hall.

Opposite
Bath. Romans used this Circular Bath as a cold plunge. It silted up, the roof collapsed and the sixteenth-century Queen's Bath was built on top. Through archway: the Great Bath. John Jones, 1572, called the waters 'swarthy, green or marble yellow ... of the brimstone, making a sussible [muddy] colour'.

Balconies had been fixed along the wall for the Court to occupy, and a stage with scenic 'houses' and a canopied chair on it for the Queen, in full view of the audience, had been built at the west end. The audience was less exclusive than at Cambridge: in Oxford, undergraduates and the general public were admitted. The elaborately lit performance began, however, with a catastrophe. When the Queen and the Court had entered, the pressure of the crowd at the entrance forced a wall protecting the staircase to collapse, killing 'three persons' whom Wood lists as:

'Walker, a scholar of St Mary Hall; one Penrice, a brewer; and John Gilbert, cook of Corpus Christi College; beside five that were hurt: which disaster coming to the Queen's knowledge, she sent forthwith the Vice-Chancellor and her surgeons to help them, and to have a care that they want nothing for their recovery.

Afterwards the actors performed their parts so well that the Queen laughed heartily thereat, and gave the author of the play great thanks for his pains.'

On Wednesday, after two days of academic events, she returned for the second part of *Palamon and Arcyte* and showed a keen interest in the characters and rewarded with eight angels the boy who played Amelia and sang sweetly. Hippolyta was played by John Reynolds who later, as a young Fellow of Queen's, turned against drama and wrote that it was as bad for students to act as to 'dance about maypoles or to rifle in ale-houses, or to carouse in taverns, or to steal deer or rob orchards'.

Opposite above
'Real' tennis, left, was played in London in the 1560s, and was very popular at Whitehall. Balls were dogskin stuffed with human hair ('the old ornament of his [Benedick's] cheek hath ...stuffed tennis balls', *Much Ado About Nothing* 3.2.42). Numbers in 1658 print: 1, court; 2, ball; 3, racket. Right: windball (4) tossed by fist (5).

Opposite below
Martyrdom, Oxford (1555): Protestants Latimer and Ridley, 'in the ditch over against Balliol College', Cranmer watching (Foxe's *Book of Martyrs*). In *Henry VI Pt i*, 5.6.56, to speed the burning of Joan la Pucelle, Warwick commands:

'Spare for no faggots. Let there be enough.
Place barrels of pitch upon the fatal stake'.

The production of *Palamon and Arcyte* was spectacular, with 'noises off' for the hunting scene provided from outside the Hall. Wood noted the response:

'In the said play was acted a cry of hounds in the Quadrant, upon the train of a fox in the hunting of Theseus, with which the young scholars, who stood in the windows, were so much taken (supposing it was real) that they cried out: "Now, now! there, there! he's caught, he's caught!" All which the Queen merrily beholding, said: "O excellent! those boys, in very troth are ready to leap out of the windows, to follow the hounds."'

At the Queen's leaving on Friday, after academic ceremonies and the giving of many pairs of gloves, walls 'were hung with innumerable sheets of verses bemoaning' her departure, 'as did the countenances of the laity (especially those of the female sex) that then beheld her'.

Twenty-six years later, in 1592, the Queen returned to Oxford to see, as Wood wrote, 'the change and amendment of learning and manners that had been in her long absence made'. She arrived on Friday 22 September at Godstow Bridge and stopped her coach 'notwithstanding the foulness of the weather' to hear the Vice-Chancellor deliver a speech, provided 'that it were not too long' – as the Cambridge commentator, Philip Stringer, drily remarks. Shortly before the Queen's previous visit she had appointed William Boonen, a Dutchman who had introduced coaches into England, to be her coachman. It was recorded that 'after a while divers great ladies, with as great jealousy of the Queen's displeasure, made them coaches, and rid them up and down the countries to the great admiration of all the beholders'.

This second visit of Elizabeth took the same shape as her first, with a succession of speeches and much ceremony. The question 'Whether that the air, or meat, or drink did most change a man?' was the topic of a disputation in Physic. She heard and saw 'a merry Doctor of that faculty, named Richard Ratcliff', show 'forth a big, large body, a great fat belly, a side waist, all, as he said, so changed by meat and drink, desiring to see any there so metamorphosed by the air'. But air, Wood says, won the debate. Next day the thorny topic in Divinity was

Christ Church, Oxford, magnificent college founded by Wolsey, 1525. His fall halted construction. Nashe's *Lenten Stuff* (1599) refers to 'imperfect works of Christ Church in Oxford' which has 'too costly large foundations to be ever finished'. The quadrangle's north (left) side was not completed until Charles II's reign.

'Whether it be lawful to dissemble in cause of religion?' The debate received 'much attention' and had its witty moment when 'her Majesty and all the auditory were very merry', but the Bishop of Hereford's speech dragged on and on, although the Queen 'sent twice to him to cut it short'. She also

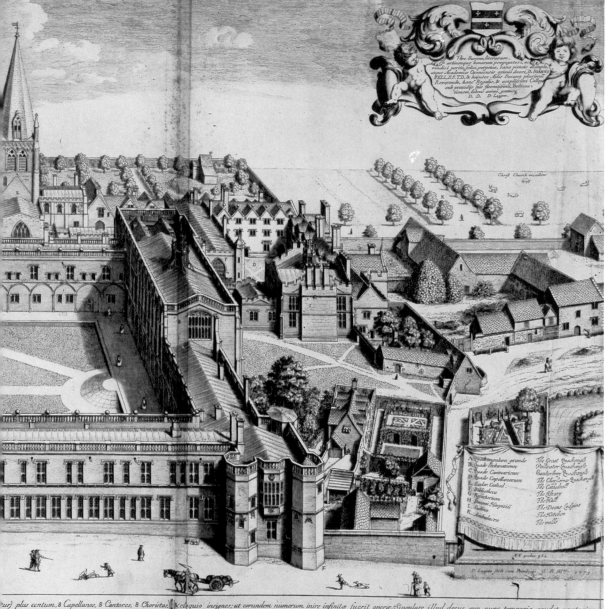

spoke her mind the next morning when, more privately, 'she schooled' Dr John Reynolds, the puritan antagonist of drama, who had in his early, profane days acted Hippolyta for her in Oxford, 'for his obstinate preciseness, willing him to follow her laws, and not run before them'. (After James's

accession, the translators of the Bible were to meet once a week at the lodgings of Reynolds, whose memory, Wood declared, was 'so prodigious ... that he might have been called a walking library'.)

The two plays which the Queen saw in Christ Church Hall, *Rivales* and *Bellum Grammaticale*, both

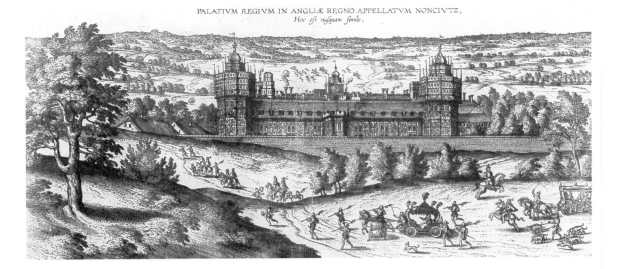

PALATIVM REGIVM IN ANGLIÆ REGNO APPELLATVM NONCIVTZ,
Hoc est nusquam simile.

Nonsuch Palace, near Epsom, built by Henry VIII. Hoefnagel's drawing 1582, shows the royal coach (foreground) and deer-hunting (background). Elizabeth I, in her later summers, spent much time at Nonsuch. Hentzner enthused about its 'parks full of deer, delicious gardens, groves ... walks ... embrowned by trees' for Pleasure herself to dwell in.

Smoking: '... this filthy custom ... loathsome to the eye, hateful to the nose, harmful to the brain, dangerous to the lungs, and in the black, stinking fume thereof nearest resembling the horrible Stygian smoke of the pit that is bottomless'. (King James I: *A Counterblast to Tobacco*, written in 1604.)

Tudor comedies in Latin, although played by the pick of the university's actors, evoked Stringer's comment: 'meanly performed (as we thought) and yet most graciously and with great patience heard by her Majesty'. She must have been positively pleased, because both Oxford and Cambridge were invited to act plays at Court during the following Christmas. However, academic plays were in Latin, but the Court required English, so the universities did not perform there.

Oxford's final offering to Elizabeth did not impress Stringer at all: on Thursday she drove away 'in her open and princely carriage' and about a mile from the city 'heard, lastly, a long, tedious oration made unto her by the Junior Proctor of the University'. Wood noted that 'she graciously received' this offering.

During the visit to Oxford of James I, Queen Anne and Prince Henry in 1605, disputations were again on the programme. One topic, of perennial interest to the King, was whether the smoking of tobacco is wholesome: another, relevant to both royal parents, was whether infants imbibe the morals of nurses with their milk.

The King was fascinated by the disputations and he chipped in with his own speeches, often interrupted by applause. When other people's speeches seemed to him 'long and not very excellent, he would say "Away away! – tush, tush!" or suchlike, but not very loud', as Philip Stringer noted. His

Majesty, according to another observer, much enjoyed being confronted at St John's College gate by 'three little boys coming forth of a castle made all of ivy, dressed like ... nymphs' who represented England, Scotland and Ireland. These national nymphs talked about 'their state' and then 'yielded up themselves to his gracious government'.

The Queen was intrigued by a Greek oration, because she had not heard Greek before. But she and her ladies much disliked the introduction of 'five or six men almost naked' into a pastoral comedy made tedious by rustic songs and dances. Two nights later, a four-hour comedy by the versatile Dr Gwyn, musicologist and physician, sent the King to sleep. Although on awakening he wished to leave – 'I marvel what they think me to be!' – he did manage to sit it out to the end, which was after 1 am.

The Bodleian Library appealed to his genuine love of books: 'Were I not a king' he declared 'I would be a university man.' At this time the hair of all the students looked 'decent and comely', but the day before James arrived over 100 of them wore their hats during a sermon in St Mary's and were therefore sent to prison. The royal visit caused prices to soar: oats were twice as expensive in Oxford as in Woodstock. At the King's departure, complimentary verses which he had disregarded when he rode by them 'were by the boys rudely pulled down' from the college walls. Students had stood to see him go, some 'orderly' in academic clothes, others dressed 'more confusedly and disorderly, without any such respect'.

SHREWSBURY

Shakespeare's company visited Shrewsbury, on the Marches, the frontier country between England and Wales, three or four times: 1602–3, official fee twenty shillings; 1609–10; perhaps 1610–11; and 1612–13. About five years before the first of those visits, *Henry IV Pt i*, in which the Battle of Shrewsbury is staged, was first performed, and Elizabethans could see Prince Hal, the future Henry V, killing Harry Hotspur and then allowing Falstaff to claim the glory of having done so. 'Many gentlemen' killed in the battle, Leland says, were buried in the Blackfriars' church, 'a little without' the town wall 'upon Severn side' at the end of Mardol Street. If Shakespeare's company acted this

play on tour at Shrewsbury, local interest would have been great: but there is no evidence that they did so. Leland wrote:

'The town of Shrewsbury standeth on a rocky hill of stone of a sad [deep] red earth, and Severn so girdeth in all the town that saving a little piece ... it were an isle. ... The town is strongly walled and defended with water, the which is to be counted in a manner for the town ditch. There be in the town three gates. The castle hath been a strong thing: it is now much a ruin. It standeth in the north part of the town. The town is more than a mile compass within the wall.'

Camden finds Shrewsbury to be 'a fine city, well inhabited and of good commerce'. It is very rich, thanks to hard work, cloth manufacture and trade with the Welsh:

' ... for hither the Welsh commodities are brought, as to the common mart of both nations. Its inhabitants are partly English and partly Welsh: they use both languages. And this, among other things, must be mentioned in their praise: that they have erected the largest school in all England for the education of youth.'

The master responsible for the success of Shrewsbury Grammar School was 'the excellent and worthy' Thomas Ashton. He and 'one other learned schoolmaster' and an usher were appointed by the town bailiffs. Ashton was a Fellow of St John's College, Cambridge, a clergyman (perhaps a Calvinist) and a skilful man of affairs, who was supported by the influential local gentry and the Corporation. The school, of which he became master in 1561, opened with 266 boys in seven classes. Half the boys came from outside the town and were boarded in local private houses; the rest of the boys lived locally. Numbers rose, and for six years were little below 400. For admission, a boy had to be able to write his name, read English perfectly and know English and Latin grammar. The only fee – for entrance – depended on status, ranging from ten shillings for a lord's son to one fifteenth of that amount for the son of an ordinary man living in Shrewsbury. Two of Ashton's pupils were Philip Sidney (the grave and brilliant son of Sir Henry

Sidney, Lord President of Wales and Lord Deputy for Ireland) and Fulke Greville. The boys, first cousins, came in the same term at the age of ten and as men they entered Queen Elizabeth's Court together.

According to the ordinances of 1578, the hours of Shrewsbury School, typical of the period, were 6 am to 5.30 pm in summer and 7 am to 4.30 pm in winter 'if daylight will serve thereunto'. Candles were forbidden in the school, for fear of 'breeding disease' or 'peril otherwise'. The dinner hour was at 11 am. On Thursdays, games were allowed but were limited to 'shooting in the long bow', 'chess play', running, wrestling and leaping. Although all betting, 'openly or covertly', was forbidden, and offenders were to be severely punished or 'expulsed for ever', boys were allowed to play their games for limited stakes: one penny a game, four pence a match. Holidays comprised eighteen days at Christmas, twelve at Easter and nine at Whitsun.

The school day began and ended with prayers, and if a sermon was being preached in any church all scholars were to 'resort thither to the hearing thereof'. Ashton was himself 'a good and godly preacher', but he was far more celebrated for his drama. Within his school, he stipulated that 'every Thursday the scholars of the first form [the top one] shall for exercise, declaim and play one act of a comedy' in Latin. Outside his school he devoted his time and energy to the Whitsun Mystery plays. These were part of Shrewsbury's lively dramatic tradition, and they were acted in a large hollowed space called 'the Quarry' where huge audiences could gather and see without obstruction. At different times, wrestling, bull-baiting, bear-baiting and cock-fighting also occupied the Quarry.

Ashton had risen from producer to author of Whitsun plays before he became a headmaster. In 1565 'Queen Elizabeth made progress as far as Coventry intending for Salop [Shropshire] to see Mr Ashton's play: but it was ended'. His greatest work seems to have been *The Passion of Christ* (since

lost) and this may have been the 'notable stage play played in ... the Quarry, which lasted all the holidays [perhaps the three days of recreation that had been customary when Corpus Christi had still been celebrated about the same time of year as Whitsun] unto the which came great number of people, of noblemen and others, the which was praised greatly'. Ashton may have acted a part himself, besides directing his pupils and the towns-folk in a mammoth show, which cost more than usual. There was room in the vast quarry for several stages; the river could have been used too. The Queen never saw an Ashton production.

After retiring from his headmastership, Ashton drew up statutes for the school. He wrote anxiously in 1573: 'You know that the school is old and inclining to ruin, also casualty of fire may happen.' The county jail stood just below the school buildings, and some fifteen years later, after Ashton's death, on a January night, the prisoners 'found means to unfasten their bolts and links and ... pulled down certain stone of the walls towards the school house'. But the prisoners could not get up there.

As in every school, a pupil's failure could be tragic. On 4 May 1590 'there was a young scholar, being about twelve or thirteen years old, being boarded at Master Hamon's ... hanged himself in the chamber where he did lie, being a Welsh boy whose name was Reece Ap John, being an idle boy and hated the school.'

The stark fact of death, less poignant when people die at a ripe age, had to be prepared for at the almshouses, administered by the Drapers' Company, on the west side of St Mary's churchyard. There was accommodation for fourteen poor people, unmarried, and for a married couple in the hall, part of whose duties was to nurse the sick. Inmates received a small stipend and firewood. Only people over the age of fifty could apply, and those who were accepted had to bring with them a winding sheet with fourpence tied up in the corner of it to pay for their burial. Thirteen one-room dwellings were provided by the Mercers' Company in their almshouses.

On a stage in the Cornmarket in July 1590 Hungarian tumblers performed 'wonderful feats and knacks', such as double somersaults in the air, both forward and backward. And then, despite each acrobat being put in a sack and its mouth being tied, the troupe again somersaulted forward and backward in the air. Nearby, on a rope fixed up outside 'Master Purser's place' one tumbler danced barefoot, holding a long pole. Then he 'put on two broad shoes of copper ... not touching them with his hands' and walked unswervingly along the rope. He put down his pole, and swung and twisted and turned on the rope, up and down, backwards and forwards, 'as if it had been an eel'. The townsfolk were amazed.

When Shakespeare's company first came to Shrewsbury the Roman Catholic mass was probably still being said in many places thereabouts. Shropshire, like Herefordshire, remained strong in the old religion. Local officials turned a blind eye, although in 1575 a member of the council of the Marches, William Gerard, of an ancient Lancashire family, was accused by a puritan draper, Thomas Browne, of slackness in prosecuting papists. The Queen asked Sir Henry Sidney to investigate the charges, which seem to have been dismissed, eventually, as frivolous.

Sidney's official residence, as the Lord President of Wales, was Ludlow Castle nearby, and he was a frequent visitor to Shrewsbury. When he came with his son Philip, who had just returned from foreign travel, the town spent seven shillings and twopence on 'wine and cakes and other things'. Shrewsbury cakes were famous. In 1602 Lord Herbert of Cherbury, aged twenty, sent a gift of them to his guardian and wrote:

'Lest you think this country [this region] ruder than it is, I have sent you some of the bread which I am sure will be dainty, howsoever it be not pleasing: it is a kind of cake which our country people use and make in no place in England but in Shrewsbury; if you vouchsafe to taste of them, you enworthy the country and sender. Measure my love not by the substance of it which is brittle, but by the form of it which is circular [that is, eternal].'

Ingredients of the cakes were flour, sugar, butter, nutmeg and rose-water, but other recipes abounded, and some included eggs and caraway seeds.

Shrewsbury was also known for its ale. Ale and beer are different drinks, though the distinction tends to be forgotten. An older drink than beer, ale was made from barley mash, yeast and water. There were no hops in that fermented malt liquor. Hops and beer were brought from the Low Countries in the fifteenth century. This liquor with hops in it kept better, and it soon rivalled ale in popularity, although ale-tasters (such as Shakespeare's father) had the task of seeing that brewers did not add 'hops nor other subtle things' to ale in the brewing. The cities first, and then the country, took to beer, but not without protest. Hops, the 'wicked weed', were said to 'spoil the taste of ale and endanger the people'. Andrew Boorde in his *Dietary* claims that the health of Englishmen is undermined by beer: 'specially it killeth them the which be troubled with the colic and the stone', Harrison writes that ale is thought of as a drink for the old and sick, and he calls the English a 'nation of malt bugs'. Not until after Shakespeare's day was ale made with hops.

In his time good drinking-water was rare (boiling was recommended) so ale and beer were drunk by everybody, from babies to dotards. Poorer people in the country drank milk, whey, buttermilk, cider, or liquors made from fermented honey – mead or metheglin. Gervase Markham wrote that those 'two compound drinks of honey and herbs ... in the places where they are made – in Wales and the Marches – are renowned for exceeding wholesome and cordial'. Many small households and most large ones brewed their own beer. In Harrison's modest Essex rectory his wife and her maids brewed 200 gallons a month and the household drank it, at a cost of little more than a penny a gallon. Household beer contained little alcohol, and it was drunk at all meals and between meals.

The third speciality of Shrewsbury was brawn, which was eaten at the main meal of the day – dinner – or at supper. For many people, dinner was the first meal: breakfast was said to be unhealthy. People who did take breakfast, however, began their day with bread and beer. If servants got anything, it was probably a piece of bread: occasionally, porridge. Wealthy homes also provided meat or fish (on fish days) and sometimes wine. The Queen's maids of honour had beef or herrings. Dinner began between 10 am and 1 pm. Harrison notes that 'the nobility, gentry and students do ordinarily go to dinner at eleven' but that farmers and London merchants seldom dine before noon. In a well-off home, when

there were guests, dinner could last as much as three hours, even if there were only two courses. An enormous variety of dishes was served, but this was so as to satisfy people's different tastes, not to encourage over-eating. No-one (not even a Falstaff) was expected to eat many of the dishes provided.

Gervase Markham advises 'any good man' providing a 'humble feast of ordinary proportion' for his family and 'his true and worthy friends' to set down:

'... the full number of his full dishes ... for one course ... as for example: first, a shield of brawn with mustard; secondly, a boiled capon; thirdly, a boiled piece of beef; fourthly, a chine of beef roasted; fifthly, a neat's tongue [beef or veal] roasted; sixthly a pig roasted; seventhly, chewets [finely chopped meat] baked; eighthly, a goose roasted; ninthly, a swan roasted; tenthly, a turkey roasted; the eleventh, a haunch of venison roasted; the twelfth, a pasty of venison; the thirteenth, a kid with a pudding in his belly; the fourteenth an olive pie [of little meat rolls]; the

Battlefield, Shrewsbury. 'Tomorrow' says the Archbishop in *Henry IV Pt i*, 4.4.9,

'the fortune of ten thousand men
Must bide the touch; for, sir, at Shrewsbury ...
The King with mighty and quick-raisèd power ...'

meets Hotspur. Here Henry IV defeated the rebels, July 1403, and the church was built in commemoration, 1408.

fifteenth, a couple of capons; the sixteenth a custard or Dousets [usually small tarts]. Now to these full dishes may be added sallets...'

and other dishes up to 'the full service of no less than two and thirty dishes'. Boiled 'sallets' used any of these vegetables (a word not yet in common use): leeks, borage, bugloss, endive, chicory, cauliflower, sorrel, marigold leaves, watercress, onions, asparagus. Green salads were coming into fashion. Gerard, in his *Herball*, recommends lettuce as a starter to stir the appetite and after supper to keep 'away drunkenness which cometh by the wine; and that is by reason that it stayeth the vapours from rising up into the head'. Supper was generally a smaller version of dinner, although wealthy households would serve a supper as large as dinner if there were guests. In a modest home, supper might consist of bread and cheese and beer, perhaps with porridge or eggs. The nobility, gentry and students supped between 5 and 6 pm, merchants seldom before 6 and farmers at 7 or 8. Candles, rush-lights and torches encouraged people to go to bed early.

Health books or 'dietaries' were popular, and they all advised temperance in eating and drinking (and in love-making). Nevertheless, English people were not generally healthy. The rich ate too much, the poor too little, and stomach troubles resulted. Spices were necessary to prevent meat going bad. Lack of hygiene and of refrigeration, and of good drinking-water, encouraged illness.

In 1593 Shrewsbury, fearing the plague, closed its wool market from mid-July until mid-August and appointed warders 'at every gate of the town' to check all arrivals. The weather – then believed to be connected with plague – was terrible that summer, and the Severn remained almost at flood level. Most people spent Sunday 11 August in St Mary's Church, fasting, praying for seasonable weather, 'lamenting their sins and calling to God' and listening to sermons 'from eight of the clock in the morning until four of the clock at night, and never came out of church until then'. God seemed to respond: 'in the end it fell out a very fair season'.

Three years later, however, in 1596, there was widespread hunger. 'Many in all countries in England die' wrote the anonymous local chronicler 'and go in great numbers miserably a-begging'. The town bakers made penny loaves for the poor 'who were not able to buy any bigger portion. They were so unruly and greedy to have it' that the six bailiffs and other officers had much ado to serve them.

At such a time of dearth, the Privy Council's demand for £400 from this inland town 'towards the furnishing of her Majesty's Royal Navy' came as a terrible blow: but patriotism had been fostered during the Queen's reign. Shows and pageants played their part in this. On St George's Day 1581 Sir Henry Sidney, as a Knight of the Garter, marched in a procession to St Chad's Church, Shrewsbury, and presided over a local version of the Garter service. A week later he attended a muster of 360 Shrewsbury schoolboys and their masters, and he listened to the head boy or 'general' and the

young 'captains' make speeches about how valiantly they would defend their country. When, after another week, the Lord President left by water, he was honoured with a pageant on an island a few hundred yards down river. Here some of the versatile schoolboys, dressed as water-nymphs in green costumes with willow head-dresses, lamented his departure in orations and songs, accompanied by a band of boy musicians. Thomas Churchyard, a local poet whom Sir Henry recommended, wrote the lyrics. In their last song, the nymphs – non-swimmers alas! – express their frustration:

> '*And will your honour needs depart,*
> *And must it needs be so?*
> *Would God we could like fishes swim,*
> *That we might with thee go!*'

This final item, says the chronicle, 'was done so pitifully that truly it made many to weep: and my lord himself to change countenance'.

By the time the King's Men came to Shrewsbury, such tearful scenes were ending. The emotional bond between the town and the Lord President became, in James I's reign, a contract with a string attached. The bailiffs, aldermen and council agreed in 1611 to pay the Lord President (who was then Ralph, third Lord Eure) 'a gratuity not exceeding twenty nobles – but only 'if it please him to keep Lent term next in this town, or else not'. Elizabethan sentiment had given place to Jacobean bargaining.

COVENTRY

There were Shakespeares living in Coventry long before Elizabeth's reign. When William was an infant, his father went there to give bail of ten pounds for a tinker of Stratford. During Shakespeare's youth, when Coventry's population was about 6,500, he and his father may have made the journey again to see one of the last performances of the Coventry cycle of Mystery plays acted by the craft guilds. The vast scale of the sequence showed that a series of plays, such as the histories that Shakespeare would eventually write, was possible. His company acted in Coventry as the King's Men in 1603 for forty shillings official pay, and at the end of October 1608 for twenty shillings. This was seventeen years after the guilds' plans to revive the Mystery plays had been finally scotched by the

Coventry authorities. Only secular drama 'shall be played on the pageants [the stages used for street theatre] at Midsummer Day and St Peter's Day next in this city, and no other plays'.

Coventry, in the middle of 'woody country' having been 'some ages since enriched with the manufacture of clothing and caps', was – according to Camden – the most successful market town of Warwickshire, and attracted more people 'than could be expected from its midland situation'. Camden's surprise was typical of an era when road transport often cost ten times as much as water transport. Coventry, served by neither sea nor navigable river, was not expected to prosper, but Camden described the town as 'large and neat; fortified with very strong walls and adorned with beautiful buildings'. The scene of *Henry VI Pt iii* (5.1) is set at Coventry, where the Earl of Warwick enters on the walls with the Mayor and other characters. Speeches about troop movements at Dunsmore and Southam – places nearby not mentioned in chronicles used as sources by Shakespeare – give the impression that Shakespeare knew the area well. Leland noted the 'many fair towers' of the city walls, built of the local 'darkish deep red' stone. He mentioned the 'fair suburbs without the walls' and 'a mint for coining'. 'The town rose by making of cloth and caps: that now decaying, the glory of the city decayeth.' Cloth caps used to be worn by all classes; but the felt hat, with a brim and a crown, became so fashionable that in 1571 a statute was imposed to boost the cappers' outmoded trade. Cap-wearing was made compulsory on holy days, but this legal measure failed. Coventry had also suffered grievously from the suppression of the monasteries, which was followed by the wanton destruction of many of the city's fine medieval buildings. Their ruins were plundered by local people, who took away stone for their own use. The dissolution of chantries and religious guilds furthered the city's decay.

About sixty years before Shakespeare's birth, Coventry began to suffer from poverty and unemployment more dire than any other town of the age experienced. Hundreds of houses stood empty and for various reasons the slump dragged on. Much trade was lost by the abolition of the Mystery plays, Catholic dramas which became unacceptable after Elizabeth's excommunication. Blue thread, used for embroidering scarves and napkins, had been one of the town's most celebrated products: its colour was called 'Coventry blue' and woad for dyeing was grown nearby, but a developing taste for foreign fashions upset local markets, as a pamphlet published in 1581 shows:

'I knew the time when men were contented with caps, hats, girdles and points, and all manner of garments made in the town next adjoining, whereby the towns were then well occupied and set a-work: and yet the money paid for the stuff remained in the country. Now, the poorest young man in a country cannot be content with a leather girdle, or leather points, knives or daggers made nigh home. And specially no gentleman can be content to have either cap, coat, doublet, hose or shirt in his country, but they must have this gear come from London. And yet many things hereof are not there made, but beyond the sea: whereby the artificers of our good towns are idle, and the occupations in London and specially of the towns beyond the seas are well set a-work, even upon our costs. I have heard say that the chief trade of Coventry was heretofore in making of blue thread, and then the town was rich even upon that trade . . . only: and now our thread comes all from beyond sea. Wherefore that trade of Coventry is decayed, and thereby the town likewise.'

Queen Elizabeth, on her way to visit the newly created Earl of Leicester at Kenilworth, had stayed at Coventry on 17 August 1566. The sheriffs in 'scarlet cloaks, and twenty young men on horseback, all in one livery of fine purple' greeted her 'at the utmost of the liberties towards Woolvey' and rode before her to the city, 'where the Mayor and his brethren' met her. The Recorder then outlined the splendid history of 'this ancient city' where now 'lamentable ruin and decay' had replaced prosperity: but her Majesty had come like the sun after a dark tempest and the streets were full of 'company of all ages' longing to see her and detain her with their 'divers shows and stages'.

To entertain her, guildsmen who were heirs to the tradition of Mystery plays had prepared their stages, the 'pageants' on which the Corpus Christi cycle had been performed. 'The Tanners' pageant stood at St John's Church; the Drapers' at the

Cross; the Smiths' at Little Park Street End; and the Weavers' at Much Park Street.' She visited the Free-school, which Henry VIII had founded, went into the library, and presented some money. 'Thence she rode unto the White Friars' where she spent two nights. After her visit, she knighted the Recorder and had a gift of venison – thirty bucks – delivered from Kenilworth to the Mayor and his brethren.

Most dietaries warned against the eating of venison, which might upset the balance of the body's four chief fluids, the 'humours'. These were believed to determine a person's temperament and health (physical and mental), one humour dominating each of the four temperaments: blood, the sanguine temperament; phlegm, the phlegmatic; red bile, choleric; and black bile – an imaginary fluid – melancholy. From the eating of venison, melancholy and choleric humours might result. But, as Dr Andrew Boorde noted, 'Englishmen have a passion for venison.' This food was not, though, for ordinary people: 'I am sure it is a lord's dish, and I am sure it is good for an Englishman, for it doth animate him to be as he is: which is strong and hardy.' But Boorde warns 'every man . . . not to kill and so eat of it, except it be legal, for it is meat for great men. And great men do not set so much by the meat as they do by the pastime of killing it'. Boorde himself finds venison irresistible: 'Although the flesh be dispraised in physic, I pray God send me part of the flesh to eat, norwithstanding.'

Thirty-five years after the Queen's visit, pioneers of the public library succeeded in Coventry in 1601: 'at the earnest suit of Mr Tony, schoolmaster, the library was begun, and he, with Mr Arnold, the usher, made such request to gentlemen, that it was quickly furnished with books'. This civilized development was particularly important in Coventry, the town which was perhaps more continuously violent than any other, with street fights and riots sparked off by such matters as religious disagreements and the enclosure of the common fields. Four years after the Queen's visit she displaced the Mayor for killing a man:

'John Harford, Mayor of Coventry, walking in the field with a couple of greyhounds, which greyhounds ran at a little spaniel of William Heley's, an embroiderer: the said Heley, meaning to save his spaniel, beat the greyhounds; for which cause the said John Harford beat the said William Heley with his walking-staff, that he died of the stroke; for which cause he was deprived of his mayoralty, and John Saunders served out his year. The said John Harford was fain to agree with Heley's wife for the pardon, and also exempted the Council of the City for ever.'

So the matter was settled out of court, at no charge to Coventry. Dogs were highly prized in Shakespeare's day. Macbeth briefly catalogued them (3.1.94–5) as 'hounds and greyhounds, mongrels, spaniels, curs' and 'shoughs' (shaggy dogs), 'water-rugs' (rough water dogs) and 'demi-wolves' (cross-breeds). Harrison classified them more amply according to the method of Dr John Caius, the Elizabethan authority, as game-dogs, house-dogs and toy-dogs.

Game-dogs consisted of two breeds of spaniel – land-spaniels and water-spaniels – and eight breeds of hound: harriers, terriers, bloodhounds, gaze-hounds (who hunt by eye), greyhounds ('cherished' says Harrison 'for strength and swiftness'), lymers (powerful in smelling and in running), tumblers (a sort of lurcher) and thieves (perhaps another sort of lurcher). These last two breeds 'incline only to deceit, wherein they are oft so skilful that few men would think so mischievous a wit to remain in such silly creatures'. Turberville writes about coursing, a sport highly popular in the Cotswolds: 'We use three manner of courses with greyhounds, here in England; that is: at the deer, at the hare, and at the fox or other vermin.' The spaniels were used for falconry: they roused the game after the hawk had driven it into some covert or into the water. Another sort of spaniel, according to Harrison, was the 'spaniel-gentle or comforter'. Such lap-dogs were 'little and pretty . . . instruments of folly' for 'dainty dames . . . to play and dally withal, in trifling away the treasures of time'.

House-dogs were either shepherds' curs, used for 'keeping the herd together' when they grazed or went before the shepherd, or mastiffs; huge, 'stub-born, ugly, eager, burdenous of body (and therefore but of little swiftness) terrible and fearful to behold'. Englishmen trained mastiffs to bait bears, bulls, lions and to be 'Fierce and cruel unto strangers . . . and the fast hold which they take with their teeth exceedeth all credit.'

THE NOBLE ART OF
VENERIE or HVNTING.

Wherein is handled and set out the Vertues, Nature, and Pro-
perties of fifteene sundry Chaces, together with the order and
manner how to Hunt and kill euery one of them.

Translated & collected for the pleasure of all Noblemen
and Gentlemen, out of the best approoued Authors, which
haue written any thing concerning the same : And reduced
into such order and proper termes as are vsed here
in this noble Realme of Great Britaine.

AT LONDON,
Printed by Thomas Purfoot.
An. Dom. 1611.

G Turberville: 'A good keeper of hounds should be gracious, courteous and gentle, loving his dogs.
. . . The first thing to do when he riseth is to go see his hounds, to make their lodging clean . . . take his
horn . . . sound three or four times the call, to . . . comfort them and call them'.

At Stratford, unmuzzled dogs, pigs and ducks were forbidden in the streets. Yet some English mastiffs were so gentle that children were said to have ridden on them, and Harrison recalls:

'I had one myself once, which would not suffer any man to bring in his weapon further than my gate: neither those that were of my house to be touched in his presence. Or if I had beaten any of my children, he would gently have essayed to

159

catch the rod in his teeth and take it out of my hand, or else pluck down their clothes to save them from the stripes.'

Toy-dogs were 'a confused company, mixed of all the rest'. There were the whippets or warners, which were good for nothing but to bark a warning 'in the night season'; and (favoured by ladies) the Iceland shoughs – or simply the Icelands – saucy, quarrelsome, with a painful bite and a love of eating candles; and, finally, the dancers: performing dogs, taught by their 'idle, roguish masters', who profit from them, to dance to music and do tricks such as 'to turn round as a ring, holding their tails in their teeth'. Dogs were more versatile than categories suggest. Both the greyhound and the spaniel were used to hunt deer and hares: so perhaps it was to save his spaniel for the chase that Heley, the embroiderer, risked – and lost – his life.

Mayor Harford's brutal attack may have typified the violence of Coventry, but the city had its humane aspect. Rich people, as in other towns of Warwickshire, bequeathed money to provide the poor with almshouses, food and fuel: but private charity could not supply the desperate needs of the time. Women were especially vulnerable to unemployment. When the manufacture of blue thread was dwindling, the men who made the thread were protected: no unmarried woman was allowed to work in the trade. Fishmongers, leather-workers, brickmakers and carpenters were subject to similar but less frequent regulations banning unmarried women. But the poor and strangers were leniently treated. If a man could work, his apprenticeship and his membership of a craft fellowship were compulsory, leading to the freedom of the city. The drifting vagrant, who survived by casual labour, begging and petty theft, was turned away from Coventry, as from other towns. For the removal of crippled vagrants, two carts were provided by the city.

By the time Shakespeare's company played in Coventry, early in James's reign, the town had no special trade of its own, although the production and sale of cloth occupied most men. There were still open spaces, and because of the decline of the cloth trade the grazing of cattle on the commons was becoming increasingly important to many freemen of this city. Coventry, though land-locked in the middle of England, had the good fortune to be the road-centre of the Midlands.

Entertainers who came in Tudor times included bear-wards, 'the Keeper of the Queen's Apes', musicians, puppeteers, morris dancers and 'the Turk', perhaps an acrobat. Other tumblers visiting Coventry 'went on the ropes', and about the time of Shakespeare's death nine shillings were paid 'to an Italian that thrust himself through the side to make experiment of his oil'. Roughly two years earlier the King's Men were paid a fee of forty shillings, although Coventry was exceptionally generous to some of the troupes who played in those times, giving £4 on a few occasions.

Coventry had its own musicians, the city waits, established more than 140 years before Shakespeare's birth. These waits, probably always four in number, were paid by the city and were often hired by guilds. The chief musician played a trumpet and the other three played pipes and probably drums and a stringed instrument: perhaps a dulcimer or a fiddle. The Coventry waits wore the city's livery: coats or cloaks of red and green, with silver escutcheons and chains. A banner of 'double taffeta sarcanet, crimson and green' hung from the trumpet. Many towns and cities had waits, among whom were some of the kingdom's finest musicians. Waits attended the mayor, played for any public festivity such as a royal visit and – in some places – were allowed to play in the streets at night. For this night music, the pay was lavish. In *Othello* (3.1.2) perhaps the musicians who play wind-instruments to bid 'Good morrow' in Cyprus are waits.

Opposite
The River Wylye, from which Wilton, one of England's oldest boroughs, was named. The Wylye, with its 'meandrous winding, watering the meadows' (Aubrey) belongs to the English landscape that King Lear describes:

'With shadowy forests and with champaigns riched,
With plenteous rivers and wide-skirted meads'.

(*King Lear* 1.1.64–5)

Overleaf
'Shakespeare's cliff', Dover. Chalk, about 350 ft high. The supposed scene of Gloster's attempted suicide in *King Lear* (Quarto Sc 20). Drayton wrote of sea-gods robbing 'Dover's neighbouring cliffs of samphire': the herb aids digestion, opens the liver, provokes urine and washes away the stone (Culpeper)'

Christ Church, Oxford, the college where Queen Elizabeth I stayed. Cornets accompanied the *Te Deum* in thanksgiving for her arrival, 1566. On Sunday morning she was unwell and stayed in her room. There 'a very pretty boy' delighted her with a Latin oration and Greek verses: she demanded an encore.

Wilton House. Fire destroyed the building visited by James I, poets and writers welcomed by the Countess of Pembroke. Samuel Daniel, her son's tutor, dedicated poems to her. 'By them, great lady, you shall then be known When Wilton shall lie level with the ground.'

11 GARDEN, COUNTRY AND COURT

CRIPPLEGATE, WILTON HOUSE
AND HAMPTON COURT

London doth mourn, Lambeth is quite forlorn,
Trades cry 'Woe worth' that ever they were born,
The want of term is town and city's harm;
Close chambers do we want, to keep us warm;
Long banished must we live from our friends;
This low-built house will bring us to our ends.
    From winter, plague and pestilence, good Lord deliver us.

THOMAS NASHE: Backwinter's Song from *Summer's Last Will and Testament*

CRIPPLEGATE

By 1604 – perhaps even as early as 1602 – Shakespeare moved from Southwark back across the Thames to the north-west part of the City of London, beyond Cheapside, into Cripplegate Ward. A few houses away from a right-angle turn in the City Wall, he lodged in a house at the north-east corner of Silver Street and Mugwell (later, 'Monkwell') Street. The house he lived in belonged to a maker of ladies' ornamental head-dresses – a 'tire-maker'. He was a Huguenot, Christopher Mountjoy by name. In the house there also lived Madame Mountjoy, their daughter Mary and Mountjoy's three apprentices. One of them, Stephen Belott, married Mary. Later, Stephen and his father-in-law quarrelled about the dowry: and eventually, in 1612, Stephen went to court. Shakespeare was said to have encouraged the match as a go-between; he was called upon to declare what he remembered, and his deposition survives in written answers. He had known Mary and Stephen 'for the space of ten years or thereabouts'.

The Mountjoys' substantial house had a shop on the ground floor and living quarters above. It was near the parish church where Shakespeare presumably went: St Olave's, at the west end of Silver Street. In Stow's opinion, this church was 'a small thing, and without any noteworthy monuments'.

Silver Street was famous for its wigs. These, with masks, muffs and fans, had been introduced into English fashion from Italy early in Elizabeth's reign. When 'every part of the town owns a piece' of a dolled-up wife then, according to Jonson's satirical catalogue, 'All her teeth were made in the Blackfriars, both her eyebrows in the Strand, and her hair in Silver Street'. The hair of fashionable ladies was dressed high and tire-makers used fabric, feathers, gems, gold and silver to ornament it. Tires designed as little jewelled ships were much admired. Mountjoy was successful enough to supply the Queen with a tire.

There were 'divers fair houses' in Silver Street. Halls belonging to a number of city companies – Plasterers, Brewers, Curriers (who dressed leather and coloured it), Bowyers (who made bows), Haberdashers and Barber-Surgeons – gave importance to the neighbourhood and it was also well supplied with almshouses.

If Shakespeare wanted to enjoy the peace of gardens, he could take a short walk from his lodgings up through the City Wall at Cripplegate (its name derived not from 'cripple' but from an Old English word implying 'sunk, covered or narrow'). Then he could turn left at the conduit, along Fore Street and Redcross Street towards the street called the Barbican. Alleys off to the left led to the Jews' Garden; once it had been the only Jewish cemetery in England. However, 300 years had passed since the Jews' 'final banishment out of England', and now the place had been 'turned into fair garden plots and summer houses for pleasure'.

Further out of the City, Shakespeare could turn slightly left towards the windmill on Mount Calvary, in the direction of Islington, or he could turn right towards Finsbury Field, part of a marsh that had been troublesome to drain. He might have met a few archers out for practice, and seen the windmills working. These, used for grinding corn, were built up on bone heaps. New, frivolous buildings caught the eye. Londoners, no longer concerned to create hospitals and almshouses, were decorating the suburban fields with 'fair summer houses ... with towers, turrets and chimney tops: not so much for use or profit' Stow grumbled, 'as for show and pleasure'; which sometimes included liaisons.

For a round walk, Shakespeare could have come back over Moorfields, where laundresses dried their washing on the grass, to Moor Lane outside Cripplegate. Craftsmen of archery – bowyers, bowstring-makers and fletchers (who made arrows) – had at one time thrived there but no longer, since

Previous page
Holbein Porch, Wilton: Sidney, greatest of poet-courtiers, would have known this building. His writings circulated in manuscript. At his sister's wedding, there was at Wilton a lavish show of noblemen and gentry tilting. Sidney devised most of the decorative shields (*imprese*). They hung in Wilton for many years.

Opposite
Copperplate map, 1553–9: Moorgate, between Bishopsgate and Cripplegate. North of the City Ditch: Moorfields; Finsbury beyond. Laundresses lay washing out, lads carry a basket on a pole, archers shoot. East of 'Dogge-hous', a domed summerhouse stands west of tenter-ground (cloth stretching). South of that, the 'Giardin di Piero' may be a bear-garden.

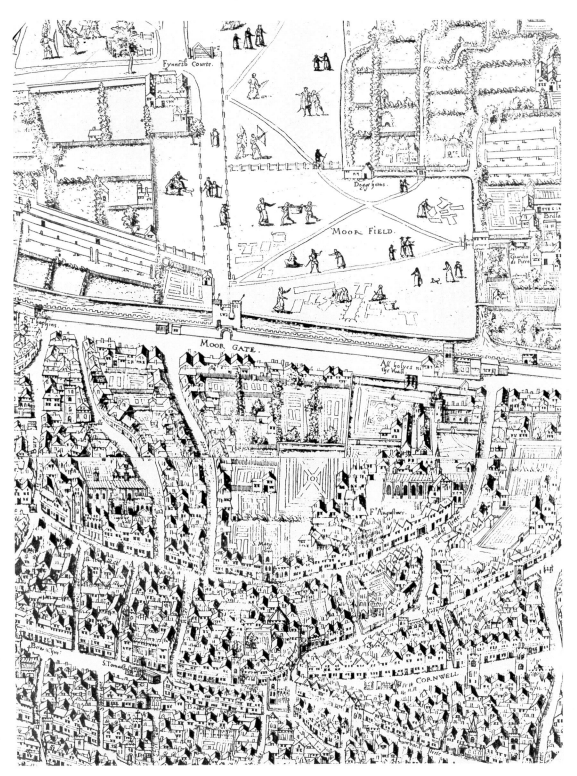

the butts were being deserted for bowling-alleys and dicing-houses, symptoms of the craze for gambling.

If, on the other hand, Shakespeare wanted a chat with his intimate friends and important colleagues in the Chamberlain's Men, John Heminges and Henry Condell, away from the playhouse, he had only a short walk from his lodgings down in the Guildhall direction: perhaps along Love Lane – 'so called of wantons', writes Stow – to Aldermanbury (in Cripplegate Ward Within) where they were pillars of the community. He could call on them in their houses, conveniently close to his own lodgings.

Some fifteen years before, Heminges had been married in St Mary Aldermanbury. Probably his wife was Rebecca, widow of a player, William Knell. Heminges was one of the original Chamberlain's Men. He had more to do with their finances than anyone else, and generally received the company's payment for Court performances. He was a churchwarden and a sidesman at St Mary's, where fourteen of his children were baptized. In the theatre world he was so important that he may have represented all the London companies in dealings with government officials. Henry Condell was another respected member of the King's Men. Perhaps young enough to have been Heminges's apprentice, as an actor Condell did not achieve fame, but he was on very good terms with his colleagues. He was a sidesman at St Mary Aldermanbury, the church in which nine of his children were baptized and he and his wife, Elizabeth, were buried. The thigh-bone of a man who had been 'full ten or eleven feet high', according to Harrison, hung in the cloister. Stow declared that it 'must needs be monstrous'.

In Shakespeare's time the rôles of girls and women were acted by boys, who were apprenticed to men players and learnt theatrical skills within the company. When a boy became an apprentice, he went to live in his master's home. John Rice, for example, as a boy-player apprenticed to John Heminges, joined the Heminges family. The domestic life of such a boy (in another company) is conjured up by a letter that John Pyk (or Pig), on tour with his master, Edward Alleyn, dictated for sending to Alleyn's wife in Southwark, about seven years before Shakespeare was living there:

'Mistress:

Your honest, ancient, and loving servant Pig hath his humble commendations to you and to my good Master Henslowe and Mistress and to my mistress' sister Bess for all her hard dealing with me I send her hearty commendations, hoping to be beholding to her again for the opening of the cupboard. And to my neighbour, Doll, for calling me up in a morning, and to my wife Sarah for making clean my shoes, and to that old gentleman Monsieur Pearl, that even fought with me for the block in the chimney corner. And though you all look for the ready return of my proper person yet I swear to you by the faith of a fustian king never to return till Fortune us bring with a joyful meeting to lovely London.

I cease, your pretty, pretty, prattling, parling pig

By me John Pyk

Mistress, I pray you keep this that my master may see it, for I got one to write it, Mr Downton, and my master knows not of it.

(addressed)

To his loving Mistress Alleyn on the Bankside over against the Clink.'

WILTON HOUSE

The plague of 1603, although probably not imported, was believed to have been brought from the Low Countries. It was particularly strong in Southwark early in the year, but the nation was preoccupied with anxiety about the Queen's dying and whatever troubles might follow. She had reigned for forty-four years and lived for sixty-nine. Suffering from fever and melancholy, for four days and nights she remained on cushions on the floor in her palace at Richmond, refusing to be moved. Then, emaciated, she was carried to her bed. She indicated the King of the Scots as her successor and on 24 March, at about 3 am, 'her Majesty', as John Manningham wrote, 'departed this life, mildly like a lamb, easily like a ripe apple from the tree'.

James VI of Scotland's peaceful accession was followed by his triumphant progress to London, where 'multitudes of people' turned out to greet him as James I of England. The crowd 'covered the beauty of the fields' and 'with much unruliness ... injured one another'. Visitors flocked from the country and so the terrifying plague increased.

Nevertheless, the King was crowned at Westminster, although his 'Triumphant Passage' through the City had to be postponed for many months. During the last week of August more than 3,000 people died of plague in panic-stricken London, where theatres were closed and would remain so for nearly a year.

The Court kept on the move, visiting Oatlands, Richmond and Woodstock – where James left all work to his Council and spent a number of weeks hunting. Then the King and his unwieldy cavalcade passed on to Southampton, Winchester and Wilton, near Salisbury. Plague struck at his sprawling retinue. 'God bless the King', wrote a loyal follower, 'for once a week, one or other dies in our tents.' Shakespeare's company too was on tour; but that winter they were back near London, probably rehearsing for a busy Christmas season at Court, when they were called from Mortlake to act before the King at the Earl of Pembroke's 'stately house or palace' at Wilton. For 'pains and expenses' in travelling from Surrey to Wiltshire, the players were paid the remarkably large sum of £30. They gave what seems to have been their first performance before their new monarch and patron and his Queen Anne, on 2 December in the delightful setting of Wilton House, home of the son of Mary Herbert, Countess of Pembroke. She and her brother, Sir Philip Sidney, had been devoted to each other; when out of favour at Court he had spent months with her at Wilton, and for her he wrote the romance, *Arcadia*. She shared his love of books and at his death she took over the patronage of the writers he had supported. Edmund Spenser and, later, Samuel Daniel and Nicholas Breton owed

W Camden: Elizabeth I's funeral cortège: her effigy, fully dressed and crowned, lying on the coffin. During her last illness, the Council suspended plays five days before she died. Her body, brought from Richmond to Whitehall by water, was buried in Westminster Abbey on 28 April 1603. There were 1,600 mourners.

much to the 'Wise and fair and good' Countess whom they all honoured. She had married Henry, the second Earl of Pembroke, and she had spent most of her time at his Wiltshire seats: Wilton, Ivychurch and Ramsbury. In James's reign she rented Crosby Hall in Bishopsgate.

Wilton House during her time, wrote Nicholas Breton, was 'a kind of little Court' in which God was 'daily served, religion truly preached, all quarrels avoided, peace carefully preserved, swearing not heard of'. Hers was 'a table fully furnished, a house richly garnished' and 'kindness was a companion in every corner'. Her son William, the third Earl, inherited her generosity towards poets and extended it to dramatists. He and his brother Philip were to become the dedicatees of Shakespeare's First Folio, where they are called 'The Most Noble and Incomparable Pair of Brethren' who had not only valued Shakespeare's plays but had honoured 'both them, and their author living, with so much favour.'

The Court was at Wilton from at least 24 October to 12 December 1603 and during that time James visited Salisbury, just over three miles away. A lost – or apocryphal – letter from the forty-two-year-old Lady Pembroke to her son, telling him to bring James from Salisbury to see *As You Like It*, is said to have included the sentence: 'we have the man Shakespeare with us'. According to stage tradition,

Shakespeare himself used to play the parts of Adam in *As You Like It* and the Ghost in *Hamlet*, parts which are important but do not keep the actor on stage for very long.

Wilton was, Camden wrote, 'once the chief town of the county, to which it gave its name'. But the town 'dwindled, by little and little, into a small village; only it hath ... the most beautiful house of the Earls of Pembroke, built out of the suppressed abbey'. William Herbert, first Earl of Pembroke, used the site and fabric of the monastic buildings, conferred on him by Henry VIII, to create this mansion. It has been greatly altered and much rebuilt, but a porch from the court-yard to the Great Hall still remains, attributed to Hans Holbein: its

Royal Picnic: in *The Noble Art of Hunting*, G Turberville recommends a site 'under shade of stately trees ... near some fountain spring' for cooling the drink in 'kilderkins ... firkins ... bottles and ... barrels' to accompany veal, capon, goose, pigeon-pies, mutton, ham and tongue. In this Jacobean edition, Elizabeth is replaced by James.

fluted columns, coat of arms, busts and shell-gables now form a garden ornament.

Jonson's *Sejanus*, produced in 1603, showed Shakespeare's name for the last time on a cast list. Perhaps from then on he acted less. Until he retired to Stratford, however, he must have continued to show some interest in provincial tours even if he did not take part in them. James's Letters Patent, naming among others 'William Shakespeare,

Richard Burbage, Augustine Phillips', gave the King's Men supreme status and was a passport and recommendation to authorities in any city, university town or borough. After Wilton, the King's Men acted at Court from Christmas into January 1604. In August, they were at Somerset House in their official capacity as Grooms of the Chamber, wearing their scarlet liveries, in attendance on the new Spanish ambassador.

The King's Men played before James at least 107 times while Shakespeare was alive: between 1 November 1604 and 31 October 1605 they acted eleven plays for him, seven of them by Shakespeare including *Othello*, *Measure for Measure*, and *The Merchant of Venice* which the King saw on Shrove Sunday and, at his command, again on Shrove Tuesday. Almost certainly in 1606 *Macbeth* was acted at Court by Burbage; he also played Lear, with Armin as the Fool, at Whitehall that December.

HAMPTON COURT

The Great Hall of Hampton Court Palace, scene of

Fanciful map of Somerset and Wiltshire, engraved by W Hole for Drayton's *Polyolbion*, 1612. There are few place-names but many masque-like figures. Chief towns are shown by crowned personages, hills are surmounted by shepherds, rivers inhabited by nymphs, and Diana hunts in the forests of this fantastic, Arcadian England.

many splendid Tudor entertainments, was not only the most spacious in England but also the most suitable for pageantry and Court gaieties. Needy adventurers, hoping for advancement from James I, the new king who was lavish with honours, flocked to Hampton Court and at Christmas 1603 the 1,200 rooms and outbuildings had to be supplemented with tents in the park for retainers and servants.

The year ended with much revelry (and with the French and Spanish ambassadors fretting about precedence), as Dudley Carleton wrote:

'We have had a merry Christmas and nothing to disquiet us save brabbles amongst our ambassadors, and one or two poor companions that

ROBIN
GOOD-FELLOW,
HIS MAD PRANKES AND MERRY IESTS.

Full of honeſt Mirth, and is a fit Medicine for Melancholy.

Printed at *London* by *Thomas Cotes*, and are to be fold by *Francis Grove*, at his ſhop on Snow-hill, neere the Sarazens-head. 1639

In *A Midsummer Night's Dream* 2.1.33 and 40, a fairy addresses Robin Goodfellow as 'that shrewd and knavish sprite' also called 'hobgoblin' and 'sweet puck': 'I am', says Robin, 'that merry wanderer of the night' (43). This woodcut of folklore character Robin Goodfellow comes from a book of his pranks and jests.

172

died of the plague. The first holidays we had every night a public play in the Great Hall, at which the King was ever present, and liked or disliked as he saw cause: but it seems he takes no extraordinary pleasure in them. The Queen and Prince were more the players' friends, for on other nights they had them privately, and have since taken them to their protection. On New Year's night we had a play of Robin Goodfellow.'

This play, featuring the prankster of folklore who was also called a puck, was acted by the King's Men; it may well have been Shakespeare's *A Midsummer Night's Dream*, originally acted in Elizabeth's reign. As a most important member of the company, Shakespeare would surely have been among the players at the first Christmas season for the new King.

Queen Elizabeth had occasionally stayed at Hampton Court, but she preferred Greenwich, her birthplace. In 1562, at the age of twenty-nine, she was at Hampton Court when she fell sick of the smallpox. That Christmas was one of the ten she spent there, and her Court amused themselves with backgammon and dancing. She was a keen and excellent dancer who, despite puritan horror of the lascivious amusement, accepted it as a pastime suitable for Sunday afternoons. So did James I. When on a Sunday in 1604 he gave a ball at Whitehall to celebrate peace with Spain, his Queen Anne excelled in the 'brawl' – a French dance from which the minuet later developed. It was in the livelier dances, such as the coranto with its leaps and running steps, varied at will by the male partner, and in the galliard, for which young courtiers removed their cloaks and rapiers and danced in doublet and hose, that Henry, Prince of Wales, distinguished himself. Dancing was generally considered to be part of a liberal education. At the age of fifty-six the gifted Queen Elizabeth used to dance half-a-dozen galliards for her morning exercise. She had 'learnt in the Italian manner to dance high', as the French ambassador noted some years later. When she was sixty-nine, only a few months before her death, she still danced the coranto.

By then, in addition to such courtly dances derived from the Continent, English country dances had climbed the social scale and become fashionable. Elizabeth watched her ladies dance country dances to the music of tabor and pipe almost every night. Folk dances ranged from the simple round or roundel (a circular dance) and the hay or hey (in which dancers wound in and out) to the morris or morisco: a dramatic dance of Moorish origin which was probably introduced into northern Europe via Spain. The morris included elements which persist in pantomime. There were such

Illustration, c1560–1623, of court dances and peasant dances, J T de Bry. Couples in the court dance, above, are probably going round in a circle, man leading lady with right hand. The Latin text contrasts courtly decorum with peasant boorishness. 'A palace differs from a sheepfold, a courtier from a peasant.'

characters as a negro or Moor, Robin Hood, Friar Tuck, Little John, Maid Marian, and dragons. A man inside a frame with horse's head, tail and trappings, pranced about as the hobby-horse. The dancers wore on their legs bells of different sizes and tones, and took part in maypole festivities in country and town.

The May revels in London, with 'warlike shows' including archery, 'stage plays, and bonfires in the streets', besides morris dancers, featured (as Stow recorded) 'the triumphant setting up of the great shaft (a principal maypole in Cornhill, before the parish church of St Andrew therefore called Undershaft)'. In Shakespeare's youth the maypole still flourished. Puritan opposition rings out in Philip Stubbes's outraged description of men, women and children – all supervised by Satan – preparing for revels in May:

'They have twenty or forty yoke of oxen, every ox having a sweet nose-gay of flowers placed on the tip of his horns: and these oxen draw home this maypole (this stinking idol, rather) which is covered all over with flowers and herbs, bound round about with strings from the top to the bottom, and sometime painted with variable colours, with two or three hundred men, women and children following it with great devotion. And thus being reared up with handkerchiefs and flags streaming on the top, they straw the ground about, bind green boughs about it, set up summer-halls, bowers and arbours hard by it; and then they fall to banquet and feast, to leap and dance about it, as the heathen people did at the dedication of their idols, whereof this is a perfect pattern, or rather the thing itself.'

The players' ability to dance was eventually put to spectacular use by a member of Shakespeare's company, Will Kemp. The parts played by Kemp, the most famous comedian of his generation, included Peter in *Romeo and Juliet* and Dogberry in *Much Ado About Nothing*. He was a 'sharer' in the Lord Chamberlain's Men, and for a renowned actor to leave this most eminent of companies was very unusual. Kemp, however, did so, about the time of his most celebrated exploit: a nine-day dance from London to Norwich. He described himself, with

justification, as 'Head Master of Morris Dancers, High Headborough of Hays'.

His place in the company was filled by Robert Armin, who presumably acted in the Robin Goodfellow play at Hampton Court. When plays were to be presented in the Great Hall, the stage was always erected at the lower end of it, in front of the screens which were surmounted by the minstrels' gallery. Players may often have made their entrances and exits through the two openings in the screens. This was the usual arrangement for theatricals in college halls and in halls of private houses. Court performances, which were the players' supreme occasions, set the pattern of staging. Performances by Shakespeare's company in public theatre, private theatre, guildhall, inn, inn-yard, church, school,

Inigo Jones: masque costume for a torchbearing, fiery spirit. Jones, born in London in 1573, became joiner's apprentice in St Paul's Churchyard. The third Earl of Pembroke sent him to study art in Italy. In James I's reign, Jones achieved great success as architect and as designer of court masques, many by Jonson.

private house or open-air arena, were all variations on that norm. Drama was ruled by Royal Command Performances.

On the same night as the professional Robin Goodfellow play, at Hampton Court there was also a show performed by aristocratic amateurs: a masque, which needed elaborate staging. In Shakespeare's time, masques became increasingly fashionable and stylish. He presents them, and entertainments like them, in a number of his plays including *Love's Labour's Lost*, *Romeo and Juliet*, *Timon of Athens* and *The Tempest* – which includes his most fully developed masque.

For the amateurs' masque at Hampton Court, as Dudley Carleton writes, 'There was a heaven built at the lower end of the hall' and from this the presenter, a Chinese magician, descended. A curtain opened to reveal the masquers 'sitting in a vaulty place with their torchbearers and the other lights, which was no unpleasing spectacle'. (The wavering flames of tapers, candles and torches must have added enchantment and warmth to any indoor performance at night in Shakespeare's day.) Music played, and the masquers 'presented themselves to the King. The first gave the King an *impresa* in a shield, with a sonnet in a paper to express this device, and presented' a very valuable jewel to him.

This shield, painted with an *impresa* or device, would probably have been made of paper. Such shields, with their allegorical or mythological designs and poetic mottoes, featured in a tourney (or tournament) at Court some ten years later to mark the anniversary of the King's accession; Shakespeare devised the *impresa* for the Earl of Rutland to carry. Richard Burbage, whose talents extended from acting to occasional painting, made it and painted it. Shakespeare and Burbage, for their *impresa* – which has not survived – were each paid a handsome fee of forty-four shillings. Ephemeral trophies of this sort were seen in Queen Elizabeth's bedroom in Whitehall Palace by the German visitor, Paul Hentzner, five years before her death: 'emblems on paper, cut in the shape of shields, with mottoes used by nobility at tilts and tournaments, hung up for a memorial'.

Of the *imprese* which the masquers gave King James at Hampton Court during the Chinese masque, Philip Herbert's *impresa* of 'a fair horse colt in a fair green field', representing a descendant of

Alexander the Great's charger, Bucephalus, particularly intrigued the King. He 'made himself merry' and cracked a joke about Banks's Horse, 'the dancing horse' of *Love's Labour's Lost* (1.2.53). This famous performing bay, named Morocco, was renowned for counting money and calculating, and was even said to have climbed St Paul's steeple.

The Chinese masque, true to form, developed into dancing, but not with complete success. The masquers' costumes were:

'. . . rich but somewhat too heavy and cumbersome for dancers, which put them besides their galliards. They had loose robes of crimson satin embroidered with gold and bordered with broad silver laces, doublets and bases of cloth of silver; buskins, swords and hats alike and in their hats each of them an Indian bird for a feather with some jewels.'

A cast supremely distinguished by the inclusion of Queen Anne herself performed a masque a week later on 8 January, a Sunday night. The King encouraged theatricals, bear-baiting, revels and archery on Sundays because, in his opinion, puritan restrictions – which, by banning public plays on Sundays, he had officially endorsed – led to 'filthy tippling and drunkenness', as he wrote in his *Book of Sports*. On that particular Sunday in the Great Hall, the show was Samuel Daniel's masque, *The Vision of the Twelve Goddesses*, performed by the Queen and eleven of her ladies under the direction of a Mr Sanford. About the costumes, Lady Arabella Stuart had written from Hampton Court before Christmas that 'my Lady Suffolk and my Lady Walsingham hath warrant to take of the late Queen's best apparel out of the Tower of their discretion'. Queen Elizabeth left at least 300 dresses at her death, many of them New Year's gifts accumulated during recent years, so their Ladyships had a rich choice.

Later in the year, disorder at supper was so riotous in Whitehall Palace when the Queen and her ladies performed a masque by Jonson, that in the scramble for food 'down went tables and trestles before one bit was touched'. According to a Court newsletter: 'There was no small loss that night of chains and jewels, and' – with much rending of cloth – 'many great ladies were made shorter by their skirts. . . .'

12 THE KING'S MEN ON TOUR

BARNSTAPLE, MAIDSTONE AND DUNWICH

When I have seen the hungry ocean gain
Advantage on the kingdom of the shore,
And the firm soil win of the wat'ry main,
Increasing store with loss and loss with store . . . .

Sonnet 64

BARNSTAPLE

In 1605, before Michaelmas, and again in 1607, the King's Men were acting in north Devon, beside the River Taw, at Barnstaple, 'a town of ancient note' according to Camden:

'... and of the first rank in these parts for beauty and populousness, built among the hills in the form of a semicircle, whose diameter is the river, which at every full and new moon, as the sea rises, overflows the country so as to make the town a peninsula.'

At ebb tide, 'the river is so small as scarce to bear little boats, losing itself in meanders among the sands'. Barnstaple was at that time a ship-building town, a major port and a centre for the textile trade. Woollen cloths, notably the coarse fabric named 'kersey' and baize, a local product, were exported to France through Barnstaple; and flax and hemp cloths, such as linen, buckram and sailcloth, were imported from Rouen, Morlaix and St Malo. Spain and Portugal, in time of peace, were important markets. Merchants of the sixteenth and seventeenth centuries are said to have sealed their bargains, in the Jewish manner, by putting a down payment on the Tome Stone on Barnstaple quay, before witnesses. The Tome Stone may still be seen in Queen Anne's Walk.

Cargoes to Milford Haven and other Welsh ports included woollen felts, calico, linen, canvas, brass and pewter pots, shoes, dried fish from Newfoundland, whale oil, soap, wine, ginger, cheese, salt, sugar and pepper (a most valuable spice, because fresh meat was scarce in winter, and pepper could both preserve and season it more reliably and palatably than salt). Little ships, a mere four tons to sixty tons, were used for this local trade. From Wales, the ships brought sheep-skins and rabbit-skins, leather, tin, barley, wheat, rye: and oysters, a cheap item in anyone's diet. This 'shelly sort' of fish was generally 'forborne' from May to August (when there is no R in the month) 'yet in some places they be continually eaten, where they be kept in pits', according to Harrison.

Opposite
In the middle of a lake near Maidstone: Leeds Castle, converted by Henry VIII from Norman fortress to palace. In Henry V's reign Sir John Oldcastle, Lollard leader, refused to come here to answer for his heresies. Later he escaped from the tower of London: by witchcraft, his enemies claimed.

Below
The Long Bridge, Barnstaple. In 1599 the Privy Council ordered the mayor to ship 200 soldiers to Ireland. During any delay, he was to give each soldier, for food, sixpence a day (the pension Bottom might have had in *A Midsummer Night's Dream* 4.2.18) and for 'their purses' tuppence.

" A Stocks to stay sure and safely detain,
Lazy leud Leuterers that laws do offend:
Impudent persons, thus punished with pain,
Hardly for all this, do mean to amend."

(From " *Miscellanea Antiqua Anglicana.*")

The Long Bridge, spanning the tidal River Taw, was about three centuries old in Shakespeare's time. Leland described it in Henry VIII's day as 'the right great and sumptuous bridge of stone, having sixteen high arches'. It was approached by a causeway. The bridge, rebuilt and widened several times, is even now impressive. Leland noted that Barnstaple's 'houses be of stone, as all houses in good towns thereabout be' and that the annual fair was at the Nativity of Our Lady.

One of the vicars, John Trender, rashly 'inveighed in his sermon against the aldermen for not coming to church'. According to the Town Clerk, 'he said they were like two fat oxen, that they would not hear when Christ called unto them, but drew backwards: and drew others from Christ'. This bold accusation was sneakily disproved: 'the aldermen were present but unseen'. There was a showdown, and the vicar 'for this and his indecent behaviour on being questioned for this abuse' was arrested. He was released the next day.

Four years later, on the night of Friday 14 November 1600, when curfew was at nine o'clock, 'Mr Mayor and aldermen going upon their search in

Stocks, much used for punishing by confinement. Their:

'... low correction
Is such as basest and contemnèd wretches
For pilf' rings and most common trespasses
Are punished with.'

(*King Lear* Quarto 7.136)

The Earl of Kent, threatened with stocks, objects 'if I were your father's dog You could not use me so' (7.130).

the evening, as usual, found the vicar, Mr Trender ... a little after nine' tippling and enjoying the frivolous music of a tabor (a little drum) and a pipe – instruments favoured by Claudio in *Much Ado About Nothing* (2.3.14): 'now had he rather hear the tabor and the pipe'. The vicar, for this and other misdemeanours, was jailed again. He appealed to the Bishop of Exeter, was duly released, and took his chilling revenge: 'Sunday following he preached two hours: being a cold day, he wearied his audience.' Conflict soon broke out again, not only with the vicar but also with other preachers, stubbornly puritanical, who refused to wear surplices: 'so' – the Town Clerk lamented – 'there is no likelihood of good government, while such dissensions last'.

A form of violence acceptable to Barnstaple, and

to England in general, was privateering, or licensed piracy. This seizing of foreign wealth at sea, besides new ventures into transatlantic fishing, brought profit to the enterprising townsmen of Barnstaple. The *White Hart*, for example, captured a load of elephants' tusks and the pinnace *Fortmouth* seized a cargo of wine. The most lavish of Barnstaple's prizes was achieved by the 100-ton *Prudence* (owned by Richard Dodderidge, merchant and, in 1589, Mayor of the town). Off the Guinea coast she seized 'four chests of gold to the value of £16,000 and divers chains of gold' – the chests and baskets of gold weighing 320 pounds – 'with civet', the costly ingredient of perfumes. All these, 'and other things of great value', instantly made Dodderidge a millionaire.

Barnstaple's armed men, local defenders against the Spanish Armada, were reviewed in the town by Sir Richard Grenville, the Cornish sea-commander and cousin of Sir Walter Raleigh. The Privy Council also demanded 'two ships and one handsome pinnace in warlike manner to be victualled for two months and to be ready ... to join with Her Majesty's Navy, under the conduct of Sir Francis Drake' at Plymouth. Barnstaple, being like other English ports extremely unwilling to provide vessels for the royal fleets, pleaded poverty and seems to have supplied only one ship.

Soldiers in transit also disturbed the peace of the town at the end of Elizabeth's reign. Barnstaple, like Bristol, was a port of embarkation for troops, not all of them from the west country, on their way to Ireland. There were 300 soldiers in the town in 1596, the same year that Barnstaple suffered 140 plague deaths. Peter Mingus, the negro servant of a Mr Morrish, was one of the victims of this, the town's most serious epidemic in Shakespeare's lifetime.

At midsummer, Ann Kemyns and 'Nicholas Gay's daughter and one Davy were all carted about the town for their filthy and lascivious life and the next day, being Friday, they sat all three at the High Cross in the stocks'. Soldiers kicking their heels in the town presumably hurled ribaldry, if nothing else. Edible food was too scarce to fling. When the harvest failed after 'continual rain day and night' £100 was raised in the town towards the sending of three ships to Danzig for rye. About five years later, at one time there were 775 soldiers in the town, on

draft to Ireland from the south and west. The clothes issued to each Devon soldier consisted of 'a coat, a doublet, two shirts, a pair of breeches, a pair of stockings, a pair of shoes'. So there was only one spare article, a shirt. A brown woollen cap, the sort worn by the leek-sporting Welsh soldiers in *Henry V* (4.7.97), was also issued. This type of cap for soldiers and sailors was originally knitted in Monmouth and hence was called 'a Monmouth cap'.

In Barnstaple, local constables had recently been told to modernize their arms. Primitive bladed weapons called 'bills' were to be replaced by pikes, and bows and arrows by portable guns: muskets and calivers. Saltpetre, the chief constituent of gunpower, began to be made.

Local records show that Barnstaple, with its share of Elizabethan and Jacobean entertainment, reflects normal theatre history. James I, at his accession, took control of drama in an autocratic way, limiting the number of London companies to three: the King's Men and, in the following months, Prince Henry's Men and Queen Anne's Men. Royal patents guaranteed these three troupes the right to perform in provincial cities. Revision of the Act concerning Rogues and Vagabonds deprived the provinces of their companies of players. This was resented and troupes from London sometimes evoked displeasure. Players, on those occasions, were paid the official fee by the local mayor, but he refused them permission to perform. The players, frustrated but fed, moved on to try their luck elsewhere.

In Elizabeth's reign, similar non-events had occurred, but for other reasons, some of which persisted in James's reign. A mayor and aldermen might be worried about players introducing plague or other infection; or the guildhall might be needed for an event already arranged; or local feeling might be strongly against plays, either because they stirred up unrest and disorder, or were regarded as sinful, or lured apprentices from work. At Canterbury in 1602–3 a performance by the Admiral's Men was refused as not 'fit' because the Queen was believed to be 'either sick or dead'. In Barnstaple, at the end of Elizabeth's reign, for whatever reason, the Mayor gave twenty shillings 'to the Earl of Worcester's players being in town to depart the town without playing'. Payment was a sign of respect to the patron, even though his players were rejected. In the early seventeenth century, when

Pikemen, musketeers (c1630), usually stayed together for mutual protection: muskets took a while to reload. The stand carried in the right hand was to support the musket when firing. From the bandolier, on the shoulder, hung separate charges of powder and a bag of bullets. Other weapons: top left, halberd; top right, spontoon; bottom right, partisan.

MAIDSTONE

In 1605–6 Shakespeare's company acted at Maidstone: there was 'paid to the King's players by Mr Mayor and to the trumpeters two pounds five shillings'. Maidstone, the shire town of Kent, with a population of no more than 2,500, living in fewer than 300 houses, was described by Leland as 'a market town on one long street well builded and full of inns', and by Camden as 'neat and populous'. The manor of Maidstone had belonged to the Archbishop of Canterbury. It was annexed by Henry VIII, and the manor house – formerly the Archbishop's Palace – in the south-west part of the town was granted by Elizabeth to the Master of her Jewels. She never visited Maidstone.

This town on the River Medway was famous for its deposits of ragstone (a type of stone which breaks in a ragged or rough way) and the river transported it from the quarries. Timber, too, was carried on the Medway for building men-of-war (armed ships). Ragstone was used to build the Tower of London, Eton College and Westminster Palace; and to fortify Calais, during English occupation; and to make cannon balls. When in 1417 Henry V ordered 7,000 of these 'gunstones' – in

puritans were very strong in the ports, players were often refused the chance to act at Barnstaple.

Previously, musicians and players had been generally welcome in the town. Various companies of actors came and performed over the years. The Queens' Players received ten shillings in 1593–4. Wear and tear also had to be made good, and sixpence was 'paid for amending the ceiling in the Guildhall that the interlude players had broken down there this year'. Perhaps they had hung overweight stage machinery from it.

A continuing expense at Barnstaple was the bull-ring and its equipment: a post, a rope of eighteen pounds in weight and a collar. Town funds paid for all these to be supplied, repaired and frequently replaced. Nearly every town and sizeable village in England had its bull-ring and no bull was allowed to be killed until it had been baited, so enabling mastiff dogs to be trained. Bull-fever was socially respectable. Much inferior was football, the rabble's game, played in the streets but acknowledged to promote health and strength. Some thirty years before Shakespeare's birth it had been dismissed by Sir Thomas Elyot as 'nothing but beastly fury and extreme violence, whereof proceedeth hurt ... wherefore it is to be put in perpetual silence'.

Overleaf
Saltwood Castle, north of Hythe, where Thomas à Becket's death was plotted. After his martyrdom at Canterbury, Hythe became a port of entry for foreign pilgrims to his shrine. Poins, proposing the Gad's Hill robbery (*Henry IV Pt i*, 1.2.124) describes potential victims: 'pilgrims going to Canterbury with rich offerings'.

Opposite
Above left
? J de Critz: Lucy Harington, Countess of Bedford, close friend of James I's Queen Anne and enthusiastic performer in court masques. Poets she patronized included Jonson and Donne. Through her influence, Daniel was employed to create *The Vision of the Twelve Goddesses*: she, a 'fine dancing dame', performed in it.

Above right
Shrewsbury: Elizabethan map. The Welsh Bridge, crossing the Severn at the north (top) of the town, has two towers with portcullises. The English Bridge, at the south end of the town, has one portcullis midway across. The Quarry (left, beside river) has seven fields. The Castle stands at the east end of the town. At the top of Pride Hill: the pyramidal Market Cross.

Below
Unidentified artist: heraldic impression of the Spanish Armada and English fleet engaged, 1588. Foreground: Spanish galleass, crowded with Spanish gentlemen, plus monks and jester, is flanked by the *Ark Royal* (right), Lord Howard of Effingham's flagship, and (left) probably Drake's *Revenge*. Beyond, lines of alternating Spanish and English ships fire broadsides.

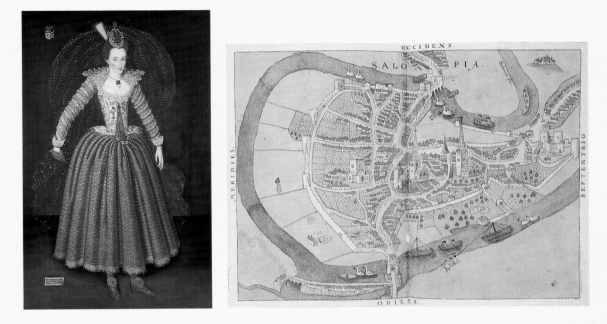

Henry V (1.2.282) to repay the Dauphin's gift of tennis-balls – John Bennett, mason of Maidstone, superintended their making. That same year, Sir John Oldcastle was required to come before the Archbishop of Canterbury at Leeds Castle, near Maidstone. He failed to appear, was excommunicated and, two years later, was martyred.

Many rebels were associated with Maidstone, including Wat Tyler, whose followers there released John Ball, imprisoned for life for proclaiming the doctrines of Wycliffe. Jack Cade, the rebel who appears in *Henry VI Pt ii*, also found supporters in Maidstone. And ten years before Shakespeare's birth, Sir Thomas Wyatt the younger (son of the poet), who lived close to Maidstone at Allington Castle, led an abortive rebellion to prevent Queen Mary from marrying the Archduke Philip of Spain.

In 1590 on the prison near the top of the High Town, now the High Street, the quarters of some traitors were set up on two poles. More than 800 people were hanged each year in England at that time, out of a population of under five million, because there were so many capital crimes.

A baker who delivered unwholesome bread to the prisoners in 1600, was put in the stocks for an hour with a sample of his bad bread in front of him. Then he had to give three shillings and fourpence to the Corporation, three shillings and four pence to the poor, and three shillings and four pence worth of good bread to the prisoners.

Kent assizes were held at various Kentish towns, including Maidstone, during Elizabeth's reign; but from the beginning of the seventeenth century Maidstone was generally chosen because it was central and accessible. When the judges came, the Corporation paid for their lodging; presented such gifts as a hogshead of beer, wine, sugar-loaves, a sheep or a calf; and provided cooks, butlers, stewards, chamberlains and criers – two of each – plus oats and fodder for thirty or forty horses.

Beside the Courthouse stairs stood 'the high cage' for rogues and vagabonds, but the highwayman Gamaliel Ratsey, who seems to have operated for a

Opposite
Shrewsbury, on Severn. After the battle in *Henry IV Pt i*, 4.1 and 3, and 5.1–5, in which Falstaff (5.4.145) claims he fought 'a long hour by Shrewsbury clock' (three and a half miles from the battlefield), Hotspur's body was hanged, drawn and quartered at the top of Pride Hill in the town.

while at Maidstone, moved on before being caught. He was hanged at Bedford.

In the worst times of plague, occupants of almshouses in the town were ordered by the Corporation to 'serve with any person' who needed them as nurses. Failure to 'comfort, help and succour the sick' would lead to ejection from the almshouse and forfeit of possessions. Occupants of the almshouses had to admit to their own rooms the sickest people and look after them there. Pigs however – linked with plague in the minds of the Mayor and Jurats – were to be banished. If people in almshouses in Stone Street, Pudding Lane and on the bridge continued to 'keep hogs or swine in rooms or houses where they lived', a fine of three shillings and fourpence would 'be levied by the sale of the said hogs or swine'.

The crafts of making wool and silk cloth and the art of dyeing were introduced into Kent from the Netherlands by the Walloons, who also brought hops to England (see page 97). Beer that had been made bitter by hops was believed to induce melancholy, and there were petitions against it in James I's reign. Hops are said to have first been grown successfully in England around Maidstone. When thousands of Walloons fled from persecution in the Netherlands by the Duke of Alva, viceroy of Philip II of Spain, Maidstone sought the Crown's permission to accept refugees: 'Dutch artificers with their families' who would set up in the town their manufacture of cloth, Spanish leather, pottery, tile, brick, paper, armour and gunpowder. Hard-working Walloons added to Maidstone's prosperity. They worshipped in St Faith's chapel, hired houses to accommodate looms, made fustian, grogram, linsey-woolsey and diaper, and employed many of the poor. Fuller's earth, which was found locally and used to scour the cloth, was so valuable that its export was prohibited. Common people spun flax, which skilled workmen made into thread. Broad-cloth, sackcloth and baize were woven and sold at local fairs, two of which had the engaging names of Runt Fair and Garlic Fair. In 1585 there were in Maidstone about 120 Dutch settlers over the age of twenty-one. Twenty years later, the cloth trade in the town had been 'learned and taken' from the settlers 'by the King's born subjects'.

Local bylaws decreed that any tradesman who opened his shop on a Sunday was liable to a fine of a shilling. Every young man 'living idly in the town' was to pay sixpence for every day he should be found 'idle and not using his art'. Failure to pay up would put him in prison 'until he should reform himself'. The same applied to every unmarried woman under forty who was out of service. Local benefactors tried to provide work. John Amye, a merchant, described how the poor 'who had not wherewithal to set them nor their children in work' became 'beggars from door to door' and being a little accustomed to begging 'did never fall to labour again, but to robberies and all other profanities'. Amye bequeathed money to buy 'hemp, flax, wool or such other wares' so 'that the poor people of the town might be set on work by dressing, spinning or repairing of the said wares or stuff' and keep 'their children ... from idleness and loitering tending to beggary'. Part of Amye's money was used to teach poor children to make 'cauls, buttons, button moulds, thread, or the winding thereof, or the like honest, easy arts'.

Leisure pursuits included bear-baiting in the Bear Ringle: an enclosed area (paved with stone from the Archbishop's Palace) in the High Street, just below the top of Mill Lane. The King's Mead, or Fair Meadow, was used 'to shoot in, and for other disport, pastimes and recreations, as well as for mustering and training of soldiers'. Performances of plays for the Mayor are likely to have been in the Lower Court House. Nearly twenty years before the visit of the King's Men, a play was acted at the Star inn 'about Christmas'.

DUNWICH

The King's Men were at Dunwich, a fishing town on the Suffolk coast four miles south of Southwold and about a hundred miles from London, between Christmas 1606 and Christmas 1607. There was 'laid out for a gratuity' to them six shillings and eightpence. Ten years earlier the Queen's Men had come to Dunwich, received six shillings and been 'much discontented' with that fee: the company, when it was founded as a troupe of stars in 1583, had received more pay in the provinces than other companies, which may have led, eventually, to a general pay-rise.

Although the population may have been less than 500 when the King's Men are first known to have come, the troupe returned three times in

Shakespeare's life: 1608–9, 1610–11 (probably between 19 and 26 October 1610) and 1614–15, so the players must have thought the earlier visits worth while.

Dunwich was described by Ralph Agas in 1589 as 'near the middle of the shire ... situate upon a cliff forty foot high, or thereabout, bounded on the east' by the North Sea. The sea is Dunwich's greatest enemy, because its surging waves easily undermine the sandy, loose cliff on which the town was built. In the past Dunwich had been a thriving port, and in Saxon and medieval times a bishopric and a prosperous town. But before Elizabeth's reign the hungry sea had encroached mercilessly, land had been swallowed up and the townsfolk, despite their bravery and resourcefulness as fishermen, were helpless. Dunwich, Camden wrote, 'lies in solitude and desolation'.

As well as bringing destruction to the town, the sea had brought wealth, some of which lingered on after the loss of the harbour. The western part of Dunwich continued for some time as a thriving market town. Dunwich shipwrights were brought to London to caulk the *Great Harry* for Henry VIII. Early in Elizabeth's reign there were still 166 sailors at Dunwich (174 at Southwold and 122 at Walberswick). The combined Suffolk fishing fleet generally sailed for Iceland in March, remained near there throughout the summer and then brought its catch of cod home. Towards the end of Elizabeth's reign, Dunwich contributed 32 of the 149 ships that formed the Iceland fleet. On the way, in 1598, the fleet plundered the Orkneys and kidnapped some Orkneymen for the voyage.

The year before, the Bishop's visitation exposed various Dunwich scandals. The curate of All Saints 'doth not instruct the youth in their catechism: he practiseth physic'. Margaret Finly was 'vehemently suspected to be a witch'. She and Thomas Deane – who confessed that he had 'two wives now living' – had been excommunicated. Probably the Bishop also heard about Amos Trewe and his three fellows, imprisoned for 'going to sea upon the Sabbath Day and following their labours'.

Elizabeth made a gesture to boost the fortunes of 'her town by rage and surges of the sea daily wasted and devoured'. In response to 'the humble suit and petition of the bailiffs and burgesses' she granted Dunwich a loan. The money for this came from the sale of 'bells, lead, iron, glass and stone' of the 'decayed church in Suffolk called "Ingate"' (materials valued at nearly £77) and of 'old lead' (value unknown) from the church at Kessingland – on the coast north of Southwold – which was being 'daily embezzled and conveyed by the inhabitants adjoining'. Eighteen years later, in 1596, the year when Raleigh and Essex took the town of Cadiz and burnt the Spanish fleet in harbour, Dunwich contributed armour, horses and money for ships in the Queen's service, and gunpowder for the town's ordnance. Essex, in the next year, sought to appoint Dunwich's two MPs himself. He had to make do with one, the appointment of the other having

already been granted to Sir Edward Coke, Attorney-General. (He was later, as judge, to preside over the trials of both Essex and Raleigh.)

An Elizabethan visitor to Dunwich, possibly Stow, mentioned in 1573 seeing:

'. . . foundations of down-fallen edifices – remains of dead exposed – naked wells divested of the ground about them by the waves of the sea – divers coins, several mill-hills and part of the old quay – seven or eight great hills there standing . . . .'

The area of the town he estimated as 200 acres, and the population 'not above 730, including strangers'.

13 CHANGING PLAYHOUSES

BLACKFRIARS AND THE GLOBE

Heaven is our heritage,
Earth but a player's stage;
Mount we unto the sky.
I am sick, I must die:
*   Lord, have mercy on us!*

THOMAS NASHE: Will Summer's Song from
Summer's Last Will and Testament

BLACKFRIARS

From 1608 Shakespeare's company was based not only at London's Globe but also at the Blackfriars Playhouse. This indoor theatre was especially useful during the winter. It was to the south-west of St Paul's and about 100 yards north of the river.

Before the Reformation, the friary had housed eighty or ninety brethren of the Dominican Order, which was distinguished by the wearing of long black cloaks over white habits, hence the name 'Blackfriars'. In 1529 the large hall upstairs at Blackfriars was used as the divorce court for Henry VIII and Katharine of Aragon. 'In the Great Hall' writes Holinshed 'was preparation made of seats, tables, and other furniture, according to such a solemn session and royal appearance.' In 'a chair royal' under 'a cloth of estate ... sat the King; and beside him, some distance from him, sat the Queen'.

Eighty-four years later, that trial was to be dramatized there, when the King's Men played *Henry VIII* at the Blackfriars Playhouse. Their theatre, which they had reconstructed after it had fallen 'far into decay for want of reparations', seems to have been housed in that very hall, upstairs in the converted friary. Nothing of the building now remains; on this site, the only visible reminder of theatrical history is the sign 'Playhouse Yard' on a wall outside.

When Henry VIII was not swiftly granted a divorce he blamed Cardinal Wolsey for the delay, charged him with treason, deprived him of the chancellorship and gave it to Sir Thomas More. The Great Hall at Blackfriars now became the scene of Wolsey's trial and condemnation. In *Henry VIII* Shakespeare or his collaborator, probably John Fletcher, a younger dramatist, was to write for Wolsey the despairing speech which includes the line 'Farewell, a long farewell, to all my greatness!' (3.2.352). In 1538, nine years after Wolsey's trial, the priory of Blackfriars – caught up in the suppression and seizure of monasteries – was dissolved and its church plate seized for the King.

Put to secular use, Blackfriars became an area of desirable apartments and houses. The Revels Office was moved into there, and provided rehearsal space for Court performances. Blackfriars Stairs, the nearby landing place, gave handy access to boats and barges on the Thames.

In Elizabeth's reign, choir boys achieved success not only as singers but also as actors. Richard Farrant, choirmaster, composer, playwright and Master of the Children of the Chapel at Windsor, set up an indoor playhouse in Blackfriars so that his young troupe could perform regularly. Although Blackfriars residents objected to the noise of play-goers' horses and coaches, Farrant's playhouse opened and flourished, with scripts by eminent dramatists (excluding Shakespeare: he never wrote for a company of boy-players). In the same year, 1576, James Burbage, a joiner who had become an actor, launched his open-air playhouse which he

John Fletcher, collaborator with Beaumont from 1609 – living on Bankside – and from ? 1612 collaborator with Shakespeare, whom he succeeded as principal dramatist to the King's Men. Fletcher was born in Rye, Sussex, 1579: son of a clergyman (later Queen's Chaplain and Bishop of London). Fletcher died of plague, 1625, in Southwark.

Opposite
The Cathedral Church of St Saviour, Southwark. Here, Shakespeare's brother Edmund was buried, 1607. Before London Bridge was built, the Priory of St Mary Overy (? 'of the ferry', 'over the river') was founded here. After Shakespeare's death, John Fletcher and Philip Massinger, chief dramatists of the King's Men, were buried in St Saviour's.

named simply 'the Theatre' as mentioned on page 41. Because it stood at Shoreditch, outside the City Walls, it was beyond the jurisdiction of the puritan City authorities. The Blackfriars and other indoor playhouses came to be called 'private'. The Theatre – later to be dismantled, transported across the Thames to Southwark, re-erected and renamed 'The Globe' – like other outdoor playhouses came to be called 'public'.

After Farrant's death, the Blackfriars Playhouse was closed for a number of years, although a fencing school on the floor below continued to flourish under the most popular fencing master in England, Rocco Bonetti. This Italian could 'hit any Englishman with a thrust, just upon any button in his doublet', as George Silver, devotee of English fencing, mentioned in *Paradoxes of Defence* (1599). Thirty-one Blackfriars residents, apprehensive of 'vagrant and lewd' crowds, of plague, and of 'the noise of the drums and trumpets' disturbing church services if the Playhouse reopened, petitioned the Privy Council to keep it shut. A ban was duly imposed on its use for plays.

Eventually, however, the Blackfriars Playhouse was reopened by Henry Evans. Success followed for a while. Frederic Gershow, from Stettin-Pomerania, much enjoyed the performance on 18 September 1602, as his diary shows. There were 'a good many people present and even many respectable women'. He says that the play was acted by artificial light:

'... which produces a great effect. For a whole hour before the play begins, one listens to a delightful instrumental concert played on organs, lutes, pandorins, mandolins, violins and flutes ... a boy using tremolo sang so charmingly to a bass-viol that we have not heard the like of it in the whole of our journey, unless perhaps the nuns at Milan may have excelled him.'

In *Hamlet* (2.2.339) Rosencrantz scornfully alludes to child actors as 'little eyases' who 'are now the fashion': their shrill voices attack public theatres, which they snootily call 'the common stages'. Evans was an unsavoury manager who put on plays which outraged the authorities. He landed his boys in prison and he clashed with the Lord Chamberlain. The company was dissolved: in 1608 Evans sur-

rendered his lease of the Blackfriars Playhouse, and the King's Men's syndicate took over.

At once, plague drove them out of London. That autumn, Shakespeare's mother died and was buried at Stratford on 9 September. On 16 October, Shakespeare became godfather to William Walker of Stratford, either in person or by proxy. The King's Men acted in Marlborough on an unspecified date and in Coventry on 29 October. They returned to London and performed a dozen plays at Court during the winter, for £120. In addition, the company received £40 for private rehearsals during the plague so as 'to perform their service before his Majesty in Christmas holidays'.

Next year, 1609, the plague grew even worse. 'Playhouses' wrote Dekker 'stand (like taverns that have cast out their masters) the doors locked up, the flags (like their bushes) [bushes were hung up as tavern-signs] taken down'. The King's Men continued to tour during most of the year, returning to London for six weeks of rehearsal in which they prepared thirteen plays for the Christmas season at Court. Payment was £130 and bonus £30; the money must have been very welcome after such a long period of touring.

The company's delayed opening at the Blackfriars Playhouse inaugurated a most successful period. Shakespeare was probably spending more and more time in Stratford, and less and less in London. As provider of scripts, he was joined by dramatists who had written for the Children at Blackfriars: Jonson, Beaumont and Fletcher. From 1610 to 1616 nearly all the plays by the best playwrights were written for the King's Men at that theatre. Moreover, the company was in great demand at Court. For six months, from 31 October 1611 to 26 April 1612, they played there almost every week, presenting *The Tempest*, *The Winter's Tale* and twenty other plays. Occasionally they gave two plays there on one day, a matinée and evening show, as on 6 and 17 January 1608.

Either because Shakespeare wanted a convenient lodging for his visits to London, or as an investment, or both, on 10 March 1613 he bought from a musician the upper floor of a gatehouse in the Blackfriars precinct, on the eastern side, abutting 'a street leading down to Puddle Wharf'. Part of this 'dwelling-house' was, the deed says, over the 'great gate', and Shakespeare also bought a plot of land on the west side of that, in 'a great piece of void ground lately used for a garden'. The Blackfriars Playhouse was only a hundred yards away. Access to the Thames, and so to the Globe at Southwark, was easy.

THE GLOBE AND BLACKFRIARS

That summer, however, the King's Men suffered a disaster when, as Thomas Lorkin wrote on 30 June 1613:

'No longer since than yesterday, while Burbage's company were acting at the Globe the play of *Henry VIII*, and there shooting off certain chambers [stage cannon, which fired wadding, for the King's entry at the masque in Cardinal Wolsey's house] in way of triumph, the fire catched and fastened upon the thatch of the house [the Playhouse], and there burned so furiously, as it consumed the whole house, all in less than two hours, the people having enough to do to save themselves.'

Two days later, Sir Henry Wotton wrote to his nephew that the only casualties were:

'... wood and straw, and a few forsaken cloaks; only one man had his breeches set on fire, that would perhaps have broiled him, if he had not by the benefit of a provident wit put it out with bottle ale.'

According to Henry Bluett, a young merchant, the Globe was 'very full' – modern research gives 3,350 as its capacity – and the only man hurt was 'scalded with the fire by adventuring in to save a child which otherwise had been burnt'. John Chamberlain, scholar and letter writer, thought 'it was a great marvel and fair grace of God that the people had so little harm, having but two narrow doors to get

Globe Playhouse commemorated. J Taylor: 'As gold is better that's in fire tried, So is the Bankside Globe that late was burned; For where before it had a thatched hide, Now to a stately theatre 'tis turned.' The new Globe was demolished, 1644, to make way for tenement houses.

HERE STOOD THE GLOBE PLAYHOUSE OF SHAKESPEARE 1598-1613

COMMEMORATED BY THE SHAKESPEARE READING SOCIETY OF LONDON AND BY SUBSCRIBERS IN THE UNITED KINGDOM AND INDIA

out'. Puritans, however, saw 'the sudden fearful burning' as God's hand at work against the sin of theatre, 'no man perceiving how' this fire came.

Thatch, an obvious fire hazard, was replaced on the new Globe by tiles. This playhouse took only a year to build and re-open, and it was 'said to be the fairest that ever was in England'.

Crowds continued to flock to the Blackfriars Playhouse. It held about 735 people and the cheapest entrance fee was sixpence, compared with one penny (two for a new play) at the Globe. A complaint written less than two years after Shakespeare died, and therefore likely to be relevant also to the last years of his life, blames the Blackfriars Playhouse for 'such resort of people' daily 'and such multitudes of coaches (whereof many are hackney coaches bringing people of all sorts) that sometimes all our streets cannot contain them, but that they clog up Ludgate also'. This traffic problem in the narrow streets 'almost every day in the winter time . . . from one or two of the clock till six at night', hindered people coming to church for 'christenings and burials and afternoon's service' and disrupted worldly life too. The coaches 'break down stalls, throw down men's goods from their shops, and the inhabitants there cannot come to their houses nor bring in their necessary provisions of beer, wood, coal or hay, not the tradesmen or shopkeepers utter [put out] their wares, nor the passengers go to the common water stairs, without danger of their lives and limbs'.

14 RETURNING TO STRATFORD

HYTHE, ROMNEY, STAFFORD AND
STRATFORD-UPON-AVON

*Sweet Swan of Avon! what a sight it were
To see thee in our waters yet appear,
And make those flights upon the banks of Thames,
That so did take Eliza, and our James!*

BEN JONSON: *To the memory of my beloved, the Author,
Mr William Shakespeare: and what he hath left us*

HYTHE AND ROMNEY

The King's Men were in Kent, playing at Hythe, one of the Cinque Ports, on 16 May 1609, and the next day at New Romney, on each occasion for an official fee of twenty shillings. (The company had played at Ipswich on 9 May.)

Hythe, moulded by 'banking of ooze and great casting up of shingle', was useful to shipping in Henry VIII's time. Leland wrote:

'The haven is a pretty road, and lieth meetly straight for passage out of Boulogne. It crooketh in so by the shore along, and is so backed from the main sea with casting of shingle, that small ships may come up a large mile toward Folkestone as in a sure gut.'

Elizabeth gave Hythe, by charter, control over its own affairs, and she encouraged the people to keep their haven scoured. A great shingle bank, however, threatened to block up the port, and an earthquake in 1580 may have hastened the coastal change. Nearly twenty years after Shakespeare's death, the entrance was 'absolutely stopped and starved up'.

South-west of Hythe in about the eleventh century, the mouth of the River Rother was so barred with sand and silt that Old Romney was abandoned and New Romney (a town already in existence, and not new) replaced it as a port about two miles nearer the sea. In the thirteenth century a storm clogged the estuary with shingle and closed the river mouth. Making a new channel out to sea at Rye, the river forsook the port and harbour of New Romney. The town continued as a fish market for porpoise, cod, herring, sprats, salmon, haddock, crab, lampreys, mackerel, conger, shrimps, whiting, tench and eels.

Camden was impressed by the use of Romney Marsh, a vast tidal marsh enclosed by shingle and silt:

Previous page
Romney Marsh: 'a marvellous rank ground for feeding of cattle ... grass groweth so plentifully upon the ooze sometime cast up there by the sea' (Leland). Long wool was the speciality. Chill winds made 'good grass under foot' easier to find than 'wholesome air above the head' (Lambarde).

'How fruitful the soil is, what herds of cattle it feeds that are sent hither from the remotest parts of England to be fatted, and with what art they raise walls to fence it against the incursions of the sea are things which one can hardly believe that has not seen them.'

Tens of thousands of sheep, besides horned cattle, grazed on the marsh. It was so exposed that Lambarde called it 'evil in winter, grievous in summer and never good'. Young sheep could not be wintered there, but were taken inland and brought back in the late spring.

To promote England's wealth through wool in Elizabeth's time, a prohibitive duty of between twenty and forty shillings a bag was imposed on fleeces for export. Contraband trade in wool – called 'owling' – flourished, despite threatened penalties of mutilation or death. Most of the rough wool from Romney Marsh was exported in French shallops by night.

Beacons were vital to England as a warning of attack. To speed the gathering of troops for defence, the Lieutenant of Kent, Sir William Brooke, Lord Cobham, had a map of the beacons drawn on card, with connecting lines to show their relative positions 'by which any man, with little labour, may be assured where the danger is, and thereof inform his neighbours'. At New Romney the church tower was the site of the main beacon. Lambarde had seen old-fashioned beacons made of 'great stacks of wood' in Wiltshire: but in Kent 'it was ordained that ... they should be high standards with their pitchpots.'

STAFFORD

In 1610 and 1613 the King's Men played in Stafford, on each occasion for an official fee of ten shillings. Smith described Stafford as 'a proper little town, walled about, standing in the midst of the shire, upon the river of Sow, which falleth into the Trent three miles east from thence'.

In Shakespeare's day Roman Catholicism persisted in Staffordshire: Philip II of Spain was correctly informed that 'the gentry and common people' were 'strong Catholics'. Men went abroad to be trained as priests and returned to make converts. A Dr Henshawe claimed to have converted 228 people in the county in two months. Robert Sutton, a carpenter's son, worked for many years in Stafford before he was caught in 1588 saying mass inside the county jail, where a number of Catholics were imprisoned. Everyone present at the mass was condemned to death. There was a public outcry: only Sutton was executed; the laymen were spared, but fined.

Shoemakers, goldsmiths and ironmasters featured in Stafford during Shakespeare's lifetime but the chief work was capping – knitting a coarse, woollen cap. When Elizabeth visited the town in August 1575, she found it suffering from a recession:

'She commended the situation of the town and asked what was the cause of the decay of the same. An answer was made that the decay of capping was one cause thereof. Another for that the assizes were taken away from the town.'

Her Majesty 'lovingly answered that she would renew and establish better the ... Statute for Capping' and she promised that the assizes 'should ever after be kept at Stafford'. The attempt to compel people to wear caps failed; but an Act, passed in the year of her visit, encouraged the establishment of Stafford as the assize town: which it became after the shire hall was rebuilt in the 1580s.

In the same year as the first recorded visit of the King's Men to Stafford, plague led to the opening of a temporary hospital with beds, fuel, two nurses and a doctor. The town already had various health regulations. No-one was allowed to 'wash clothes, fish or any other thing, water horses, wash their hands' or prepare parsnips ('shrag' and wash them) 'in or at any common well or bucket'. The jailer was not to 'suffer his prisoners to lay their dung or filth near the prison' or within forty foot of any street or of the town ditch, but to bury it in a 'convenient pit or place to be made in one of his gardens, as no man may be annoyed with the savour thereof'.

Regulations extended into the tricky area of sexual morality. No householder was to keep in his house anyone 'suspected to be of evil demeanour or of unchaste living' nor 'any woman of light disposition'. The bailiff was to 'cause diligent search to be made through all the town and see that all houses be cleansed of light suspect women and single women gotten with child or to be gotten with child'. (The gossips of Stafford must have relished this order.)

Some regulations show how rural the town was. Anyone winnowing corn or malt in street, gate or churchyard had to carry away the 'chaff and dust' forthwith. No-one was to 'hurl, sling or cast any stone or shoot in any bow or gun at any doves or other fowls about the church or in the town'. In Tudor Stafford, the hobby-horse dance was used to raise money for the church, but the town was not a lively social centre. A grim aspect of local behaviour, likely to dismay strangers, is indicated in the order to the jailer not to allow more than 'two prisoners to stand upon the chain to beg, neither at any time to make any fire under the gates'.

STRATFORD-UPON-AVON

The King's Men returned to Kent and performed again in New Romney for an official fee of twenty shillings on 21 April, 1612. By that time, however, Shakespeare had virtually retired. From about 1611 he seems to have spent most of his time at Stratford, visiting London occasionally: for instance, in 1612 to give evidence in the Belott-Mountjoy suit, and in 1613 and 1615 to deal with the lease of his property at Blackfriars. He was still writing: *The Tempest* was performed on Hallowmas Night 1611, in the Banqueting House at Whitehall. *Henry VIII* was being acted in 1613 when the Globe burnt down; and about that year there were performances of *Cardenio*, a lost play ascribed to Shakespeare and Fletcher, and of Fletcher's *Two Noble Kinsmen*, a play in which Shakespeare probably had a hand. He is not known to have written for the stage after that. Nor, after 1611, is he at all likely to have been involved in provincial performances of the King's Men, who visited Winchester, Folkestone and Nottingham, places not apparently visited by the troupe in earlier years.

There is no record that Shakespeare contributed, with other sharers, to the rebuilding of the Globe after the fire of 1613. He had worked for nearly twenty years with the company: now he seems to have left its future to more active men. In Stratford, he was a person of substance, owning the Birthplace in Henley Street and the Great House of New Place, with other purchases: the copyhold of a cottage opposite New Place garden; arable land and pasture rights in Old Stratford; and a half interest in the lease of tithes in the hamlets of Old Stratford, Welcombe and Bishopton.

Over the years, family·events must have called Shakespeare home to Stratford. In 1607 his daughter Susanna married John Hall, an excellent and dedicated physician who had graduated at Queen's College, Cambridge, and settled in Stratford. Susanna had been in trouble the year before her marriage for not attending Easter Communion: perhaps a sign of Roman Catholic tendencies, though John was a protestant. They are said to have lived in the half-timbered house in Old Town, near New Place and Holy Trinity Church. Now called Hall's Croft, the house had a large garden where Hall could grow some of the plants he used in his medicine.

Shakespeare's own house, New Place, was the second largest in Stratford (the largest was the old monastic college). There were probably more than ten rooms in New Place, which had a frontage of over sixty foot in Chapel Street and a depth of about seventy foot along Chapel Lane. There appear to have been three storeys, five gables, ornamental beams, a small courtyard and a garden to which Shakespeare added land to the east, in Chapel Lane, to form the Great Garden, now a feature of Stratford. New Place was noted for its vines and Shakespeare is said to have planted a mulberry tree. His properties were spared by the terrible Stratford fire of 9 July 1614, but the house was pulled down in the eighteenth century. Some foundations, the well and the garden remain, with a mulberry tree reputed to have been grown from a scion of Shakespeare's own tree.

Of Anne, his wife, little is known between the baptism of their children and the drawing up of his will, in which her rights as widow did not need to be stated. She would inherit a life interest of a third of her husband's estate, and residence in the family house. Shakespeare's brother Gilbert was buried at Stratford in 1612 and his last brother, Richard, in 1613. Of John's eight sons and daughters, now only William and his sister Joan remained.

In February 1616 Shakespeare's daughter Judith, aged thirty-one, married Thomas Quiney, vintner, aged twenty-seven. He ran a tavern near the top of the High Street. They married during the prohibited Lenten season and when summoned to the consistory court at Worcester they failed to appear. Quiney was excommunicated. In July the couple moved into a bigger house, the Cage, at the corner of the High Street and Bridge Street. Quiney kept a vintner's shop on the upper floor and dealt in tobacco.

Shakespeare died on 23 April 1616. The Stratford vicar and physician, John Ward, wrote half a century later – presumably quoting a local legend – that the cause was a fever, contracted after drinking with Drayton and Jonson. Shakespeare was buried in the chancel of Holy Trinity Church, Stratford, and his widow was buried beside him seven years later.

Holy Trinity Church, Stratford-upon-Avon, north door: sanctuary knocker (thirteenth-century) on the inner door (fifteenth-century). Any criminal who reached it could claim protection for thirty-seven days. Durham Cathedral has a similar sanctuary knocker: there, criminals who took sanctuary had forty days to leave the country.

SHAKESPEARE'S WRITINGS

In this list, much of the dating is conjectural.

Late 1580s	*Two Gentlemen of Verona*	**1598–9**	*Much Ado About Nothing*
1590–1	*Henry VI Pt ii*; *Henry VI Pt iii*	**1599**	*Henry V*; *Julius Caesar*
1591–2	*Henry VI Pt i*	**1599–1600**	*As You Like It*
1592	*Venus and Adonis*	**1600**	*Hamlet*
1592–3	*Richard III*	**1601**	*Twelfth Night*
1593	*The Rape of Lucrece*	**1601–2**	*Troilus and Cressida*
1593–4	*Titus Andronicus*; *The Taming of the Shrew*; *The Comedy of Errors*; *Love's Labour's Lost*	**1602–3**	*All's Well That Ends Well*
		1603–4	*Othello*
1594–5	*Romeo and Juliet*; *A Midsummer Night's Dream*	**1604**	*Measure for Measure*; *Timon of Athens*
		1606	*Macbeth*; *Antony and Cleopatra*
1595–6	*Richard II*	**1607–8**	*Pericles*
1595–1600	Sonnets	**1608**	*King Lear* (Quarto); *Coriolanus*
1596	*Henry IV Pt i*	**1608–16**	*King Lear* (Folio)
1596–7	*King John*; *The Merchant of Venice*; *Henry IV Pt ii*	**1609–10**	*The Winter's Tale*
		1610–11	*Cymbeline*; *The Tempest*
1597	*The Merry Wives of Windsor*	**1613**	*Henry VIII*; *Two Noble Kinsmen*

THE LORD CHAMBERLAIN'S/KING'S MEN ON TOUR

VENUES MENTIONED IN THIS BOOK

Because of the incompleteness of the records and the imprecision of dates, this list is tentative and marred by gaps: but at least it shows the mobility of Shakespeare's players.

1594	Marlborough	**1606**	Marlborough
1594–5	Ipswich. Cambridge	**1606–7**	Dunwich
1596	Faversham	**1607**	Oxford. Barnstaple
1597	Marlborough. Bristol. Bath. Rye. Dover	**1608**	Marlborough. Coventry
		1608–9	Dunwich
1600–01	Oxford	**1609**	Ipswich. Hythe. New Romney
1601	Cambridge?	**1609–10**	Oxford. Shrewsbury
1602–3	Ipswich. Shrewsbury. Bath	**1610**	Stafford. Dover
1603	Coventry. Wilton	**1610–11**	Dunwich. Shrewsbury?
1603–4	Oxford	**1611–12**	Winchester
1605	Oxford. Barnstaple	**1612**	New Romney
1605–6	Maidstone. Oxford. Cambridge (or 1606–7)	**1612–13**	Oxford. Shrewsbury. Folkestone
		1613	Stafford
		1614	Coventry
		1614–15	Dunwich
		1615	Nottingham

TIME CHART

EVENTS IN THE FAMILY LIFE OF SHAKESPEARE

These occur in or near Stratford-upon-Avon, unless a different place is named.

Year	Family Life	General Events
1564	23 Apr. Shakespeare's 'official' birthday: his date of birth is uncertain. The son of John and Mary Shakespeare (she was formerly Arden), William is born at their home in Henley St. 26 Apr. He is christened.	Death of Calvin. War ends between France and England.
1565	4 Sept. Shakespeare's father is elected alderman.	
1566		Birth of future King of England, James I. Gresham founds Royal Exchange.
1567		Darnley is murdered. Alva arrives in the Netherlands.
1568	4 Sept. Shakespeare's father is elected bailiff.	Mary, Queen of Scots, flees to England. Birth of William Harvey
1569		Rebellion of northern Earls.
1570		Pope Pius V excommunicates Elizabeth I.
1571		Elizabeth approves the Thirty-Nine Articles.
1572		Burghley becomes Lord Treasurer. Massacre of St Bartholomew Birth of Donne.
1573		Walsingham becomes Principal Secretary.
1574		First seminary priests arrive in England. Henry III of France succeeded by Charles IX.
1575		Grindal succeeds Parker as Archbishop of Canterbury.
1576		Poor Law Act. (1576–8) Frobisher's voyages.
1577	Shakespeare's father stops attending council meetings.	Don John of Austria arrives in Netherlands. (1577–80) Drake sails round the world.
1578		Don John dies: Parma takes over.
1579	4 Apr. Shakespeare's sister, Anne, is buried.	Desmond rebellion in Munster.
1580		First Jesuit mission arrives in England. Montaigne publishes Essa in France.
1581		Levant Company is founded.
1582	28 Nov. In Worcester, a licence is issued for Shakespeare and Anne Hathaway to marry. Where the wedding takes place is uncertain: perhaps in a village near Stratford. They live in his parental home in Henley St.	
1583	26 May. Their daughter, Susanna, is christened.	Whitgift becomes Archbishop of Canterbury.
1584		Throckmorton Plot. William of Orange assassinated.
1585	2 Feb. Their son, Hamnet, and daughter, Judith, twins, are christened. Between 1585 and 1593, Shakespeare leaves his family in Stratford and establishes himself in London, becoming a house-holder there by the mid-nineties, but returning annually to Stratford.	Leicester is sent to Netherlands, Drake to West Indies. War of the Three Henries begins. (1585–7) John Davis's voyages.
1586		Treaty of Berwick. Babington Plot. Sidney, wounded at Zutphen, dies.
1587		Mary, Queen of Scots, is executed. Drake attacks Cadiz.
1588		Spanish Armada is defeated. Death of Leicester.
1589		Drake's expedition to Portugal. Henry III of France assassinated: succeeded by Henry IV.
1590		Walsingham dies. At Ivry, Henry IV defeats Catholic League.
1591		Elizabeth sends troops to Brittany and Normandy.

THEATRICAL AFFAIRS

Marlowe born.

Alleyn born. Elizabeth sees plays on 'pageants' at Coventry.

Richard Burbage born. Nashe born.

Jonson born.

City of London protects against players. Act authorizes Master of Revels to license acting companies.

Elizabeth sees shows at Kenilworth. Cambridge bans players.

James Burbage opens The Theatre, Shoreditch.

Curtain opened.

Tilney becomes Master of Revels. Gosson's *School of Abuse* published. Fletcher born.

Stubbes published *Anatomy of Abuses*.

Whit Monday riot at The Theatre.

Leicester's Men act in the Netherlands.

Henslowe opens Rose Playhouse, Bankside.

Tarlton dies.

About now, Alleyn becomes leading actor of Admiral's Men: continues to 1597.

EVENTS IN THE FAMILY LIFE OF SHAKESPEARE	GENERAL EVENTS
1592	Parma dies.
1593	Henry IV becomes Roman Catholic. Hooker's *Ecclesiastical Polity* is published.
1594	Rebellion of Hugh O'Neill in Ireland.
1595	Hawkins dies.
1596 — 11 Aug. Hamnet is buried. Shakespeare is living in parish of St Helen's, Bishopsgate, London. 20 Oct. London: Grant of Arms to Shakespeare's father.	Drake dies. Essex and Howard attack Cadiz. Robert Cecil becomes Secretary of State.
1597 — 4 May. Shakespeare buys New Place.	Essex's raid on the Axores fails. Poor Law codified.
1598	Burghley dies. Revolt in Ireland. Peace of Vervins. Philip II of Spain succeeded by Philip III.
1599	Essex is sent to Ireland. Edmund Spenser dies. Oliver Cromwell born.
1600 — Shakespeare is living in liberty of the Clink, Southwark, London,	East India company founded.
1601 — 8 Sept. His father is buried.	Essex is executed. Battle of Kinsale. Poor Law renewed. Monopolies debate. Madrigals: *The Triumphs of Oriana*.
1602 — Shakespeare buys land in Old Stratford, and opposite New Place in Stratford.	
1603	Elizabeth dies: James VI of Scotland succeeds her as James I of England. Raleigh imprisoned.
1604 — (?1602/3) He is living in parish of St Olave, Cripplegate, London.	Hampton Court Conference. End of war with Spain. Bancroft becomes Archbishop of Canterbury.
1605 — 24 July. He buys a lease of tithes in Stratford and in three hamlets nearby.	Gunpowder Plot is foiled. Cervantes publishes first part of *Don Quixote* in Spain.
1606	Trial of Henry Garnet, Jesuit.
1607 — 5 June. Susanna Shakespeare and John Hall marry. 31 Dec. Shakespeare's youngest brother, Edmund, is buried in Southwark.	Commons reject proposed Union with Scotland.
1608 — 21 Feb. Elizabeth Hall, Susanna's daughter, is christened. 9 Sept. Shakespeare's mother is buried. During the rest of Shakespeare's life, he spends more time in Stratford.	Birth of Milton.
1609	Galileo makes his first telescope.
1610	
1611 — By now, he has reduced his work-load in the theatre, and he lives almost entirely in Stratford in retirement, although he still writes some plays.	Abbot becomes Archbishop of Canterbury. 'Authorized Version' of Bible is published. James dissolves Parliament.
1612 — 3 Feb. His eldest brother, Gilbert, is buried.	Prince Henry dies. Cecil dies.
1613 — 4 Feb. The last of Shakespeare's brothers, Richard, is buried. 10 Mar. Shakespeare buys a property in Blackfriars, probably as an investment.	Princess Elizabeth and the Elector Palatine marry. Francis Bacon becomes Attorney General.
1614 — 9 July. His Stratford properties escape burning in a terrible fire.	Parliament, summoned by James, refuses to grant him subsidies. Raleigh's *History of the World* is published.
1615	Thomas Wentworth is imprisoned.
1616 — 10 Feb. Judith Shakespeare and Thomas Quiney marry. 25 Mar. Shakespeare's will. 23 Apr. Shakespeare dies.	Lord Chief Justice Coke is dismissed.
1623 — 6 Aug. His widow, Anne, dies. 8 Nov. The First Folio is entered in the Stationers' Register, London.	

THEATRICAL AFFAIRS

Greene dies. Cambridge renews ban on players.

Marlowe dies.

Chamberlain's Men, newly formed, play mainly at The Theatre: Shakespeare is a leading sharer in the company. Admiral's Men at Rose Playhouse.

Swan Playhouse built on Bankside.

James Burbage buys Blackfriars property.

James Burbage dies: Richard inherits his property. Theatres are closed after Nashe's *Isles of Dogs*. Alleyn sells stock in Admiral's Men.

Jonson's *Every Man in His Humour* acted by Chamberlain's Men. December: The Theatre is pulled down; timbers ferried to Bankside for building Globe.

By May, Globe opens.

Henslowe builds Fortune at Finsbury, for Admiral's Men: Alleyn stars there till 1605. Children of the Chapel act at Blackfriars. Jonson's *Every Man out of His Humour* starts 'war of the theatres' which ends in 1602. Kemp dances from London to Norwich.

Chamberlain's Men become King's Men. Theatres closed by plague.

Alleyn and Henslowe become Masters of the Royal Game. Children of the Queen's Revels act at Blackfriars.

Eastward Ho! puts Jonson and Chapman in prison.

Red Bull Playhouse opens in Clerkenwell. King's Men act Jonson's *Volpone* at Globe.

King's Men take over Blackfriars from Children of Revels, for use as winter house.

Beaumont and Fletcher collaborate.

Jonson's *The Alchemist*.

Thomas Heywood publishes *Apology for Actors*.

Shakespeare and Fletcher collaborate. Globe is burnt down: rebuilding starts at once.

Globe, rebuilt, opens by 30 June. Webster's *Duchess of Malfi*.

Jonson publishes his *Works*, the first 'collected plays' by any dramatist.

BIBLIOGRAPHY

Indispensable to the author throughout:

Bentley, Gerald Eades: *The Profession of Dramatist in Shakespeare's Time*, Princeton University Press, 1971
 The Profession of Player in Shakespeare's Time, Princeton University Press, 1984
Byrne, Muriel St Clare: *Elizabethan Life in Town and Country*, Methuen, 1925, revised 1961
Camden, William: *Britannia*, 1586, fourth edn, 1722
Chambers, Sir EK: *The Elizabethan Stage*, 4 vols, OUP, 1923
 William Shakespeare, OUP, 1930
ed. Darby, HC: *An Historical Geography of England before 1800*, CUP, 1936, reprinted 1963
Foakes, RA: *Illustrations of the English Stage 1580–1642*, Scolar Press, 1985
Furnivall, Frederick J: *Harrison's Description of England* London, 1877
ed. Lee, Sir Sidney and Onions, CT: *Shakespeare's England*, Clarendon Press, Oxford, 1916
Lorwin, Madge: *Dining with William Shakespeare*, Atheneum, New York, 1976
Malone Society: *Collections*, OUP
Murray, JT: *English Dramatic Companies, 1558–1642*, 2 vols, 1910
Nichols, John: *The Progresses and Public Processions of Queen Elizabeth*, 3 vols, 1788–1821
 The Progresses, Processions and Magnificent Festivities of King James the First, 4 vols, 1828
Rye, WB: *England as seen by Foreigners*, London, 1865
Schoenbaum, S:
 William Shakespeare. A Documentary Life, Clarendon Press, Oxford, with Scolar Press, 1975
Sugden, EH: *A Topographical Dictionary to the Works of Shakespeare*, Manchester, 1925
ed. Toulmin Smith, Lucy: *Leland's*

Itinerary, Centaur, 1964
The Victoria History of the Counties of England, Oxford (1899–)
Wickham, Glynne: *Early English Stages 1300 to 1660*, Routledge and Kegan Paul, 1959–72

In passages about London:
Barker, Felix and Jackson, Peter: *London: 2,000 years of a city and its people*, Cassell, London, 1974
Holmes, Martin: *Elizabethan London*, Cassell, 1969
Rutter, Carol Chillington: *Documents of the Rose Playhouse*, Manchester University Press, 1984
Stow, John: *A Survey of London*, ed. CL Kingsford, Oxford, 1908
Thomas, David: *Shakespeare in the Public Records*, HMSO, 1985

In particular chapters:

Chapter 1
Baker, Oliver: *In Shakespeare's Warwickshire and the Unknown Years*, Simkin Marshall, London, 1937
Eccles, Mark: *Shakespeare in Warwickshire*, The University of Wisconsin Press, 1963
Fripp, Edgar I: *Introduction and Notes to Minutes and Accounts of the Corporation of Stratford-upon-Avon and Other Records*, OUP, 1921 and 1924

Chapter 2
Hart Milman, Henry: *Annals of St. Paul's Cathedral*, London, 1868
Kemp, Will: *Kemp's Nine Days Wonder*, Kylin Press, Waddesdon, 1983
Moryson, Fynes: *An Itinerary*, London, 1617

Chapter 3
Bentley, Gerald Eades: *The Jacobean and Caroline Stage*, OUP, 1941
Cardigan, Earl of: *The Wardens of Savernake Forest*, London, 1949
Dawson, Giles: Introduction to Malone Society *Collections*, vol. VII
Hotson, Leslie: *Shakespeare's Sonnets Dated*, Hart-Davis, 1949

Kempson, EGH: manuscript notes on the history of Marlborough
Stedman, AR: *Marlborough and the Upper Kennet Country*, 1960

Chapter 4
anon.: *The Honourable Society of Gray's Inn*, 1969, second edition 1976
Dalzell, WR: *The Shell Guide to the History of London*, Book Club Associates, 1981
Harwood, TA: *Windsor Old and New*, London, 1929
Hughes, GM: *A History of Windsor Forest*, 1890
Jenkins, Simon: *The Companion Guide to Outer London*, Collins, 1981
Lee, Albert: *The Story of Royal Windsor*, 1910
Piper, David: *The Companion Guide to London*, Collins, sixth edition, 1977
Prockter, Adrian and Taylor, Robert: *The A to Z of Elizabethan London*, London Topographical Society, 1979
Thorne, James: *Handbook to the Environs of London*, 2 vols, 1876

Chapter 5
Bacon, Nathaniel: *The Annals of Ipswich*, 1654 and 1884
Harrison, AD: 'Thomas Eldred: Merchant', *Mariner's Mirror*, 1929
Malster, Robert: *Ipswich, town on the Orwell*, Lavenham, 1978
Redstone, Lilian J: *Ipswich through the Ages*, Ipswich, 1948
Smith, William: *The Particular Description of England*, London, 1879
Taylor, Gary: 'The Fortunes of Oldcastle', *Shakespeare Survey* no. 38, CUP, 1985
Webb, John: *Great Tooley of Ipswich*, Suffolk, 1962
White, William: *History, Gazetteer and Directory of Suffolk*, 1844
Boas, Frederick S: *University Drama in the Tudor Age*, New York, 1914
Cooper, Charles Henry: *Annals of Cambridge*, Cambridge, 1843
Gray, Arthur: 'Shakespeare and

Cambridge', *The Cam*, February 1937
Moore Smith, GC: *College Plays performed in the University of Cambridge*, CUP, 1923
Power, Eileen: 'Stourbridge Fair', NUT Cambridge Souvenir, 1928

Chapter 6
Boas, Frederick S: 'Queen Elizabeth The Revels Office And Edmund Tilney', Howland Lecture, OUP, 1938
Pinks, WI: *The History of Clerkenwell*, London, 1881

Chapter 7
Brentnall, Margaret: *The Cinque Ports and Romney Marsh*, John Gifford, 1972
Burrows, Montague: *Cinque Ports*, Longmans Green, 1888
Holt, Anita: *Arden of Feversham*, The Faversham Society, 1970
Jessup, Frank W: *A History of Kent*, Darwen Finlayson, 1958
Lambarde, WM: *A Perambulation of Kent*, Chatham, 1826
Percival, Arthur: *The Faversham Gunpowder Industry and its Development*, Faversham Papers, 1969
Bagley, Geoffrey Spink: *The Book of Rye*, Barracuda, Buckingham, 1982
Holloway, William: *The History and Antiquities of the Ancient Town and Port of Rye*, London, 1847
Hueffer, Ford Maddox: *The Cinque Ports*, Blackwood, 1900
Jones, J Bavington: *Annals of Dover*, Dover, 1916, second edn, 1938

Chapter 8
Barker, Dr Kathleen MD: *Bristol at Play*, Moonraker, 1976
Green, Emanuel: 'Did Queen Elizabeth visit Bath in the Years 1574 and 1592?', *Bath Natural History and Antiquarian Field Club*, 1879
Latimer, John: *The Annals of Bristol in the Sixteenth Century*, Bristol, 1970
ed. MacInnes, CM and Whittard, WF: *Bristol and its Adjoining Counties*, Bristol, 1955 (especially McGrath, Patrick: 'Bristol Since 1497')

Warner, R: *The history of Bath*, 1801
BMA: *The Book of Bath*, 1925
Hamilton, M: *Bath before Beau Nash*, 1978
James, P Rowland: *The Baths of Bath in the Sixteenth and Early Seventeenth Centuries*, Bristol, 1938
Matthews, Leslie G: *The Antiques of Perfume*
ed. Piesse, Charles H: *The Art of Perfumery*, 1891
Smith, RAL: *Bath*, Batsford, 1944

Chapter 9
Foakes, RA and Rickert, RT: *Henslowe's Diary*, CUP, 1961

Chapter 10
Boas, Frederick S: *University Drama in the Tudor Age*, New York, 1914
Wilson, FP: *The Plague in Shakespeare's London*, OUP, 1927
ed. Leighton, Rev. WA: *A History of Shrewsbury School 1551–1888*, from the Blakeway Manuscript, 1889
Fisher, George W: *Annals of Shrewsbury Schools*, London, 1899
Owen, H and Blakeway, JB: *A History of Shrewsbury*, London, 1825
Vail Motter, TH: *The School Drama in England*, 1929
Dyer, Alan: 'Warwickshire Towns under the Tudors and Stuarts', *Warwickshire History*, vol. 3, no. 4
Fox, Levi: *Coventry's Heritage*, 1947
Poole, Benjamin and Taunton, W Frederic: *Coventry, its History and Antiquities*, Coventry, 1869
Williamson, Ward: 'Notes on the Decline of the Provincial Drama in England, 1530–1642', *Educational Theatre Journal*, USA, 1961

Chapter 11
Pevsner, Nikolaus, rev. Cherry, Bridget: *The Buildings of England: Wiltshire*, Penguin, 1975
Strong, Roy: *Elizabeth R*, Book Club Associates, 1971
Whitlock, Ralph: *Salisbury Plain*, Robert Hale, 1955
Law, Ernest: *The History of Hampton Court Palace*, London, 1885
Thorne, James: *Handbook to the*

Environs of London, 2 vols, 1876
Winwood, Ralph: *Memorials*, 1725

Chapter 12
Bates, Darrell: *The Companion Guide to Devon and Cornwall*, Collins, 1976
Chanter, JR: *Sketches of the Literary History of Barnstaple*, 1866
        and Wainwright, Thomas: *Reprint of the Barnstaple Records*, 1900
Morris, Christopher: *The Tudors*, Batsford, 1955, Fontana, 1966
Lamplugh, Lois: *Barnstaple: Town on the Taw*, Phillimore, Chichester, 1983
Powell, JW Damer: *Bristol Privateers and Ships of War*, Bristol, 1930
Grove, LRA and Joyce, Alfred: *Maidstone Guide*, London, 1973/4
Russell, JM: *The History of Maidstone*, Maidstone, 1881
Cooper, Ernest Read: *Memories of Bygone Dunwich*, Ipswich, 1948
Gardner, Thomas: *The Historical Account of Dunwich*, London, 1754
Parker, Rowland: *Men of Dunwich*, Collins, 1978, Granada, 1980

Chapter 13
Adams, JC: *The Globe Playhouse*, Constable, 1961
Orrell, John: *The Quest for Shakespeare's Globe*, CUP, 1983
Smith, Irwin: *Shakespeare's Blackfriars Playhouse*, New York University, 1964, Peter Owen, 1966

Chapter 14
Bowden, Peter J: *The Wool Trade in Tudor and Stuart England*, Macmillan, 1962
Hinings, Edward: *History, People and Places in the Cinque Ports*, Spurbooks, Bourne End, 1975
Hueffer, Ford Maddox: *The Cinque Ports*, Blackwood, 1900
Roper, Anne: *The Gift of the Sea*, Ashford, 1953
Calvert, Charles: *History of Stafford and Guide to the Neighbourhood*, 1886
Greenslade MW and Stuart, DG: *A History of Staffordshire*, Beaconsfield, 1965
Kettle, Anne J: 'The Black Book of Stafford', '*The Stafford Historical and Civic Society*' Transaction, 1965–7

INDEX

Numbers in italics refer to illustrations. For London's best-known landmarks, see general index; for its others, see under 'London'. The edition of Shakespeare referred to is *William Shakespeare: the Complete Works* (Clarendon Press, 1986), General Editors: Stanley Wells and Gary Taylor.

Acknowledgements

The author would like to thank the following for their help:

Mr Christopher Morris and Dr Stanley Wells, who read all the manuscript and offered constructive criticism with suggestions for development; Ms M Connatty, Mr J Cooper, Mr N J Fogg, Mr W Fowkes, Mr I Green, Mr A Grove, Mr G Heath, Ms L Lamplugh, Mr J B Lawson, Mr B Little, Ms M MacDonald, Mr G Mayhew, Ms C Morris, Mr J Munby, Mr A Percival, Dr O G Pickard, Mr DJ Rimmer, Ms A Roper, Ms P Rundle, Ms R Serjeant, Ms R Trapnell, Ms R Weinstein and Ms HM Wills who each read and criticized very helpfully a section of the manuscript, giving generously of their time and knowledge; librarians at many libraries including the Bodleian; Guildhall, London; Library of the Museum of London; Reference Library, Bath; Central Library, Bristol; Shakespeare Centre, Stratford-upon-Avon; Central Library, Oxford, and the Marlborough Library, who supplied books and information; many other librarians who helpfully answered queries; the staffs of the National Portrait Gallery and the Museum of London; and a host of other people who gave help in many varied ways. Among these helpers were: Mr R Avery, Ms D Banerjee, Mr GR Cannon, Mr MAN Coker, The Rev. DJ Dales, Mr RW Ellis, Dr & Mrs K Fincham, Ms K Folkard, Mr DJ Green, Mr B Guthrie, Mr RR Harris, Ms A Hart, Dr M Henig, Mr C Johnston, Mr CA Joseph, Mr EGH Kempson, Mr WJ Latham, Mr & Mrs M Laughton, Mr R Ormond, Mr CJ Rogers, Mr P Spottiswoode, Ms G Stephenson, Mr J D Stuart, Mr R Upton, Mr R Watkins, Mr D Whiting and Mr ARD Wright.

Gratitude is also due for permission to quote from *William Shakespeare: The Complete Works* (Clarendon Press, 1986), General Editors: Stanley Wells and Gary Taylor.

Finally, the author wishes to thank Mr Andrew Best, of Curtis Brown, for his useful suggestions; Ms Anne-Marie Ehrlich for her very helpful picture researches; Mr Simon McBride for his excellent photographs; and his wife, Elaine Davis, for her practical help and wise comments.

The publishers would like to thank the following for supplying illustrations:

Colour
British Library 181 (above right); Marquess of Bath 28, 40, 141 (below); Marquess of Salisbury 48 (above); Marquess of Tavistock and the Trustees of the Bedford Estates 181 (above left); Simon McBride 25, 26–7, 28 (above), 45 (above), 46–7, 65, 66–7, 101, 102–3, 104, 113, 131, 132 (by kind permission of the President and Fellows of Queens' College), 144, 161, 162–3, 164, 184; Museum of London 48 (below); National Maritime Museum 114 (below), 182–3; National Portrait Gallery 68, 142–3; Royal Collection 141 (above).

Black and White
British Library 7, 17, 36–7, 41, 51, 53, 69 (below), 75, 93, 97, 98, 119 (below), 159, 169, 170, 172; Courtauld Institute of Art 76, 84, 174, 189; ET Archive 20, 30, 72, 78, 106, 108, 128–9, 134, 140, 146 (below), 180; Fitzwilliam Museum, Cambridge 63; Fotomas Index 12, 21, 24, 85, 90 (above), 118, 119 (above), 146 (above), 148–9, 150, 173; John R Freeman 167; Governors of Dulwich Picture Gallery 54, 115, 116; Guildhall Library, London 89; Her Majesty the Queen 70; Lord Sackville 189; Simon McBride 8, 11, 18, 32, 43, 49, 58, 64, 73, 76, 83, 88, 96, 100, 111, 126, 138, 155, 165, 176, 177, 188, 191, 193, 196; Mansell Collection 90 (below), 178; Mercer's Company 86; Museum of London 130; National Portrait Gallery 9, 23, 36, 62, 123, 152; Private Collection 69 (above); Rijksuniversiteit Utrecht 42; Society of Antiquaries 34; Victoria and Albert Museum 15, 99; Viscount De L'Isle VC KG 60.